**Stitches, Patterns and Projects
for Crochet**

A7786

Other titles in this series

Stitches, Patterns and Projects
for Knitting

Stitches, Patterns and Projects
for Embroidery

Stitches, Patterns & Projects for

Crochet

Wanda Bonando

MACDONALD & CO
London & Sydney

A MACDONALD BOOK

© Arnoldo Mondadori Editore S.p.A. Milan 1978
English translation © Arnoldo Mondadori Editore S.p.A., Milan 1984

First published in Great Britain in 1984
by Macdonald & Co (Publishers) Ltd
London & Sydney

A member of BPCC plc

ISBN 0 356 11029 X (cased)
ISBN 0 356 11032 X (limp)

Translated by Sylvia Mulcahy

English edition revised by Barbara Clarkson.
Charts on pages 116, 125, 126, 136, 147, 151, 154, 156,
160, 198, 202-3, 204, 210 and the key on page 113
by Barbara Clarkson.

Filmset by
SX Composing Ltd, Rayleigh, Essex
Printed and bound in Italy by
Officine Grafiche
Arnoldo Mondadori Editore, Verona
Macdonald & Co (Publishers) Ltd
Maxwell House
74 Worship Street
London EC2A 2EN

CONTENTS

7 Introductory notes

15 **Stitches**

16 *Basic stitches, increasing, decreasing and finishing off*
16 Basic steps
24 Increasing, decreasing, finishing off
36 *Close-textured stitches and their uses*
64 *Openwork stitches*
64 Dress elegantly with crochet

89 **Motifs, medallions and patchwork**

90 *Strips and geometric shapes*
90 Stitches for medallions to build into rugs, curtains, bed-coverings, tablecloths, etc.
91 Stitches in wool for bedspreads, cot-covers, etc.
94 Square shapes from circles
109 Round and square medallions for curtains, coverlets and tablecloths
113 Hexagons, flowers, squares and stars in cotton

132 *Borders, edgings and insertions*
132 Crochet for the finishing touches
133 Borders
143 Trimmings
148 Edgings
155 Insertions

163 **Complete patterns**

164 *Garments and accessories*
164 Creating things to wear

192 *Tablemats, tablecloths and bedspreads*
192 The fascination of tradition

234 *Gifts and things*
234 Easy-to-make patterns and practical ideas

251 **Index**

Chart of corresponding crochet hook sizes

English	1	2	3	4	5	6	7
American		K/10¼	J/10	I/9	H/8	H/8	G/6
European	7.50	7	6.50	6	5.50	5	4.50

English	8	9	10	11	12	13	14
American	F/5	E/4	D/3	C/2	B/1		
European	4	3.50	3.25	3	2.50	2.25	2

The author wishes to thank:
Signora Graziella Mentasti, Mrs Ruth Olson and the
Ghelfi brothers, 'Casa della Lana', Como, Italy, for their
kind collaboration; and The Vergottini Tricot Boutique,
Milan, for the Lurex cap described on page 179.

The asterisk (*) is used to indicate a group of stitches to
be repeated throughout all the instructions for stitches,
motifs and patterns. Groups contained between two
asterisks (**) are to be repeated as many times as
indicated or for the whole row or round.
Brackets are also used, especially where groups are to be
repeated within other groups.

INTRODUCTION

The history and art of crochet

The origins of crochet are obscure. While discoveries of hooked needles dating from biblical times suggest that the ancient civilizations of the southern Mediterranean seaboard knew of knitting crafts, exactly how they were used is not clear. Some historians believe crochet was used as early as 1200 BC and that the Israelites took the skill with them when they fled from Egypt during the Great Exodus, using camel and sheep wool spun and worked in simple crochet stitches during the long trek across the Sinai desert. Just as Egypt was known for its fine woven linen, Babylon – now Iraq – became the centre of woollen crafts. The Babylonians liked to decorate their clothes with complicated embellishments, although later there was a reaction against such things and plain woollen 'sacks' were frequently made from knitting or crochet.

All the countries in North Africa developed the craft and even today the patterns created by the Muslims are echoed in some parts of India, where the skill was brought along with increased trade. It is believed that crochet has been worked continuously for thousands of years in the Middle East and that what we now know as Tunisian crochet could be the missing link between knitting and crochet.

There are other crafts whose influence must have contributed to the spread of crochet. One of these was macramé, which seems to have originated and developed in France and

Italy, where evidence has been found dating from the sixteenth century. It was a popular pastime among sailors who, in their leisure hours, would demonstrate their skill at making knots by producing all kinds of useful objects.

The knotting of various thicknesses of ropes of differing lengths to form squared fabrics and patterns similar to those of needle- and pillow-lace was widely practised in North, Central and South America. Although the results were much cruder than lace, any material could be used, such as strips of leather, straw, wool and cotton, and some of the products were just as delightful. It is thought that crochet spread in the wake of missionary advance. The religious sisters of Spain introduced crochet to South America and some of the earliest and best preserved examples are the decorative head and wrist bands woven for ceremonial wear.

Part of the difficulty in tracing the development of crochet in Europe is that it is referred to only as a type of lace. But we do know that its history is closely linked to its more illustrious ancestors, the embroidery needle and the bobbin. A craft that is almost unknown today but from which crochet undoubtedly grew was tambour embroidery, which developed in the early Middle Ages. This was worked with a hooked stick similar to the modern crochet hook, which was used to draw loops of linen through a background mesh. It is suggested that at some point the mesh was discarded and the crochet hook was used independently to create a lace fabric from a series of chains. This type of work became highly prized by kings and queens, who used it on their clothes and furnishings.

It was in Venice in the fifteenth and sixteenth centuries that needle-lace – another precursor of crochet – emerged. Like all crafts whose origins are unknown, it has its own special legends. One of the most evocative tells of a young Venetian sailor who, on the day of his marriage, gave his bride a piece of rare seaweed. Its delicate tracery and frills were so beautiful that when the groom had to return to his ship soon after the wedding, his young wife – seeking to record his symbolic gift forever – tried to imitate the intricate forms by translating them into embroidery. Using fine thread and a sewing needle, she thus became the inventor of needle-lace.

In the sixteenth century the demand for lace in Venice became so great that the governors had to issue laws prohibiting its immoderate use. However, lacemaking developed into one of the most prosperous cottage industries in the islands of the lagoon, and the work was highly prized. A history of the great Sforza family mentions lacemaking from 1493, and two hundred years later the ladies of all the great families were still adorning themselves with beautiful and valuable examples of the craft. Lace collars, cuffs and shawls enhanced the beauty of their wearers both in public and private, while the long hair of girls was interwoven with gold and silver lace ribbons. When the Doge made his annual visit to the Convent of the Virgins, he was always presented with a posy of flowers wrapped in an exquisite piece of lace.

In France lacemaking in the Italian style was learnt by French women from the entourage of Catherine de Medici. Louis XIV in particular adored the lavish use of lace, and encouraged Italian workers to start lace production in his country. French women soon become so proficient at the skill that French lace threatened to rival Venetian and the Venetian government found it necessary to intervene. Lacemakers were forbidden to work outside the boundaries of the Republic under pain of imprisonment or, should this not prove a sufficient deterrent, death. Despite these measures, as the fortunes of Venice declined in the seventeenth century its lace industry was almost completely taken over by France, and French lacemakers furthered its growth with the development of pillow-lace, which reached its peak in Belgium.

Pillow-lace involves a rather different technique from that of needle-lace, the thread being wound on bobbins that are woven in and out of pins stuck into a small cushion to delineate a design rather than using a needle and cloth. Exactly when this variation started is not known although there are, as usual, some delightful legends. It is said that the Prince of Bruges decided to hold an embroidery competition in which all of the most skilled workers were to participate. Many pieces of linen were embroidered with costly threads in complicated patterns, but all were rejected. One young lacemaker, who had no money to buy linen or to hire an artist to draw a design for her, was desperately unhappy at not being able to enter the competition. Gazing sadly at her needle, pins, wooden bobbins and ball of thread, she was suddenly inspired: the frost had made a delicate and enchanting design on the windowpanes and the little lacemaker worked night and day to reproduce the pattern with her simple thread pillow, bobbins and pins. When she presented her work to the judges, the decision was unanimous – she was awarded first prize and pillow-lace had arrived.

Within a short time lacemaking became part of the education of Flemish girls in all the schools and convents. This was especially useful because the garments and trimmings produced by the nuns and their pupils could be sold and the proceeds used to help support the Church. Lacemaking became known as 'nuns' work' or 'shepherds work', the latter because during a poor farming season shepherds were given a hook and spun wool with which to make garments to sell in the market so that they were not idle as they watched their flocks.

In the next few centuries the lacemaking industry reached new heights of perfection, although the price for the lacemakers themselves was high. In the outskirts of Courtrai a special flax was grown that was so fine and delicate that it had to be worked in a damp atmosphere because dry air would cause it to break. Lacemakers therefore had to work in cellars, barely able to see, using only their sense of touch to avoid making costly mistakes. This demanding work – tedious and unhealthy as it was – was very poorly paid: it took ten months to make a pair of cuffs, working fifteen hours a day. Needless to say, the price for such adornment was high, but the highest price was paid by the workers themselves.

The popularity of crochet in Britain from the beginning of the nineteenth century was largely due to the Industrial Revolution, when cotton mills, recently established in the north country, began to produce fine cotton thread that was cheaper than

Lace ruff featured in a portrait by Rubens

linen. Prince Albert was indirectly responsible for the growth in demand for crochet work: at the Great Exhibition of 1851, which was largely his brainchild, this cottage industry was well represented, and manufacturers and designers from all parts of the world became aware of its potential. But the term 'nuns' work' had taken on a slightly derogatory note; perhaps people had become tired of seeing everything covered in crochet: during the latter part of Queen Victoria's reign, even the legs of pianos and tables were covered in crocheted pantaloons.

The greatest exponents of crochet were probably the Irish, who introduced the craft into their country about 1820. Although crochet was already widely used there, at the time it had little artistic merit, being limited to a few basic stitches. It was due to the terrible potato famines between 1840 and 1860 that crochet was brought to distinction, as the women of Ireland sought to compensate for the tragic loss of revenue by perfecting the craft. It is almost certain that the refinement of crocheting was brought there from France when a young Irish woman, Honoria Nagle, who had been sent to Paris to complete her education, became aware of the dire poverty in her own country. With a few friends she learnt the intricacies of crochet from French Carmelite nuns and when the women felt sufficiently competent they returned to Ireland and began teaching it to anyone who wished to learn. They began in their home districts – Cork in southern Ireland and Monaghan in the north – which became the main centres of the craft. Although derived from Continental examples, the Irish introduced a new range of naturalistic decoration and design. Using a very delicate, fine thread, they created a series of shamrock leaves, the symbol of Ireland, set with raised rosettes and rings on a background of chain stitch lace and small 'picots'. The rosettes of Ireland became famous for their whiteness and the delicacy of their design, especially when combined with the beautiful linen fabric for which the country has long been renowned. These exquisite and original productions earned Irish crochet the great name that it still holds, and the money brought in by this easily accessible craft did much to alleviate Ireland's poverty. Even today 'Irish point' is among the most highly valued crochet work.

By about 1870 there were approximately 20,000 women engaged in crochet work, adapting patterns from as far afield as Italy and Greece. As the skill was perfected, the demand grew as ladies' fashions became increasingly smothered in frills, jabots, collars and cuffs and similar trimmings which, when worked in crochet, were less costly than lace.

With the expansion of colonialism and missionary work in the nineteenth and twentieth centuries, crochet was soon being taught in remote parts of the world. In the heart of Africa, in the Azores and the West Indies, the influence of industrious religious sisters can still be seen – a little touch of shamrock in Jamaica, an imitation of Flemish lace in the Azores, a piece of Greman 'filet' in South America. One important aspect of this is that crochet, being such a flexible medium, is susceptible to local influence and so we find local flowers and fruits, such as poinsettias, hibiscus and pineapples being introduced, exotic butterflies seem to land on delicate openwork table centrepieces and even appliqué work is reproduced by the Seminole Indians.

Crochet work continued to be extremely popular until the outbreak of the First World War when fashion took a more practical turn and, with the development of the sewing machine, dresses could be made and trimmed so quickly and prettily that hand-crocheted trimmings seemed outmoded.

Today the fashions of yesteryear are being rediscovered and, in an age of mass-production, the charm of individually worked trimmings is appreciated. New, wide-reaching possibilities are being discovered to utilize crochet – the craft of the people – in even broader areas than before, from clothes to furnishings. And, as always, when an old art or craft form re-emerges, the only limiting factor is individual imagination.

Variations of basic crochet

While all types of crochet are based on the chain stitch, there are slightly differing techniques which are divided into two main groups: Common, or German, crochet and Tunisian crochet. Common crochet is further divided according to the working technique: filet or openwork crochet – in which square, open spaces are interspersed with blocks – Irish, Friulian (an area of northeastern Italy) and Hairpin crochet are the main variations.

In Common crochet a short stick with a hook at one end is used. It is this that does all the work, picking up, holding and guiding the thread. The material from which it is made varies according to the type of thread or yarn to be used and the type of work to be done. It is usually about 12¾ cm (5 in) long but the size of the hook itself may be very tiny, if, for example, a fine cotton (no. 60) is to be used, or very thick if a chunky

triple knitting wool is employed. Finer hooks are generally made of stainless steel while thicker ones are usually made of aluminium, plastic, wood or, in the case of very old hooks, ivory or bone.

The distinguishing feature of Common crochet is that the basic stitches are linked into a ring and the subsequent rows are then built up on this in increasingly large rounds, either going continuously round and round or back and forth. This system does not necessarily mean that the finished article will be circular (it may be square, triangular or any other shape) but it does mean that each

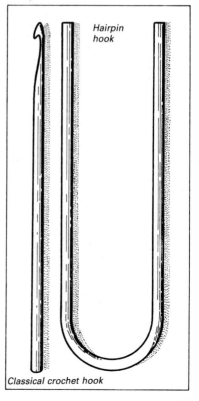

Hairpin hook

Classical crochet hook

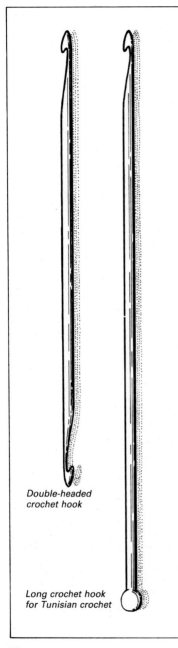

*Double-headed
crochet hook*

*Long crochet hook
for Tunisian crochet*

'round' will start and finish at the same point.

Filet or trellis stitch is usually worked back and forth in rows, the open mesh acting as a background for the pattern which is worked in blocks.

Irish crochet consists of a simple background consisting of chain lace with raised flowers and shapes of various kinds forming a three-dimensional design. In this type of work the raised decorations are sometimes made first and then linked into the work gradually as the pattern is built up.

Friulian crochet is similar to Irish but less delicate, with a rather rustic appearance.

Hairpin crochet involves the use of a U-shaped tool rather like a hairpin, from which it derives its name. This comes in several sizes and is used to control the length of the stitches which are worked with a normal crochet hook. As it is not possible to increase or decrease in hairpin crochet, it is usual to make strips of different lengths and then join them together, or they can be used individually as decorative edgings or insertions.

Tunisian crochet is also called tricot or crochet-knitting because all the stitches remain on the hook during the first stage of each row, just as with knitting, while in the second stage they are worked off until only the last stitch remains. A Tunisian crochet hook is therefore the same thickness for its full length, which is usually between 30-40 cm (12-16 in) with a knob at one end to prevent the stitches from falling off. Sometimes there is a hook at both ends to allow for two threads to be worked simultaneously.

Beginning to crochet

For some reason crochet has acquired the reputation of being difficult. This may be because for a long time it was practised almost exclusively within cloistered walls, by girls who would not need to earn their living by it, instead of being a skill attainable by anyone. Perhaps, too, some of the delightful and intricate designs produced give the impression that it is much harder to do than is really the case. In fact, it is easier than knitting, less tiring, and has the great advantage that size can be adjusted easily as the work progresses, whereas in knitting until all of the stitches have been cast off it is difficult to assess the final dimensions. There is always some caution when embarking on a new craft, and mastering the art of crochet depends on being able to overcome the initial problems. Naturally, concentration is needed in the early stages, combined with patience and determination. Once the hook is well under control and the fingers of the left hand (for a right-handed person) or the right hand (for a left-handed person) have learnt how to release the yarn at the correct tension, the hand movements will become automatic. What advice should be given to a beginner? The first thing is to be comfortable and relaxed. In the early stages the hook may seem to have a life of its own and the yarn to be totally disobedient. This is a feeling everyone has at first but if a slow, rhythmical movement is aimed at rather than jerky, aggressive jabs, your speed will develop very soon. If your hands feel tired it is only because you are using muscles that are not normally used much and some physical tension will pass as you become more confident.

After a surprisingly short time you will feel ready to tackle what at one time seemed to be quite difficult undertakings. If you wish to follow a pattern rather than experiment, do not be put off by what may look like complicated instructions. The apparently complicated stitches are merely combinations of two or more basic stitches, apart from some small variations in technique, as you will quickly see if you read the instructions before tackling them. If you read one row at a time – even covering the rest up with a sheet of paper if this helps – it is surprising how after the first time even a sequence of fifteen or twenty rows will seem quite simple because you will discover that they follow a logical system. The old maxim 'work well

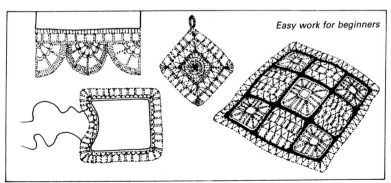

Easy work for beginners

started is already half finished' could not be more applicable, and the first chapter of this book will help you to get started in the right direction. Soon you will be able to do any kind of crochet you wish.

Once you have mastered the wayward hook, there are only a few basic stitches to be learnt. They are all that are needed to be able to make delightful articles for the home, fashion, children's and babies' clothes, men's and boy's ties, sweaters, pullovers, soft toys, rugs – the list is endless.

One last and important word of advice: the basic stitches should always be worked as evenly as possible. This not only makes the work easier to do but also gives a more professional finish. The secret is to control the tension as the yarn passes through the fingers. It is far better to proceed slowly and steadily at first, making sure that all of the stitches are the same size. Each of your fingers can be moved separately but as you may never have asked them to do this sort of thing before, they may take a little time to get the hang of it. So be patient. They will soon learn and, one day, as you are speeding along, you will find that you have forgotten you ever learnt to crochet, it will seem so natural.

THE STITCHES

Abbreviations

sl st	*slip stitch*
dc	*double crochet*
htr	*half treble*
tr	*treble*
dtr	*double treble*
tr tr	*triple treble*
fwd tr	*forward treble*
bk tr	*back treble*

beg	*beginning*
cm	*centimetres*
ch	*chain*
col	*colour*
cont	*continue*
dec	*decrease*
foll	*following*
g	*grammes*
in	*inch*
inc	*increase*
rep	*repeat*
rem	*remain*
rnd	*round*
sp	*space*
t-ch	*turning chain*
unfin	*unfinished*
yoh	*yarn over hook*

Turning chains

As explained in the book, in order to keep all of the sides of the work straight, a certain number of chain stitches must be added at the end of each row to bring the work into position for the next row. The work is then turned so that the reverse side is towards you. The number of turning chains required depends upon the type of stitch with which you will begin the next row. The following table gives the number of turning chains for each type of stitch used when the next row is to be worked in the same stitch:

Double crochet – 1 chain
Half treble – 2 chains
Treble – 3 chains
Double treble – 4 chains
Triple treble – 5 chains

In these cases, the turning chains also form the first stitch of the next row.

The Stitches

BASIC STITCHES, INCREASING, DECREASING AND FINISHING OFF

BASIC STEPS

Holding the hook

For right-handed people the hook is held in the right hand between the thumb and forefinger, just like a pen. It rests on the middle finger which acts as a guide. The thread or yarn is controlled by the left hand, passing over the index finger, under the middle (2nd) and ring-finger (3rd) and round the little finger (4th). The 2nd and 3rd fingers are kept slightly crooked inwards, towards the palm.
(Left-handed people find crochet just as easy as right-handed. The above applies, except for 'left' read 'right' and for 'right' read 'left'.)

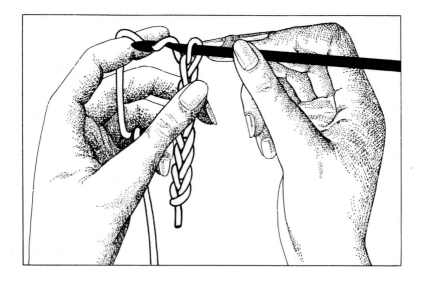

Starting to work

To begin, make a slip knot and put the hook through, as shown in the diagram, and pass the hook under the yarn which is resting on the index finger. The instruction for this movement is 'yarn over hook' (yoh), pick

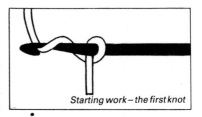

Starting work – the first knot

up the yarn with the hook and pull it through the loop already on the hook. This makes the first chain.

Chain stitch (ch)

The simple chain stitch is not only the basis of any piece of crochet work but is also an integral part of the makeup of many other stitches.
Having made the initial knot, take the yarn over the hook (yoh) and draw it through the preceding loop until the chain is a reasonable length, in relation to the type of yarn being used. It is important to remember that to make a good basis to the work the links of the chain must be of equal size, neither too loose nor too tight. For circular work, or any shape that is worked continuously rather than back and forth, the length of the chain is joined by the hook into the first stitch, taking the yarn over the hook and drawing it back through both loops.

Double chain stitch (dch)

Double chain stitch makes an excellent basis for crochet work. It is firmer than single chain stitch and can even be treated as a decorative edging.
Work 2 chains (ch), ✳ insert hook into first ch, yarn over hook (yoh) and draw a loop through, yoh and draw through both loops on hook ✳. Stitch completed. Rep from ✳ to ✳, inserting hook into back of left loop of the stitch previously completed until a chain of required length is obtained.

Slip stitch (sl st)

This is the simplest of crochet stitches and is usually used as a finishing

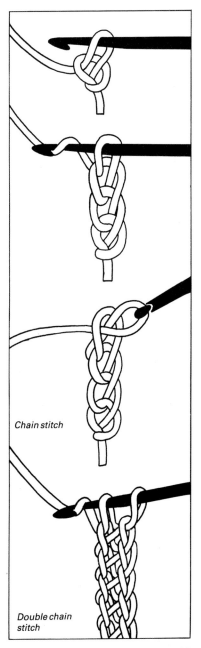

Chain stitch

Double chain stitch

17

edge or to close a round before beginning the next one. It is worked from right to left, or back and forth. Work required length of chain.

∗ Insert hook into top loop of 2nd chain (ch) from hook, yarn over hook (yoh), draw a loop through both loops on hook. Rep from ∗ to ∗ end of ch. Work 1 ch, turn.

This turning chain (t-ch) forms the first stitch.

Miss first slip stitch (sl st), rep from ∗ to end of row.

Slip stitch or single crochet (sl st)

Double crochet (dc)

Although it is simple, this stitch is most effective for many kinds of work. It is a close stitch and, worked in wool, its fabric-like texture lends itself to sweaters, jackets, skirts, capes and the like, while in cotton useful things can be made for the home.

Work required length of chain.

Insert hook under the top loop of 2nd chain (ch) from hook.

Yarn over hook (yoh) and draw a loop through ch. There are now 2 loops on hook. Yoh and draw a loop through both loops on hook. This completed one dc.

Insert hook into next ch. ∗ Rep from ∗ to ∗, working a dc into each ch to end of row. Work 1 ch.

Turn work, insert hook into first stitch of previous row and rep from ∗ to ∗ working dc into each stitch to end of row. Work 1 ch, turn.

Half treble (htr)

This stitch is widely used for all kinds of work, either by itself or as part of composite stitches.

Work required length of chain plus 2 chains (ch).

Miss first 2 turning-chains (t-ch), ∗

Double crochet (dc)

yarn over hook (yoh), insert hook from front to back under top loop of next ch, yoh, draw a loop through (3 loops on hook), yoh, draw a loop through all 3 loops on hook. This completes one htr and 1 loop is left to start next stitch. Rep from * to end of ch, 2 ch, turn.

The last 2 ch form first stitch of next row.

Work following rows, back and forth, in the same way but on next and subsequent rows miss the first htr from hook and insert hook under both loops at top of each stitch on previous row. The last stitch of each row is worked into the t-ch of previous row.

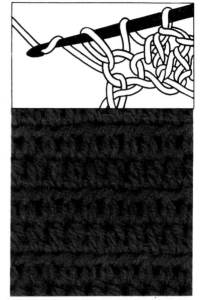

Half treble (htr)

Treble (tr)

A very useful basic stitch, used in many composite stitches both in filet crochet and in wool for all kinds of garments.

Work required length of chain plus 3 chains (ch).

Miss first 3 (turning) ch, * yarn over hook (yoh), insert hook from front to back under top loop of next ch, yoh, draw a loop through (3 loops on hook), yoh, draw a loop through first 2 loops on hook (2 loops now on hook), yoh, draw loop through 2 remaining loops on hook. This completes one tr and one loop is left to start a new stitch.

Rep from * to end of ch, 3 ch, turn.

Work following rows, back and forth, in the same way but on next and subsequent rows miss the first tr from hook and insert hook under *both* loops at top of each stitch on previous row. The last stitch of each row is worked into the turning chain (t-ch) of previous row.

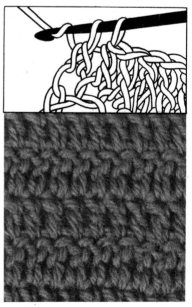

Treble (tr)

Double treble (dtr)

Work required length of chain plus 4 chains (ch)
Miss first 4 turning chains (t-ch), *
yarn over hook (yoh) twice, insert hook from front to back under top loop of next ch, yoh, draw a loop through (4 loops on hook), yoh, draw a loop through first 2 loops on hook (3 loops on hook), yoh, draw a loop through next 2 loops on hook (2 loops on hook), yoh, draw a loop through 2 remaining loops on hook. This completes one dtr and one loop is left to start new stitch. Rep from * to end of ch, 4 ch, turn.
Work following rows, back and forth, in the same way but on next and subsequent rows miss the first dtr from hook and insert hook under *both* loops at top of each stitch on previous row. The last stitch of each row is worked into the t-ch of previous row.

Double treble (dtr)

Triple treble (tr tr)

Work required length of chain plus 5 chain (ch).
Miss first 5 turning chain (t-ch), *
yarn over hook (yoh) 3 times, insert hook from front to back under top loop of next chain, yoh, draw a loop through (5 loops on hook), yoh, draw loop through first 2 loops on hook (4 loops on hook), yoh, draw a loop through next 2 loops on hook (3 loops on hook), yoh, draw a loop through next 2 loops on hook (2 loops on hook), yoh, draw a loop through 2 remaining loops on hook. This completes one tr tr and one loop is left to start new stitch.
Rep from * to end of ch, 5 ch, turn.
Work following rows, back and forth in the same way but on next and subsequent rows miss the first tr tr from hook and insert hook under

Triple treble (tr tr)

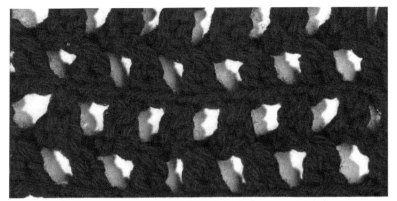

Crossed treble

both loops at top of each stitch on previous row. The last stitch of each row is worked into the t-ch of previous row.

Crossed treble

This is a very simple stitch to do but very effective if worked neatly and is especially suitable for shawls, stoles and scarves.

Make foundation ch in multiples of 3 plus 2.

Row 1: 1 tr into 5th ch from hook (the first 3 ch count as first tr), crossing back over tr just made work 1 tr into 4th ch from beginning, * 2 ch, miss 2 ch, 1 tr into next ch, crossing back over tr just made work 1 tr into 2nd of 2 ch missed *. Rep from * to * ending with 1 tr into last ch, 4 ch turn.

Row 2: Miss first 3 tr, * 1 tr into 2nd of 2 ch, crossing back over tr just made work 1 tr into first ch, miss 2 tr *. Rep from * to * ending with 1 tr into 3rd of t-ch, 3 ch, turn.

Row 3: Miss 1 tr, 1 tr into 2nd of 2 ch, crossing back over tr just made work 1 tr into first ch, * 2 ch, miss 2 tr, 1 tr into 2nd of 2 ch, crossing back over tr just made work 1 tr into first ch *.

Rep from * to * ending with 1 tr into 3rd of 4 t-ch, 5 ch, turn.

Rows 2 and 3 form the pattern and are repeated as required.

Lattice stitch

This is also an effective but simple stitch when worked neatly. It can be incorporated with other stitches or used by itself for table or cushion covers. It can be worked in a circle

Lattice stitch

21

providing that the last lattice at the end of each round is carefully linked to the first lattice with a slip stitch (sl st).

Make foundation ch in multiples of 4 plus 2.

Row 1: 1 dc into 2nd ch from hook, ∗ 5 ch, miss 3 ch, 1 dc into next ch. Rep from ∗ to ∗, 5 ch, turn.

Row 2: ∗ 1 dc into 3rd ch of 5-ch loop, 5 ch ∗ to ∗ ending with 2 ch, 1 tr into next dc, 1 ch, turn.

Row 3: 1 dc in tr, ∗ 5 ch, 1 dc in 3rd ch of 5-ch loop ∗. Rep from ∗ to ∗, 5 ch, turn.

Rows 2 and 3 form the pattern and are repeated as required.

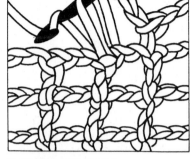

Trellis (Filet or Mesh) stitch

Trellis (or filet or mesh) stitch

This is the foundation on which filet crochet is based. By filling in the spaces, ie with trebles, representational or geometrical patterns can easily be created.

Make foundation ch in multiples of 3 plus 2.

Row 1: Miss 7 ch, 1 tr into next ch. ∗ 2 ch, miss 2 ch, 1 tr into next ch, rep from ∗ to end of row, 5 ch, turn.

Row 2: Miss 1 tr and 2 ch, ∗ 1 tr into next tr, 2 ch, miss 2 ch. Rep from ∗ to last pattern, miss 2 ch, 1 tr into next ch, 5 ch, turn.

Row 2 forms the pattern and is repeated as required.

A smaller basic mesh can be obtained by following these instructions but working 1 ch instead of 2 and missing 1 ch only. In this case, only 4 ch will be required at row endings to turn.

Blocks and spaces in mesh stitch

Two or 3 trebles (tr) worked over 2 or 3 chains is called a block. Two or 3 chains carried over a block and finished with a tr is called a space (sp).

Blocks and spaces in Mesh stitch

It is important to remember that the turning chain (t-ch) of previous row counts as the last stitch to be worked at end of each row. This is standard and is seldom specified in patterns as it is assumed that the worker has already mastered the basic technique.

Having made a practice piece in Mesh stitch, now make some blocks over some of the spaces as follows: 1 tr into tr of previous row, 2 tr into ch sp, 1 tr into next tr of previous row. Practise making spaces and blocks to end of row, 3 ch turn. Rep as required.

To make blocks on blocks, 1 tr is worked into each of the 4 tr of previous row.

Very attractive designs can be made in filet crochet by drawing up a pattern or even a picture on graph paper. Each square on the paper will represent one block or space.

Tunisian stitch

A Tunisian hook is used for this stitch and the technique varies from ordinary crochet in that all the stitches are left on the hook in the first stage (A) of each row and then worked off the hook in the second stage (B). *At no time is the work turned.*

Work required length of chain. (On first row *only*, insert hook under *one* top loop only instead of two.)

Foundation row 1: (A) Insert hook under one top loop of 2nd ch from hook, yoh, draw a loop through, leaving all loops on hook. Rep into each ch st to end.

Foundation row 2: (B) Work all loops off hook by working * yoh and drawing through first 2 loops on hook. Rep from * until only 1 loop remains on hook which becomes the first stitch of next row.

(A) Row 1: Insert hook under top loop

Tunisian stitch

of 2nd ch from hook, yoh, draw a loop through, * insert hook into next *vertical* bar, yoh, draw a loop through. Rep from * to end, finishing by inserting hook under last bar and the stitch immediately behind it, yoh, draw a loop through (this makes a firm edge).

(B) Row 2: * Yoh and draw through 2 loops on hook, rep from * until only 1 loop remains on hook.

The last 2 rows form the pattern and are repeated as required.

To finish off neatly, work 1 sl st into each bar across work.

Increasing, decreasing and finishing off

Increasing, decreasing and completing (buttonholes, edgings, etc) are the only techniques left to be learned in order to be able to follow any pattern or to make up your own designs. There is nothing difficult about these skills – all that is needed is a little patience at first and your work will soon have that neat and regular appearance that everyone admires so much in crocheted garments or articles for the home. The finishing is particularly important as an irregular line of increasing or decreasing, a buttonhole that is too small or too large or an untidy edge will ruin the final result of any piece of work. Precision is essential in increasing and decreasing as the ultimate shape of the article depends upon it.

Increasing

This is done when more stitches are required to widen the work. It may be done on the outside edges or within the working of a row or round.

Increasing on outside edges

At the end of each row where an increase is required, work as many additional chain stitches as necessary, plus the usual number of turning chains, depending upon which stitch you are using.

Increasing within rows or rounds

Perfect internal increasing is obtained by ensuring that all increases are carefully worked above one another and in the same direction. It is a good idea to thread pieces of coloured cotton in the positions where increases are to be worked. Thus, if the shaping is to be made towards the right, 2 stitches must be worked into the stitch preceding the cotton marking. If the shaping is to be towards the left, the extra stitch must be worked after the marking. A double increase can be made by

Increasing on outside edges

Increasing within rows

working 3 stitches into one instead of 2 stitches into one.

Decreasing

This is done when fewer stitches are required to narrow the work. This may be done on the outside edges or within the working of a row or round. Decreasing is involved especially in the making of garments for shaping arm holes, necklines and flares.

Decreasing on outside edges

If a sharp decrease is required (ie for a square neckline), simply omit the required number of stitches at the end of one row, or, for a sloping effect, single stitches at the ends of several rows.

To avoid irregularity, work a slip stitch (sl st) into stitch after last stitch worked, make required number of turning chains and work first stitch of new row in stitch following the slip stitch.

For example, if you wish to decrease 2 stitches, work to within last 2 stitches; work 1 sl st into next stitch, work turning chain, turn, miss sl st just worked, work next stitch into following stitch, then continue as required.

Decreasing on outside edges

Decreasing within rows or rounds

Decreasing within rows or rounds

As with increasing, internal decreases must be carefully worked above one another. Pieces of coloured cotton should be threaded in the exact positions where decreases are to be worked. In the next row (or round), insert the hook into stitch preceding the marking, yoh, draw a loop through, insert hook into stitch immediately following the marking, draw a loop through all 3 loops on hook. This completes one decrease.

Increasing of spaces on mesh or filet with 1 treble, 2 chain pattern

To increase the number of spaces at the beginning of a row to be worked, make a chain consisting of three times as many stitches as the number of new spaces you wish to make, plus 3 chains. Work back, incorporating the chain stitches as though they were part of the previous row.

To increase one space at the end of a row, work 2 chains and a triple treble (tr tr) as follows: yoh 3 times, insert

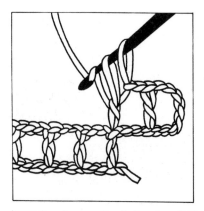 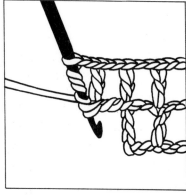

Increasing of spaces at beginning of row (left) and at end of row (right) on mesh

hook into base of last tr worked, draw a loop through ✳ yoh, draw through 2 loops. Rep from ✳ until all loops have been worked off the hook. Repeat entire process for each additional space required.

Decreasing of spaces on mesh or filet with 1 treble, 2 chain pattern

To decrease the number of spaces at the end of a row, it is only necessary to continue on the row being worked up to the width required, make the necessary 3 turning chain, turn and start the new row.

To decrease the number of spaces at the beginning of a row, work slip stitches (sl st) into the first stitches of previous row until required point is reached to start new row of spaces, work (turning) chain to replace first stitch and continue.

For example, if only one square is to be decreased, work 4 sl st over previous space, 8 sl st if two squares are to be decreased and so on until the required width of work is achieved.

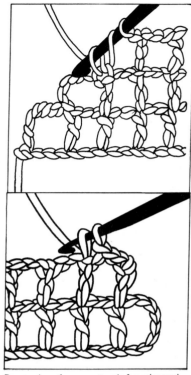

Decreasing of spaces at end of row (upper) and at beginning of row (lower) on mesh

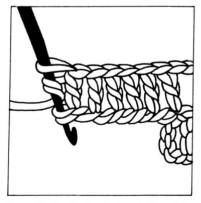
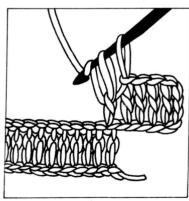

Increasing blocks at end of row (left) and at beginning of row (right)

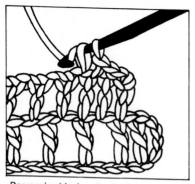 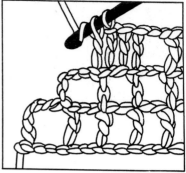

Decreasing blocks at beginning of row (left) and at end of row (right)

Increasing of blocks on mesh or filet

To increase the number of blocks at the end of a row, work a treble into the base of the last treble worked then each newly worked stitch until the required number of blocks has been reached.

To increase the number of blocks at the beginning of a row, make a chain consisting of three times as many stitches as the number of new blocks you wish to make, plus 2 turning chains. Work back, making the new blocks on the chain just made.

Decreasing of blocks on mesh or filet

To decrease one or more blocks at the end of a row, simply continue on the row being worked up to the point required, work 2 turning chains, turn and work back over previous row.

To decrease blocks at the beginning of a row, work slip stitches into the first stitches of previous row until required point is reached to start new row of blocks.

Increasing on outside edges on Tunisian crochet

To increase one stitch at beginning of a row, insert hook into chain between the 2 vertical bars of the chain stitch on previous row, yoh, draw a loop through and the extra stitch is formed.

To increase one stitch at end of a row, make 2 chain stitches and include the *first* of these (ie the one furthest from the hook) on the return row, thus forming an extra stitch.

Increasing within rows on Tunisian crochet

Mark the exact spot with a piece of coloured cotton where you wish to have the internal widening.

For shaping towards the left, pick up a stitch from the chain which links the stitch you have marked to the following stitch.

For shaping towards the right, pick up a stitch linking the one you have marked to the preceding stitch.

Increasing on outside edges on Tunisian crochet

Increasing within rows on Tunisian crochet

Decreasing on outside edges on Tunisian crochet

Decreasing within rows on Tunisian crochet

Decreasing on outside edges on Tunisian crochet

To decrease a stitch at the end of each row, merely leave the last stitch of the first row unworked; work the second (return) row as usual, draw the yarn through the last 3 stitches together.

If it is necessary to decrease more than one stitch at a time, merely work as many slip stitches as necessary from the beginning of the row.

Decreasing within rows on Tunisian crochet

Mark the exact spot with a piece of coloured cotton where you wish to have the internal narrowing.

For shaping towards the left, pick up the two vertical bars of the 2 stitches which precede the marking, yoh, and draw yarn through to make one loop. For shaping towards the right, work 2 stitches together immediately after the marking.

Buttonholes

Buttonholes are easy to do but it is important to know how to do them well as a garment may be spoilt if the buttonholes are untidy.

Horizontal buttonholes

Work 2 or more chain stitches fairly loosely at the exact point in your work where you wish to have a horizontal buttonhole. The length of chain will depend upon the size of the button. Miss as many stitches of the previous row as you have made chain stitches and continue to work normally to the end of the row. On the return row, work your pattern into the chain stitches previously made, instead of into the solid fabric.

Vertical buttonholes

These are a little more complicated as the work has to be split into two parts until the required length for each hole is achieved. Make sure you work exactly the same number of rows in each part and when the necessary height of the space has been reached, the work can then be joined into one piece, as before. The work must be divided in this way, each time a buttonhole has to be worked.

Horizontal buttonhole

Vertical buttonhole

Horizontal buttonhole in Tunisian crochet

Horizontal buttonholes in Tunisian crochet

At the point in the work where a buttonhole is required, wind the yarn round the hook two, three or four times, according to the length of but-

Vertical buttonhole in Tunisian crochet

Patch pocket

tonhole to be made. Miss the same number of stitches of the previous row and continue with the work. On the return row, work each of the loops off the hook one by one in the normal way.

Vertical buttonholes in Tunisian crochet

These are made exactly as for ordinary crochet, by dividing the work as each buttonhole is reached. (See instructions for vertical buttonholes.)

Patch pockets

When you have completed a garment, pockets may be made to what-

ever size you choose, in the same colour or in a contrasting colour. They may even have several colours, to tone with the main article. They may, therefore, blend completely with the garment or be a striking feature. In any case, the same stitch is normally used as that in which the whole garment is made or in which the edgings have been completed.

Integral pockets

In this case, the exact positioning of the pockets must be decided before the work on the garment is too advanced. When the point is reached where the pocket is to start, ie, where the slit is to come, discon-

Integral pocket

Edging in crab stitch

tinue working. Decide on the width you wish the pocket to be and, if required, work an edging, such as you will ultimately have on the edges of the main parts of the garment. When this is complete, break off the yarn and fasten off. Now make the pocket lining. Make a loose chain of the same number of stitches as you have worked on the pocket edging, working in double crochet to the required depth of the pocket (this is usually square). Insert this piece of fabric where the work has been discontinued and continue working, as before, incorporating the stitches at the top of the pocket lining.

Crab stitch

This is a very popular finish. It is hardwearing as it not only decorates an edge but reinforces it and helps to prevent stretching or bagginess. It may also be used to finish off a knitted garment.

Scalloped edging

Working into the edge of the main fabric, ensuring that the stitches are regularly spaced, work 1 row in dc for the full length. Do not turn.
Now work in dc from left to right of the work.

Scalloped edging

This is very simple but gives an attractive finish to almost any work. It consists of only one row. Working into the edge of the main fabric, start with a sl st and work *3 ch, miss 2 sts, 1 dc into next st, rep from * to end. Fasten off.

Shell edging

There are several variations of shell edges. This is the simplest and consists of only one row.
Work 1 sl st into first st, *3 ch, 3 tr into next st, miss 2 sts. Rep from * to end. Fasten off.

Twisted cord edging

This edging gives an elastic but firm finish. It consists of two rows.
Row 1: Work 1 dc into each st to end, 1 ch, turn.
Row 2: * insert hook into first st of previous row, yoh, draw loop through keeping it fairly loose, turn the hook round so that the 2 loops on

it are twisted, yoh, complete st like a normal dc. Rep from * to end. Fasten off.

Picot edging

There are many ways to make picot edgings but this is the simplest and most popular. It consists of one row only.
Work 1 sl st into first st, *5 ch, sl st into 3rd ch from hook, (this makes a picot), 2 ch, miss 2 sts, 1 dc into next st. Rep from * to end. Fasten off.

IMPORTANT – Working a sample piece

With the yarn and hook of your choice, make 12 chains or a number appropriate to the stitch you have selected. Work a few rows in the stitch you wish to use and, if the texture is right, you can calculate the number of stitches you will need for the measurements required. If the texture is too close, a larger hook is needed; if the texture is too open, then a smaller hook should be tried. When you have achieved the correct texture and you are sure it is suitable for the article you wish to make, you can calculate the number of stitches required to work 10 cm (4 in) and the number of rows to work 10 cm (4 in). Having made a note of this, you can begin work from a measured design.

Shell edging

Twisted cord edging

Picot edging

35

CLOSE-TEXTURED STITCHES
AND THEIR USES

All crochet stitches are merely combinations of the basic stitches already described. The closely worked stitches give a firm fabric and are particularly suitable for thicker garments in wool. Of course, finer yarns can also be used. The firm texture is hard-wearing and such thing as jackets, coats, capes, skirts and even trousers can be made very successfully.

The stitches described here are especially effective when worked in a tightly spun double-knitting wool with a 4.00 mm (8) hook, but this will depend upon individual working tension to a great extent. Double crêpe and manmade fibres are very suitable, too, as they are inclined to be less fluffy than wool, with less tendency for the hook to slip between the threads of the yarn.

Crossed double crochet

Make foundation ch with an even no. of sts.

Row 1: Insert hook into 4th ch from hook (first 2 ch count as 1 dc), yoh, draw loop through, miss 1 ch, insert hook into next ch, yoh, draw loop through (3 loops on hook), yoh and draw loop through all 3 loops on hook, 1 ch, * insert hook into st just worked, yoh, draw loop through, miss 1 ch, insert hook into next ch, yoh, draw loop through, yoh and draw loop through all 3 loops on hook, 1 ch *. Rep from * to * ending with 1 dc into last st worked, 2 ch, turn.

Row 2: Insert hook under 1-ch of previous row, yoh, draw loop through, insert hook under next 1-ch, yoh, draw loop through, yoh and draw loop through all 3 loops on hook, 1 ch, * insert hook under 1-ch just worked, yoh, draw loop through, insert hook under next 1-ch, yoh and draw loop through all 3 loops on hook, 1 ch *. Rep from * to * ending with 1 dc, 2 ch, turn.

Row 2 forms the pattern and is repeated as required.

Crossed double crochet

36

Elongated double crochet

Make foundation ch with an odd no. of sts.
Row 1: ✱ 1 dc into 2nd ch from hook, 1 ch, miss 1 ch ✱. Rep from ✱ to ✱ ending with 1 ch, turn.
Row 2: ✱ Insert hook under 1-ch of previous row and work 1 dc into back loop of foundation ch missed on Row 1, 1 ch ✱. Rep from ✱ to ✱, 1 ch, turn.
Row 3: ✱ Insert hook under 1-ch of previous row and work 1 dc into back loop of dc worked 2 rows below, 1 ch. ✱ Rep from ✱ to ✱, 1 ch, turn.
Row 3 forms the pattern and is repeated as required.

Ridge stitch

Make foundation ch with any no of sts.
Row 1: 1 dc into 2nd ch from hook, 1 dc into each ch to end of row, 1 ch, turn.
Row 2: ✱ Inserting hook into *back* horizontal thread at top of st of previous row, work in dc. Rep from ✱ to end, 1 ch, turn.
Row 2 forms the pattern and is repeated as required.

Elongated double crochet

Fancy double crochet

Ridge stitch

Fancy double crochet

Make foundation ch in multiples of 3 plus 1.
Row 1: Starting in 3rd ch from hook, * work 3 dc into next ch, miss 2 ch *. Rep from * to * ending with 3 dc into next-to-last ch, 1 ch, turn.
Row 2: * 3 dc into 2nd dc of 3-dc group of previous row. * Rep from * to * to end, 1 ch, turn.
Row 2 forms the pattern and is repeated as required.

Alternating stitch no. 1

Alternating stitch no. 1

Make foundation ch with an odd no. of sts plus 3.
Row 1: 1 dc into 4th ch from hook, * 1 tr, 1 dc *. Rep from * to *, 3 ch, turn.
Row 2: Work 1 tr into each dc of previous row and 1 dc into each tr.
Row 2 forms the pattern and is repeated as required.

Alternating stitch no. 2

Make foundation ch in multiples of 3 plus 1.
Row 1: 1 dc into 2nd ch from hook, 1 htr, 1 tr, * 1 dc, 1 htr, 1 tr *. Rep from * to *, 1 ch, turn.

Alternating stitch no. 2

Row 2: * 1 dc, 1 tr, 1 htr *. Rep from * to *, 3 ch, turn.
Row 3: Miss first st, 1 dc, 1 htr, * 1 tr, 1 dc, 1 htr *. Rep from * to *, 3 ch, turn.
Row 4: Miss first st, 1 htr, 1 dc, * 1 tr, 1 htr, 1 dc *. Rep from * to *, 2 ch, turn.
Row 5: Miss first st, 1 tr, 1 dc, * 1 htr, 1 tr, 1 dc *. Rep from * to *, 2 ch turn.
Row 6: Miss first st, 1 dc, 1 tr, * 1 htr, 1 dc, 1 tr *. Rep from * to *, 1 ch, turn.
Rows 1 to 6 form the pattern and are repeated as required.

Ridged alternating stitch

Ridged alternating stitch

Make foundation ch with an odd no. of sts.
Row 1: 1 tr into 4th ch from hook, 1 tr into each ch to end, 2 ch, turn.
Row 2: Miss first st, 1 forward raised tr (=yoh, insert hook behind vertical bar of first tr in previous row, draw loop through and finish as for normal tr), * 1 back raised tr (=yoh, insert hook into front of vertical bar of next tr in previous row, draw loop through and finish as for normal tr), 1 forward raised tr *. Rep from * to * ending with 1 htr into turning ch at beg of previous row, 2 ch, turn.
Row 2 forms the pattern and is repeated as required.

Basketweave stitch

Make foundation ch in multiples of 8 plus 2.
Row 1: 1 tr into 4th ch from hook, 1 tr into each ch to end, 2 t-ch, turn.
Row 2: * 4 bk tr, 4 fwd tr (counting 2 ch at beg of row as first bk tr). * Rep from * to *, 2 ch, turn.
Rows 3 and 4: As Row 2.
Row 5: * 4 fwd tr, 4 bk tr (counting 2 ch at beg of row as first fwd tr). * Rep from * to *, 2 ch, turn.
Rows 6 & 7: As Row 5.
Rows 2 to 7 form the pattern and are repeated as required.

Ridged treble no. 1

Make foundation ch with any no. of sts.
Row 1 and every alternate row: 1 tr into 4th ch from hook, 1 tr into each ch to end, 2 ch, turn.
Row 2 and every alternate row (right side of work): * 1 ridged tr (=yoh, insert hook horizontally behind the bar between first and 2nd sts of pre-

Basketweave stitch

Ridged treble no. 1

Ridged treble no. 2

vious row, bringing it forward through space between 2nd and 3rd sts of previous row and complete as for normal tr). * Rep from * to *, 2 ch, turn.

These 2 rows form the pattern and are repeated as required.

Ridged treble no. 2

Make foundation ch with an even no. of sts.

Row 1 (wrong side): Starting in 4th ch from hook, work in tr to end, 1 ch, turn.

Row 2: * 1 dc, 1 fwd tr (see instruction for Ridged treble no. 1). * Rep from * to *, 3 ch, turn.

Row 3: 1 tr into each st to end, 2 ch, turn.

Row 4: * 1 fwd tr, 1 dc. * Rep from * to *, 3 ch, turn.

Row 5: 1 tr into each st to end, 1 ch, turn.

Rows 2 to 5 form the pattern and are repeated as required.

Ridge stitch with chain

Ridge stitch with chain

Make foundation ch in multiples of 3.

Row 1: Starting in 2nd ch from hook, work in dc, ending with 1 ch, turn.

Row 2: 1 dc into each st, 1 ch, turn.

Row 3: * 2 dc, insert hook from back to front round 3rd dc of first row, yoh and draw loop through, elongating it to the same level as row on which you are working. Complete st as for normal dc. * Rep from * to * ending with 2 dc, 1 ch, turn.

Row 4: Work in dc, ending with 1 ch, turn.

Row 5: As Row 3, making sure that the picked up st is always directly over the previously elongated st, thus giving a vertical chain effect.

Rows 4 and 5 form the pattern and are repeated as required.

Fancy stitch no. 1

Fancy stitch no. 1

Make foundation ch with an even no. of sts.
Row 1: Starting in 2nd ch from hook, work in dc, ending with 1 ch, turn.
Row 2: * 1 dc, 1 htr. * Rep from * to * ending with 1 dc, 1 ch, turn.
Row 3: Work 1 dc into *both* loops of each st of previous row, ending with 1 ch, turn.
Rows 2 and 3 form the pattern and are repeated as required.

Fancy stitch no. 2

Make foundation ch in multiples of 4 plus 5 (3 ch at beg of row count as 1 tr).
Row 1: 1 tr into 4th ch from hook, 1 tr into each ch, ending with 3 ch, turn.
Row 2: 1 tr into each tr, 3 ch, turn.
Row 3: * 3 tr, ** yoh, insert hook round 4th tr of Row 2, draw yarn through and elongate loop to about 2.5 cm (1 in) **. Rep from ** to ** twice round same st, yoh and draw through first 4 loops on hook, yoh and draw through rem 2 loops. This makes one cluster. * Rep from * to * ending with 3 tr, 3 ch, turn.
Row 4: 1 tr into each tr and 1 tr into each cluster, 3 ch, turn.
Row 5: 1 tr, * 1 cluster, working round 2nd tr of Row 3, 3 tr. Rep from * ending with 1 cluster, 1 tr, 3 ch, turn.
Row 6: As Row 4.
Rows 3 to 6 form the pattern and are repeated as required.

Fancy stitch no. 2

Fancy stitch no. 3

Make foundation ch with any no. of sts.
Row 1: 1 tr into 4th ch from hook, 1 tr into each ch to end, 2 ch, turn.
Row 2: (right side) Miss first tr of previous row, * yoh, insert hook

Fancy stitch no. 3

under 2nd st of previous row (insert hook from front to back between first and 2nd sts, bringing it out between 2nd and 3rd sts from back to front); draw yarn through, elongating loop to about 1 cm (½ in), yoh and complete st as for tr *. Rep from * to *, 2 ch, turn.

Row 3: As Row 2 except that hook is inserted from the back to the front between first and 2nd tr of previous row, bringing it out towards the back between 2nd and 3rd sts.

Rows 2 and 3 form the pattern and are repeated as required.

Crazy double crochet

Make foundation ch in multiples of 3 plus 2.

Row 1: Starting in 2nd ch from hook * (1 dc, 1 ch, 1 dc), miss 2 ch *. Rep from * to * ending with (1 dc, 1 ch, 1 dc) into last ch, 1 ch, turn.

Row 2: * 1 dc, 1 ch, 1 dc into each 1-ch sp of previous row. * Rep from * to *, 1 ch, turn.

Row 2 forms the pattern and is repeated as required.

Ridged crazy double crochet

Make foundation ch with an odd no of sts.

Row 1: Starting in 2nd ch from hook, work in dc ending with 1 ch, turn.

Row 2: * 1 dc, 1 raised tr (= insert hook into st just worked, bringing it forward through 2nd dc of previous row). * Rep from * to * ending with 1 ch, turn.

These 2 rows form the pattern and are repeated as required.

Close bobble stitch

Make foundation ch in multiples of 3 plus 2.

Crazy double crochet

Ridged crazy double crochet

Row 1: 1 dc into 2nd ch from hook, *
3 ch, miss 2 ch, 1 dc. * Rep from * to
*, ending with 2 ch, turn.
Row 2: * 1 bobble in 3-ch sp (= **
yoh, insert hook under ch of previous
row and draw yarn through. Rep
from ** 4 times altogether. There
are now 9 loops on hook. Yoh, draw
yarn through 8 loops. 2 loops now on
hook. Yoh, draw yarn through both
loops), 3 ch, 1 dc into next dc of
previous row, 1 ch. * Rep from * to
* ending with 2 ch, turn.
Row 3: * 1 bobble into 3-ch sp, 3 ch,
1 dc into bobble of previous row, 1
ch. * Rep from * to * ending with 2
ch, turn.
Row 3 forms the pattern and is repeated as required.

Ridged basketweave

See Ridged alternating stitch for ex-
planation of forward treble (fwd tr)
and back treble (bk tr).
Make foundation ch in multiples of 6
plus 3.
Row 1: (wrong side) 1 tr into 4th ch
from hook, 1 tr into each ch to end, 2
ch, turn.
Row 2: * 3 fwd tr (counting 2 ch at
beg of row as first fwd tr), 2 bk tr. *
Rep from * to *, 2 ch, turn.
Row 3: 2 fwd tr (counting 2 ch at beg
of row as first fwd tr), * 3 bk tr, 3 fwd
tr *. Rep from * to * ending with 3
bk tr, 1 fwd tr, 2 ch, turn.
Row 4: 2 bk tr (counting 2 ch at beg
of row as first bk tr), * 3 fwd tr, 3 bk tr
*. Rep from * to * ending with 3 fwd
tr, 1 bk tr, 2 ch, turn.
Row 5: 3 bk tr (counting 2 ch at beg
of row as first bk tr), 3 fwd tr, 3 bk tr
*. Rep from * to * ending with 3 fwd
tr, 2 ch, turn.
Continue in this way, moving the rib
one st to the right on right side of
work and one st to the left on wrong
side.

Close bobble stitch

Ridged basketweave

Shell stitch

A shell is made by working 5 tr into 1 ch or 1 dc. Make foundation ch in multiples of 6 plus 2.
Row 1: 2 tr into 4th ch from hook, * miss 2 ch, 1 dc into next ch, miss 2 ch, shell into next ch *. Rep from * to * ending with miss 2 ch, 1 dc into last ch, 3 ch, turn.
Row 2: 2 tr into dc, * dc into centre of shell, shell into next dc *. Rep from * to * ending with 1 dc into top of t-ch, 3 ch, turn.
Row 2 forms the pattern and is repeated as required.

Shell stitch

V-stitch

Make foundation ch in multiples of 3. To make a V-motif: * yoh, insert hook into st, draw yarn through making a loose loop. Rep from * twice more into same st, yoh, draw yarn through all loops on hook *, 1 ch, rep from * to * into same st.
Row 1: Starting in 3rd ch from hook, * work 1 V-motif, miss 2 sts *. Rep from * to * ending with 1 V-motif, 2 ch, turn.
Row 2: Work a motif into each 1-ch sp of previous row, ending with 2 ch, turn.
Row 2 forms the pattern and is repeated as required.

V-stitch

Cornflower stitch

Make foundation ch in multiples of 4 plus 2.
Row 1: 2 tr into 4th ch from hook, miss 1 ch, * 1 dc, miss 1 ch, 3 tr into next ch, miss 1 ch *. Rep from * to * ending with 1 dc into last ch, 3 ch, turn.
Row 2: 2 tr into dc, * 1 dc between first and 2nd tr of 3-tr group of previous row, 3 tr into dc *. Rep from *

Cornflower stitch

to * ending with 1 dc into top of t-ch, 3 ch, turn.
Row 2 forms the pattern and is repeated as required.

Double flower stitch

Make foundation ch with an even no. of sts.
Row 1 and every alternate row (right side): Insert hook into 2nd ch from hook, yoh, draw yarn through, insert hook into next ch, yoh, draw yarn through, miss next st, insert hook into following st, yoh, draw yarn through, yoh, draw yarn through all loops on hook. (This completes one flower.) Work 1 ch fairly loosely. Insert hook into closing st at top of flower just worked, yoh, draw yarn through, insert hook into foundation ch just worked, yoh, draw yarn through, miss 1 ch, insert hook into next ch, yoh, draw yarn through, yoh and draw through all loops on hook, 1 loose ch. Rep from * ending with 1 dc, 2 ch, turn.

Double flower stitch

Row 2 and every alternate row: * Work 2 double dc into closing st of flower motif in previous row (a double dc is made by inserting hook into st, yoh, draw yarn through, yoh, draw yarn through one loop, yoh, draw through both loops). Rep from * ending with 1 dc, 2 ch, turn.
These 2 rows form the pattern and are repeated as required.

Daisy stitch

Make foundation ch in multiples of 8 plus 2.
Row 1: Starting in 2nd ch from hook, * 1 dc, miss 3 ch, (3 tr, 1 dtr, 3 tr) into next ch, miss 3 ch. Rep from * ending 1 dc into last ch, 3 ch, turn.
Row 2: Without drawing yarn through last loop (unfin tr), work 1

Daisy stitch

unfin tr into each of next 3 tr, yoh and draw through all 4 loops on hook, * 2 ch, 1 dc in dtr, 2 ch, 1 unfin tr into each of next 3 tr, 1 unfin dtr into dc, 1 unfin tr into each of next 3 tr, yoh and draw through all 8 loops on hook *. Rep from * to * ending with 2 ch, 1 dc into dtr, 2 ch, 1 unfin tr into each of next 3 tr, 1 unfin dtr into last dc, yoh and draw yarn through all 5 loops on hook, 3 ch, turn.

Row 3: 3 tr into st at base of t-ch, * 1 dc into next dc, (3 tr, 1 dtr, 3 tr) in closing st of unfin sts of previous row *. Rep from * to * ending with 1 dc into next dc, (3 tr, 1 dtr) into t-ch of previous row, 3 ch, turn.

Row 4: * 1 unfin tr into each of next 3 tr, 1 unfin dtr into next dc, 1 unfin tr into each of next 3 tr, yoh and draw through all 8 loops on hook, 2 ch, 1 dc into dtr, 2 ch *. Rep from * to * ending last dc of repeat into t-ch of previous row, 1 ch, turn.

Row 5: 1 dc into first dc, * (3 tr, 1 dtr, 3 tr) into closing st of unfin sts of previous row, 1 dc into dc *. Rep from * to * ending last dc of repeat into t-ch, 3 ch, turn.

Rows 2 to 5 form the pattern and are repeated as required.

Forget-me-not stitch

Forget-me-not stitch

Make foundation ch with an odd no. of sts.

Row 1 (wrong side): Starting in 2nd ch from hook, work in dc, ending with 2 ch, turn.

Row 2: Insert hook into first ch worked, yoh, draw yarn through, insert hook into first st, yoh, draw yarn through, insert hook into 2nd st, yoh, draw yarn through (4 loops on hook), yoh and draw yarn through all loops on hook (1 opening forget-me-not completed), 1 ch, * insert hook into st which closes opening flower, yoh, draw yarn through, insert hook into st

Crossed bar stitch

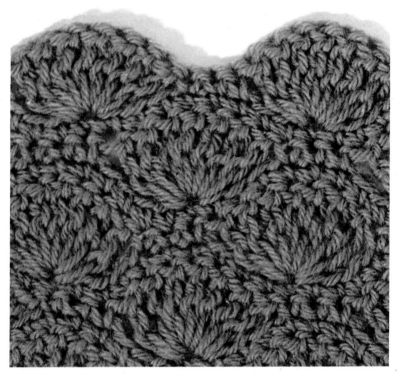

Fan stitch

already worked, yoh, draw yarn through, similarly work 1 half-finished dc into each of next 2 sts (5 loops on hook), yoh and draw yarn through all 5 loops (this completes one whole forget-me-not) *. Rep from * to *, 1 ch, turn.

Row 3: 2 dc into each st that closes forget-me-nots in previous row, ending with 2 ch, turn.

Rows 2 and 3 form the the pattern and are repeated as required.

Crossed bar stitch

Make loose foundation ch in multiples of 3 plus 1.

Row 1: 1 htr into 2nd ch from hook, 1 ch, * 1 unfin htr into same ch (= yoh, insert hook into next ch, yoh, draw yarn through), miss 1 ch, 1 unfin htr, yoh, draw yarn through all 5 loops on hook, 1 ch *. Rep from * to * ending with 1 htr, 2 ch, turn.

Row 2: 1 htr into 1-ch loop of previous row, 1 ch, * 1 unfin htr into same ch loop, 1 unfin htr into next ch loop, yoh, draw yarn through all 5 loops on hook, 1 ch. Rep from * ending with 1 htr, 2 ch, turn.

Row 2 forms the pattern and is repeated as required.

Fan stitch

Make foundation ch in multiples of 10 plus 4.

Row 1 (wrong side): Starting in 2nd

ch from hook, work in dc, ending with 1 ch, turn.
Row 2: * 3 dc, miss 3 dc, 7 dtr into next dc, miss 3 dc. * Rep from * to * ending with 3 dc, 1 ch, turn.
Row 3: Work in dc, ending with 3 ch, turn.
Row 4: Miss first dc of previous row, 4 dtr into next st, * miss 3 sts of previous row, 1 dc into each of next 3 sts, (over 3rd, 4th and 5th sts of the fan), miss 3 sts, 7 dtr into next st *. Rep from * to * ending with 5 dtr into second-to-last st, 1 ch, turn.
These 4 rows form the pattern and are repeated as required.

Alternating popcorn stitch

Alternating popcorn stitch

Make foundation ch in multiples of 3 plus 1.
Row 1: Starting in 2nd ch from hook, work in dc ending with 1 ch, turn.
Row 2: 1 dc, * 1 popcorn (= 5 unfinished tr into same st as dc just worked, yoh and draw yarn through all 6 loops on hook. 1 unfin tr = yoh, insert hook, yoh, draw yarn through, yoh, draw yarn through 2 loops only), 2 dc *. Rep from * to * ending with 1 popcorn, 1 ch, turn.
Row 3: Work in dc (1 dc into each popcorn and 1 dc into dc in between), ending with 1 ch, turn.
Row 4: 2 dc, * 1 popcorn, 2 dc *. Rep from * to * ending with 1 popcorn, 1 dc, 1 ch, turn.
These 4 rows form the pattern and are repeated as required.

Knotted double crochet

Knotted double crochet

Make foundation ch with any no. of sts.
Row 1: * 1 dc into 2nd ch from hook, insert hook into same ch, yoh, draw yarn through, insert hook into next ch, draw yarn through, yoh, draw

Antonella's stitch

Rib stitch

yarn through all 3 loops. Rep from ✳ ending with 2 ch, turn.

Row 2: 1 dc into first st, ✳ insert hook into same st as st just worked, yoh, draw yarn through, insert hook into next st, yoh, draw yarn through, yoh, draw yarn through all 3 loops on hook ✳. Rep from ✳ to ✳, 1 ch, turn.

Row 2 forms the pattern and is repeated as required.

Antonella's stitch

Make foundation ch with an odd no. of sts.

Row 1: Starting in 2nd ch from hook, work in dc, ending with 1 ch, turn.

Row 2: ✳ Insert hook into first st, yoh, draw yarn through, insert hook into next st, yoh, draw yarn through, yoh, draw yarn through 2 loops, yoh, keeping closing st loose draw yarn through rem 2 loops ✳. Rep from ✳ to ✳ ending with 1 ch, turn.

Row 3: 1 dc into front loop and 1 dc into back loop of each closing st of previous row, ending with 2 ch, turn.

Rows 2 and 3 form the pattern and are repeated as required.

Rib stitch

Make foundation ch in multiples of 6.

Row 1 (wrong side): Starting in 2nd ch from hook, ✳ 5 dc, 1 tr. ✳ Rep from ✳ to ✳ ending with 5 dc, 1 ch, turn.

Row 2 and every alternate row: ✳ 1 dc into each dc of previous row, 1 fwd tr (= yoh, insert hook from front

Column stitch

Plaited stitch

to back of horizontal bar of tr in previous row, bringing it forward to complete stitch as for normal tr). * Rep from * to * ending with 1 ch, turn. Row 3 and every alternate row: * 1 dc into each dc of previous row, 1 bk tr (= yoh, insert hook from back to front of horizontal bar of tr in previous row, taking it towards the back to complete as for normal tr). Rep from * to * ending with 1 ch, turn.
Rows 2 and 3 form the pattern and are repeated as required.

Column stitch

Make foundation ch with even no. of sts.
Row 1: Starting in 2nd ch from hook, * 1 double dc (insert hook into st, yoh, draw yarn through, yoh, draw yarn through 1 loop, yoh and draw through both loops), 1 ch, miss 1 ch *. Rep from * to * ending with an extra ch to form 2 ch, turn.
Row 2: Miss first double dc, * 1 double dc into double dc and 1 ch over 1-ch sp of previous row *. Rep from * to * ending with 1 double dc into first of t-ch, 2 ch, turn.
Row 2 forms the pattern and is repeated as required.

Plaited stitch

Make foundation ch in multiples of 4 plus 1.
Row 1: Starting in 4th ch from hook, 2 tr, * 1 ch, miss 1 ch, 3 tr *. Rep from * to *, 4 ch, turn.
Row 2: * Miss 3 tr, 1 tr into 1-ch loop, 1 tr into ch missed on Row 1, 1 tr into same 1-ch loop, 1 ch. * Rep from * to * ending with 1 tr into t-ch, 3 ch, turn.
Row 3: 1 tr into 2nd tr of 3-tr group of Row 1, 1 tr into 1-ch loop, * 1 ch, miss 3 tr, 1 tr into 1-ch loop, 1 tr into

Transverse stitch

2nd tr of 3-tr group, 1 tr into same 1-ch loop *. Rep from * to * ending with 1 tr into t-ch, 1 tr into centre of 3-tr group, 1 tr into t-ch, 4 ch, turn.
Row 4: * Miss 3 tr, 1 tr into 1-ch loop, 1 tr into 3-tr group of Row 2, 1 tr into same 1-ch loop, 1 ch. * Rep from * to * ending with 1 tr into t-ch, 3 ch, turn.
Rows 3 and 4 form the pattern and are repeated as required.

Transverse stitch

Make foundation ch in multiples of 3 plus 2.
(This stitch is worked from the *right side* throughout.)
Row 1: Starting in 2nd ch from hook, * 1 dc, 2 ch, miss 2 ch. * Rep from * to * ending with 1 dc.
Row 2: Without turning work, 1 ch, * 1 crab st into first dc (= insert hook between vertical bars of dc in previous row, yoh, draw yarn through, yoh, draw yarn through both loops), 2 ch *. Working from left to right, rep from * to * ending with 1 crab st.
Row 3: Without turning work, 2 ch, * 1 dc into 2-ch loop, 2 ch *. Rep from * to * ending with 1 dc into 2-ch loop, 1 ch, 1 dc into last crab st.

Vera's stitch

Row 4: Without turning work, 2 ch, miss first dc in previous row, * 1 crab st into next dc, 2 ch *. Rep from * to * ending with 1 crab st into last dc, 2 ch, turn.
Rows 1 to 4 form the pattern and are repeated as required.

Vera's stitch

Make foundation ch with an even no. of sts.
Row 1: Starting in 2nd ch from hook, work in dc, ending with 2 ch, turn.
Row 2: * Insert hook into first st,

Two-colour interweave

yoh, draw yarn through, insert hook into 2nd st, draw yarn through, yoh, draw yarn through 2 loops, yoh, draw yarn through rem 2 loops, keeping st very long. * Rep from * to * ending with 1 dc, 1 ch, turn.

Row 3: 1 dc into first st, 2 dc into each long st of previous row, ending with 2 ch, turn.

Rows 2 and 3 form the pattern and are repeated as required.

Two-colour interweave

Make foundation ch in first colour in multiples of 5.

Row 1 (first col): Starting in 5th ch from hook, * 1 shell (= 2 tr, 1 ch, 2 tr) into same st, 2 ch, miss 4 ch. Rep from * ending with 1 dc and 1 ch, turn.

Row 2 (2nd col): 1 dc, * 5 ch, 1 dc into 4-ch loop in foundation ch, keeping each shell in first col towards back of work *. Rep from * to * ending with 1 dc into 3rd of t-ch, 4 ch, turn.

Row 3 (2nd col): * 1 shell by inserting hook under l-ch st in top of first col shell and the 5-ch loop in 2nd col,

Two-colour trebles

2 ch. * Rep from * to * ending with 1 dc, 1 ch, turn.

Row 4 (first col): 1 dc, * 5 ch, 1 dc through 2-ch loop in first col (3 rows back), keeping shells of previous row towards back of work *. Rep from * to * ending with 1 dc into 3rd of t-ch, 1 ch, turn.

Rows 3 and 4 form the pattern and are repeated in colours, as required.

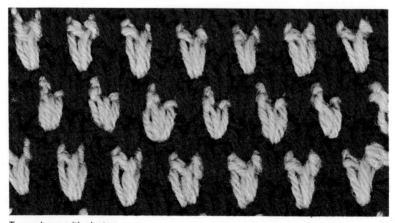

Two colours with clusters

Two-colour wavy chevrons

Two colours with clusters

Make foundation ch in first colour with an even no. of sts.

Row 1 (right side – first colour): Starting in 3rd ch from hook, work in htr, ending with 2 ch, turn.

Row 2: 1 fwd htr into each htr (= yoh, insert hook horizontally from front to back behind bar between first and 2nd sts of previous row, bringing it out in sp between 2nd and 3rd sts, draw yarn through, yoh, draw yarn through all 3 loops; the base ridge will form on right side of work), ending with 1 ch, turn.

Row 3 (2nd col): Work in dc, ending with 1 ch, turn.

Row 4: * 1 dc, 1 tr cluster into next st (** yoh, insert hook, draw yarn through, yoh, drawn yarn through 2 loops. ** Rep from ** to ** twice more, yoh, close by drawing yarn through all 4 loops), 1 ch. * Rep from * to * ending with 1 extra ch into first col.

Row 5 (first col): * 1 htr into dc and 1 htr into 1-ch sp of previous row. * Rep from * to * ending with 2 ch, turn.

Rows 2 to 5 form the pattern and are repeated as required.

Two-colour trebles

Make foundation ch in first col in multiples of 4 plus 2.

Row 1 (first col): Starting in 2nd ch from hook, work in dc, ending with 3 ch, turn.

53

Row 2: 1 tr into first dc, * miss 3 dc, 2 tr into next dc *. Rep from * to * ending with 2 tr into last dc, 2 ch, turn.

Row 3: * 2 tr into 2nd of the 3 missed dc of Row 1. * Rep from * to * ending with 1 tr into 2nd t-ch of Row 1, 2 ch, turn.

Row 4 (2nd col): 2 tr *between* each 2-tr of Row 2, ending with 2 ch, turn.

Row 5 (first col): 2 tr *between* each 2-tr of Row 3, ending with 2 ch, turn.

Row 6: As Row 5, working between each 2-tr of Row 4.

Row 7 (2nd col): 2 tr *between* each 2-tr of Row 5.

Rows 4 to 7 form the pattern and are repeated as required.

Two-colour wavy chevrons

Make foundation ch in first colour in multiples of 14 plus 1.

Row 1 (first col – wrong side): Starting in 2nd ch from hook work 1 group over each 14 sts (= 1 dc, 2 htr, 2 tr, 3 dtr, 2 tr, 2 htr, 2 dc) ending with 1 ch, turn.

Row 2: Starting in first st of previous row, dc, ending with 4 ch in 2nd col, turn.

Row 3 (2nd col): Starting on 2nd st, work 1 reverse group over each 14 sts (= 1 dtr, 2 tr, 2 htr, 3 dc, 2 htr, 2 tr, 2 dtr) ending with 1 ch, turn.

Row 4: As Row 2.

Rows 1-4 form the pattern and are repeated as required, changing col every 2 rows.

Star stitch

Make a foundation ch in first col in multiples of 6 plus 2.

Row 1: Starting in 2nd ch from hook, work in dc ending with 1 ch, turn.

Star stitch

Row 2: ✳ 1 dc, miss 2 dc, 7 tr into next dc, miss 2 dc. ✳ Rep from ✳ to ✳ ending with 2 dc, 3 ch in 2nd col (these 3 ch form first tr of first star in next row), turn.

Row 3 (2nd col): 1 unfin tr into each of next 3 tr of previous row (= yoh, insert hook, draw yarn through, yoh, draw yarn through 2 loops), yoh, draw yarn through all 4 loops. ✳ 4 ch, 1 dc into next tr (this is the central tr of 7 tr in previous row), 3 ch, 1 unfin tr into each of next 3 tr, 1 unfin tr into next dc, 1 unfin tr into each of next 3 tr, yoh, draw yarn through all 8 loops. ✳ Rep from ✳ to ✳ ending with a half star (1 unfin tr into each of last 3 tr and 1 unfin tr into last dc, yoh, draw yarn through all 5 loops), 3 ch, turn.

Row 4: 3 tr into st closing last 4-tr group of previous row, ✳ 1 dc into dc of previous row, 7 tr into st closing 7-tr group of previous row ✳. Rep from ✳ to ✳ ending with 4 tr into st closing last half star of previous row, 3 ch in first col, turn.

Row 5: 1 dc into first dc, 3 ch, ✳ 1 unfin tr into each of next 3 tr, 1 unfin tr into next dc, 1 unfin tr into each of next 3 tr, yoh, draw yarn through all 8 loops, 4 ch, 1 dc into next tr, 3 ch ✳. Rep from ✳ to ✳ ending with 1 dc into last tr, 1 ch, turn.

Row 6: 1 dc into first st, ✳ 7 tr into st closing 7-tr group of previous row, 1 dc into next dc ✳. Rep from ✳ to ✳ ending with 1 dc, 3 ch into 2nd col, turn.

Rows 3 to 6 form the pattern and are repeated as required, changing col every 2 rows.

Houndstooth check in two colours

Make foundation ch in main col with an odd no. of sts.

Row 1 (wrong side – first col): Starting in 2nd ch from hook, work in dc, ending with 1 ch, turn.

Row 2 (right side – 2nd col): ✳ 1 dc, 1

Houndstooth check in two colours

Houndstooth check in three colours

55

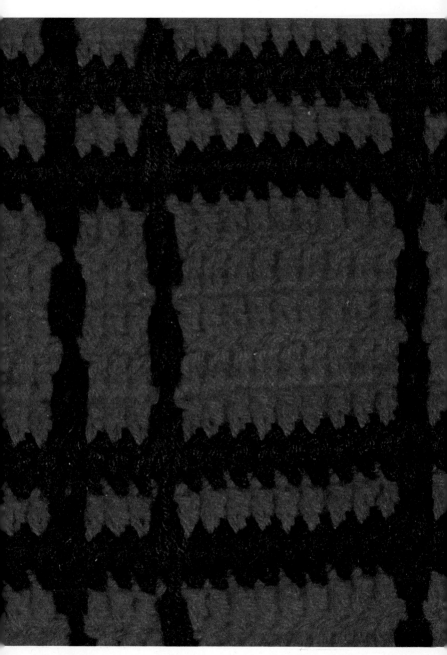

long dc (work dc by picking up st from foundation ch. * Rep from * to * ending with 1 ch, turn.

Row 3 (2nd col): Work in dc, ending with 1 ch, turn.

Row 4 (first col): * 1 long dc worked in st 2 rows below, 1 dc. * Rep. from * to * ending with 1 ch, turn.

Row 5 (first col): Work in dc, ending with 1 ch, turn.

Rows 2 to 4 form the pattern and are repeated as required, changing col every 2 rows.

Houndstooth check in three colours

Make a foundation ch in first col with an even no. of sts.

Row 1 (first col): Starting in 2nd ch from hook, work in dc, ending with 4 ch, turn.

Row 2 (first col): Miss first 2 dc, * 1 tr, 1 ch, miss 1 dc. Rep from * ending with 1 tr, 2 ch in 2nd col, turn.

Row 3 (2nd col): * 1 tr into st missed 2 rows below (= trb), 1 ch, miss 1 st of previous row. * Rep from * to * ending with 1 t-ch, 1 ch in 3rd col, turn.

Row 4 (3rd col): * Miss 1 st, 1 trb, 1 ch. * Rep from * to * ending with 1 trb and 1 t-ch in first col.

Rows 3 and 4 form the pattern and are repeated as required, changing col on each row.

Scottish tartan in two colours

Make foundation ch in first col in multiples of 14 plus 11 (last 11 sts include 1 t-ch and 2 ch to form first tr of 4 tr group in Row 1).

Row 1: Starting in 4th ch from hook work 3 tr, * 1 ch, miss 1 ch, 3 tr, 1 ch, miss 1 ch, 9 tr *. Rep from * to * ending with 1 ch, miss 1 ch, 4 tr., 3 ch, turn.

Scottish tartan in two colours

Row 2: Miss first tr of previous row, 1 tr into each tr and 1 ch over each ch, ending with 3 ch in next col, turn.

From this point, the sequence of cols is 1 row in 2nd col, 1 row in first col, 1 row in 2nd col, 5 rows in first col. When work has reached the required length, fasten off. Take a length of yarn in 2nd col, thread it into a needle and using double, work into the first line of vertical holes, weaving under and over each ch st. When one line has been woven, return, weaving through the same holes but going over instead of under, etc. When second line is finished, return through the same holes as in first line. Work through next line of holes in the same way using 2nd col and similarly across whole width of fabric.

Three-colour stitch no. 1

Make foundation ch in first col in multiples of 3 plus 1.
Row 1 (first col): Starting in 2nd ch from hook, work in dc, ending with 1 ch, turn.
Row 2 (right side): ∗ 2 dc, 1 tr ∗. Rep from ∗ to ∗ ending with 1 ch turn.
Row 3: As Row 1.
Row 4 (2nd col): ∗ 2 dc, 1 fwd tr (worked round vertical bar of tr in Row 2 ∗. Rep from ∗ to ∗ ending with 1 ch, turn.
Row 5: As Row 1.
Row 6 (3rd col): As Row 4.
Row 7: As Row 1.
Rows 2 to 7 form the pattern and are repeated as required.

Three-colour stitch no. 2

Make foundation ch in first col in multiples of 4 plus 5.
Row 1 (first col): Starting from 4th ch from hook work 2 tr, ∗ 1 ch, miss 1 ch, 3 tr ∗. Rep from ∗ to ∗ ending with 1 ch, turn.
Row 2 (2nd col): 2 ch, ∗ 3 tr into missed foundation ch, 1 ch ∗. Rep from ∗ to ∗ ending with 1 ch, 1 tr into t-ch, 1 ch, turn.

Three-colour stitch no. 1

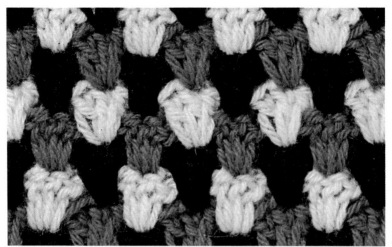

Three-colour stitch no. 2

Fancy Tunisian stitch

Row 3 (3rd col): ✳ 3 tr into 2nd tr of 3-tr group 2 rows back, 1 ch. ✳ Rep from ✳ to ✳ ending with 1 ch and 1 tr into t-ch of Row 1.
Row 3 forms the pattern and is repeated as required, changing col on each row.

This type of work tends to contract and should be worked loosely. When working stitches off hook, begin by drawing yarn through first loop on hook and then in pairs. Finish with a sl-st row beginning with 1 ch, a sl st into 2nd bar and into each following bar. Fasten off.

Fancy Tunisian stitch

Make foundation ch with an odd no of sts.
Row 1: Simple Tunisian st (insert hook through *one* top loop of basic ch instead of two). (A) and (B)=one row.
Row 2: (A) ✳ insert hook under two vertical bars (starting with first and 2nd bars), yoh, draw yarn through, insert hook into next horizontal st between two vertical bars, yoh, draw yarn through. Rep from ✳ to end.
(B) As Row 1 (B).
Row 2 forms the pattern and is repeated as required.
To finish, work 1 ch, then 1 sl st into each vertical bar of previous row.

Tunisian rib

Make foundation ch in multiples of 6 plus 4.
Row 1: (A) and (B) Work in simple Tunisian st.
Row 2: (A) ✳ 3 Tunisian sts, miss next sp between 2 vertical threads 3 ribbed Tunisian sts (= insert hook into sp *between* 2 vertical threads of st in previous row). Rep from ✳ to end.

Tunisian rib

Kairomanta stitch

(B) Work loops off in usual way.
Row 2 forms the pattern and is repeated as required.

Kairomanta stitch

Make foundation ch with an odd no. of sts.
Row 1: (A) and (B) Work in simple Tunisian st, 1 ch.
Row 2: (A) Miss first vertical bar, insert hook under next vertical bar, yoh, draw yarn through, * place hook behind yarn, yoh twice, insert hook under next 2 vertical bars in previous row, bring yarn forward under hook, yoh, draw yarn through 2 vertical bars *. Rep from * to * ending with yoh, insert hook under last vertical bar, draw through.
(B) 1 ch, * yoh, work 2 sts off. Rep from * to end, 1 ch.
Row 3: (A) Rep from * to * of Row 2.
(B) As Row 2 (B).
Rows 2 and 3 form the pattern and are repeated as required.

Tunisian check

Tunisian houndstooth stitch

Tunisian check

Make foundation ch in first col in multiples of 5.
Row 1: (first col) (A) and (B) Work in simple Tunisian st.
Row 2: (2nd col) (A) * Miss 2 sts, work 3 sts. Rep from * to end.
(B) * Work 3 sts off, 2 ch. Rep from * ending with 2 ch, join to edge of work.
Row 3: (2nd col) As Row 2, (A) & (B).
Row 4: (first col) (A) * 1 unfin tr into each of 2 vertical bars (in first col) missed in Row 2, work 3 sts. Rep from * to end.
(B) 1 ch, work sts off as usual.
Rows 2 to 4 form the pattern and are repeated as required.

Tunisian houndstooth stitch

Make foundation ch in first col with an odd no. of sts.
Row 1 (first col): (A) and (B) Work in simple Tunisian stitch.
Row 2 (2nd col): (A) * Work 1 st, miss 1 st. Rep from *, end with 1 st.
(First col): (B) 1 ch, * work 1 st off, 1 ch. Rep from * until 1 st remains.
Row 3 (first col): (A) * Miss 1 st, 1 unfin tr into single vertical bar of st (in first col) missed in Row 2 (A). Rep from * but leave last st unworked.
(2nd col): (B) 1 ch, * work 1 st off, 1 ch. Rep from * until 1 st remains.
Row 4 (2nd col): (A) * 1 unfin tr into single vertical bar of st (in same col) missed in Row 3(A), miss 1 st. Rep

Broken Tunisian stitch

from *, end with 1 unfin tr into last st.
(First col): (B) 1 ch, * work 1 st off, 1
ch. Rep from * until 1 st remains.
Rows 3 and 4 form the pattern and
are repeated as required.

Broken Tunisian stitch

Make foundation ch with an even no.
of sts.
Row 1: (A) and (B) Work in simple
Tunisian st.
Row 2: (A) Miss 1 st, * insert hook
under 1 vertical bar and 1 horizontal
thread to left of vertical bar, yoh, draw
yarn through. Rep from * to end.
(B) 1 ch, * work loops off in usual
way. Row 2 forms the pattern and is
repeated as required.

Loop stitch

Make foundation ch (any no. of sts).
Row 1: 1 dc into 2nd ch from hook, 1
dc into each ch to end, 1 ch, turn.
Row 2 (wrong side): Instead of passing over first finger, go underneath.
* Insert hook into next st, yoh (pick
yarn from over middle finger, form a
loop the size of first finger), draw
through, yoh, draw through both
loops, work a tight ch to lock st (this
does not count as a st), slip loop from
finger. * Rep from * to * ending
with 1 ch, turn.
Row 3: 1 dc in base of each loop st,
ending with 1 ch, turn.
Rows 2 and 3 form the pattern and
are repeated as required.

Loop stitch

OPENWORK STITCHES

Dress elegantly with crochet

Openwork stitches can create a light, decorative effect and even uncomplicated designs have a delicate air about them. With a little imagination, there is almost no limit to the ways in which these stitches can be utilized. Especially suitable for evening wear, summer sweaters, shawls, stoles and bed-jackets, the general effect is romantic and gracefully elegant. Baby clothes, too, lend themselves to this style of work. Manys kind of materials can be used, depending on the article to be worked, but the main requirement is that the twist should be firm, as in wool crêpe or manmade crêpe and crochet cottons. Fine mohair mixtures are also very effective although mohair by itself tends to be too soft and stretchy.

Simple shell stitch

Make foundation ch with an odd no. of sts. (T-ch counts as first tr.)
Row 1: (1 tr, 1 ch, 1 tr) into 3rd ch from hook, ✻ miss 1 ch, (1 tr, 1 ch, 1 tr) into next ch ✻. Rep from ✻ to ✻ ending with 3 ch, turn.
Row 2: ✻ (1 tr, 1 ch, 1 tr) into next 1-ch sp. ✻ Rep from ✻ to ✻ ending with 3 ch, turn.
Row 2 forms the pattern and is repeated as required.

Simple Shell stitch

Shell stitch no. 1

Make foundation ch with an odd no. of sts.
Row 1: 1 htr into 3rd ch from hook, ✻ miss 1 ch, 2 htr into next ch ✻. Rep from ✻ to ✻ ending with 3 ch, turn.
Row 2: 1 htr between first 2 htr in previous row, ✻ 2 htr between each 2-htr group ✻. Rep from ✻ to ✻ ending with 2 htr between last htr and t-ch of previous row, 3 ch, turn.
Row 2 forms the pattern and is repeated as required.

Shell stitch no. 1

Shell stitch no. 2

Make a very loose foundation ch in multiples of 12 plus 6.
Row 1: 1 tr into 3rd ch from hook, * 2 ch, miss 2 ch, 1 tr into next ch *. Rep from * to * ending with 3 ch, turn.
Row 2: (1 tr, 2 ch, 1 tr into first 2-ch loop, * 2 ch, miss 1 2-ch loop, 5 tr into next 2-ch loop, 2 ch, miss 1 ch loop, (1 tr, 2 ch, 1 tr) into next ch loop *. Rep from * to * ending with 3 ch, turn.
Row 3: * 5 tr into 2-ch loop between 2-tr of previous row, 2 ch, (1 tr, 2 ch, 1 tr) into 3rd tr of 5-tr group of previous row, 2 ch *. Rep from * to * ending with 5 tr into last 2-ch loop, 3 ch, turn.
Row 4: * (1 tr, 2 ch, 1 tr) into 3rd tr of 5-tr group, 2 ch, 5 tr into 2-ch loop, 2 ch *. Rep from * to * ending with (1 tr, 2 ch, 1 tr) into last 5-tr group, 3 ch, turn.
Rows 3 and 4 form the pattern and are repeated as required.

Shell stitch no. 2

Shell stitch no. 3

Make foundation ch in multiples of 7 plus 4 (t-ch counts as first tr).
Row 1: 1 tr into 3rd ch from hook, 1 tr, * miss 2 ch, (3 tr, 1 ch, 3 tr) into next ch, miss 2 ch, 2 tr *. Rep from * to * ending with 3 ch, turn.
Row 2: * 2 tr into 2-tr of previous row, (3 tr, 1 ch, 3 tr) into 1-ch sp in centre of shell. * Rep from * to * ending with 3 ch, turn.
Row 2 forms the pattern and is repeated as required.

Shell stitch no. 3

Shell stitch no. 4

Make foundation ch in multiples of 3 plus 1.
Row 1: Starting in 2nd ch from hook, work in dc, ending with 3 ch, turn.

Shell stitch no. 4

Row 2: * Miss 2 dc, (2 tr, 1 dc) into next dc. Rep from * ending with (1 tr, 1 dc) into last st, 3 ch, turn.
Row 3 (1 tr, 1 dc) into first tr, * miss next tr, (2 tr, 1 dc) into next tr *. Rep from * to * ending with (1 tr, 1 dc) into last st, 3 ch, turn.
Row 3 forms the pattern and is repeated as required.

Alternating shell stitch

Make foundation ch in multiples of 5.
Row 1: 2 tr into 3rd ch from hook, miss 1 ch, 1 dc, * 3 ch, miss 2 ch, 4 tr into next ch, miss 1 ch, 1 dc *. Rep

from * to * ending with 3 ch, turn.
Row 2: 2 tr into last dc worked in previous row, 1 dc into ch loop (to left of shell in previous row), * 3 ch, 4 tr into dc, 1 dc into ch loop. Rep from * ending with 1 dc into t-ch of previous row, 3 ch, turn.
Row 2 forms the pattern and is repeated as required.

Diagonal treble blocks

Make foundation ch in multiples of 12 plus 2. (From Rows 2 to 6, the t-ch of previous row forms the first tr of each row.)

Alternating shell stitch

Diagonal treble blocks

Row 1: 1 tr into 8th ch from hook, * 2 ch, miss 2 ch, 1 tr *. Rep from * to * ending with 3 ch, turn.

Row 2: * 2 tr into first 2-ch loop, 1 tr into 2nd tr, 2 tr into next 2-ch loop, 1 tr into 3rd tr, 2 tr into next 2-ch loop, 1 tr into 4th tr (10-tr group), 2 ch. * Cont with 1 tr into next tr and rep from * to * ending with 2 tr into 7-ch loop, 1 tr into 3rd ch, 3 ch, turn.

Row 3: 1 tr into 2nd to 6th tr of previous row, 2 ch, miss 2 tr. Cont with 1 tr into 10th tr of same group, working blocks of 10 tr with 2 ch between and ending with 2 ch, 1 tr into t-ch, 3 ch, turn.

Row 4: 2 tr into first 2-ch loop, 1 tr into tr, * 2 ch, miss 2 tr, 7 tr, 2 tr into 2-ch loop, 1 tr into tr *. Rep from * to * ending with 2 ch, miss 2 tr, 3 tr, 1 tr into t-ch, 5 ch, turn.

Row 5: 1 tr into 4th tr, * 2 tr into 2-ch loop, 7 tr, 2 ch, miss 2 tr, 1 tr into tr *. Rep from * to * ending with 2 tr into 2-ch loop, 3 tr, 1 tr into ch, 3 ch, turn.

Row 6: Miss first tr, * 6 tr, 2 tr into 2-ch loop, 1 tr into tr, 2 ch, miss 2 tr, 1 tr into tr *. Rep from * to * ending with 6 tr, 2 tr into 5-ch loop, 1 tr into 3rd ch, 3 ch, turn.

Rows 3 to 6 form the pattern and are repeated as required.

Treble pyramid stitch

Make foundation ch in multiples of 14 plus 1. (On Rows 2 to 4 t-ch of previous row counts as first tr of next row; last tr of row is always worked in t-ch).

Row 1: Starting in 4th ch from hook, 3 tr, * (1 ch, miss 1 ch, 1 tr) twice, 1 ch, miss 1 ch, 9 tr *. Rep from * to * ending with 4 tr, 3 ch, turn.

Row 2: 4 tr, * 1 tr into 1-ch loop, (1 ch, miss 1 tr, 1 tr into 1-ch loop) twice, 9 tr *. Rep from * to * ending with 4 tr, 3 ch, turn.

Row 3: 5 tr, * 1 tr into 1-ch loop, 1 ch, miss 1 tr, 1 tr into 2nd 1-ch loop, 3 tr, (1 ch, miss 1 tr, 1 tr) 3 times, 2 tr *. Rep from * to * ending with 5 tr, 3 ch, turn.

Row 4: 6 tr, * 1 tr into 1-ch loop, 4 tr, (1 tr into 1-ch loop, 1 ch, miss 1 tr) twice, 1 tr into 1-ch loop, 4 tr *. Rep from * to * ending with 6 tr, 3 ch, turn.

Row 5: 4 tr, * (1 ch, miss 1 tr, 1 tr) 3 times, 2 tr, 1 tr into 1-ch loop, 1 ch, miss 1 tr, 1 tr into 1-ch loop, 3 tr *. Rep from * to * ending with 4 tr, 3 ch, turn.

Row 6: 4 tr, * (1 tr into 1-ch loop, 1 ch, miss 1 tr) twice, 1 tr into 1-ch loop, 4 tr, 1 tr into 1-ch loop, 4 tr *.

Treble pyramid stitch

Rep from * to * ending with 3 ch, turn.
Rows 3 to 6 form the pattern and are repeated as required.

Four-leaf clover stitch

Make foundation ch in multiples of 8 plus 7. (See note on Treble pyramid stitch).
Row 1: 1 tr into 4th ch from hook, 3 tr, * (1 ch, miss 1 ch, 1 tr into next ch) twice, 4 tr *. Rep from * to * ending with 4 tr, 3 ch, turn.
Row 2: * 5 tr, 1 ch, 1 tr into tr, 1 ch. * Rep from * to * ending with 5 tr, 4 ch, turn.
Row 3: Miss 2 tr, 1 tr, 1 ch, miss 1 tr, 1 tr, * (1 tr into 1-ch loop, 1 tr) twice, (1 ch, miss 1 tr, 1 tr into next tr) twice *. Rep from * to * ending with 4 ch, turn.
Row 4: Miss 1 tr and 1 ch, 1 tr into tr, 1 ch, * 5 tr, 1 ch, 1 tr into tr, 1 ch *. Rep from * to * ending with 1 tr into 3rd t-ch, 3 ch, turn.
Rows 1 to 4 form the pattern and are repeated as required.

Block and cluster stitch

Make foundation ch in multiples of 9 plus 1. (See note on Treble pyramid stitch.)
Row 1: 1 tr into 4th ch from hook, 1 tr, * 2 ch, miss 2 ch, 7 tr *. Rep from * to * ending with 2 ch, miss 2 ch, 3 tr, 3 ch, turn.
Row 2: 3 tr, * 2 ch, 2 tr, 1 ch, miss 1 st, make a cluster in 4th tr (yoh, insert hook, draw yarn through) six times in same st, yoh, draw yarn through all 13 loops on hook), 1 ch, miss 1 st, 2 tr *. Rep from * to * ending with 3 tr, 3 ch, turn.
Row 3: 3 tr, * 2 ch, 2 tr, 1 tr into 1-ch loop, 1 tr into cluster, 1 tr into 1-ch loop, 2 tr *. Rep from * to * ending with 2 ch, 3 tr, 4 ch, turn.
Row 4: Miss 2 sts, 1 tr into tr, * 2 ch, (1 tr, 1 ch, miss 1 st) 3 times, 1 tr *. Rep from * to * ending with 2 ch, 1 tr, 1 ch, miss 1 st, 1 tr into last st, 3 ch, turn.
Rows 1 to 4 form the pattern and are repeated as required.

Four-leaf clover stitch

Block and cluster stitch

Open flower stitch

Make foundation ch in multiples of 10 plus 7.
Row 1: Starting in 6th ch from hook, * 1 tr, 2 ch, miss 2 ch *. Rep from * to * ending with 1 tr into last ch, 5 ch, turn.
Row 2: Miss first tr, * 1 tr, 2 ch and 2 unfin dtr into next tr, miss 1 tr, 2 unfin dtr into next tr, yoh, draw yarn through all loops on hook, 2 ch, 1 tr into same st as last 2 dtr, 2 ch *. Rep from * to * ending with 1 tr into 4th t-ch, 1 ch, turn.
Row 3: * 1 dc, 2 ch, miss 2 ch, * Rep from * to * ending with 1 dc into 3rd ch, 5 ch, turn.
Row 4: Miss first dc, 1 tr into next dc, * (2 unfin dtr and then finished tog, 3 ch, 2 unfin dtr and then finished tog) into centre of 4-dtr group, 1 tr into next dc, 2 ch, 1 tr into next dc *. Rep from * to * ending with 5 ch, turn.
Rows 1 to 4 form the pattern and are repeated as required.

Open flower stitch

Netting stitch

Make foundation ch in multiples of 12 plus 5. (On Rows 2 to 6 t-ch of previous row forms first tr of next row.)

Row 1: Starting in 3rd ch from hook, * 1 tr, 1 ch, miss 1 ch, 1 tr, 3 ch, miss 1 ch, (1 dtr, miss 1 ch) 3 times, 1 dtr, 3 ch, miss 1 ch *. Rep from * to * ending with 1 tr, 1 ch, miss 1 ch, 1 tr, 3 ch, turn.

Row 2: * 1 tr into first tr, 1 ch, 1 tr into 2nd tr, 3 ch, 4 dc into 4 dtr, 3 ch. * Rep from * to * ending with 1 tr, 1 ch, 1 tr, 3 ch, turn.

Row 3: * 1 tr into first tr, 1 ch, 1 tr into 2nd tr, 3 ch, 4 dc into 4 dc, 3 ch. * Rep from * to * ending with 1 tr, 1 ch, 1 tr, 3 ch, turn.

Row 4: * 1 tr, 1 ch, 1 tr, 1 ch, 4 dtr separated by 1 ch into the 4 dc, 1 ch. Rep from * ending with 1 tr, 1 ch, 1 tr, 3 ch, turn.

Row 5: * 1 tr, 1 ch, 1 tr, 1 ch, 4 tr separated by 1 ch into the 4 dtr, 1 ch. * Rep from * to * ending with 1 tr, 1 ch, 1 tr, 3 ch, turn.

Row 6: * 1 tr, 1 ch, 1 tr, 3 ch, 4 dtr into the 4 tr, 3 ch. * Rep from * to * ending with 1 tr, 1 ch, 1 tr, 3 ch, turn.
Rows 2 to 6 form the pattern and are repeated as required.

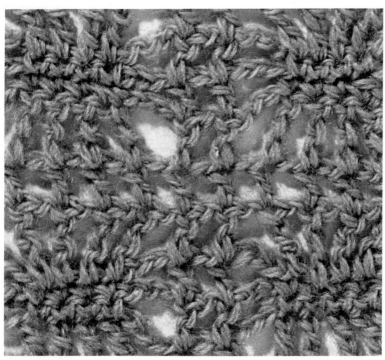

Netting stitch

Mesh stitch with picots

Make foundation ch in multiples of 3.
T-ch of row counts as 1 tr, 1-ch loop
on foll row.)
Row 1: Starting in 3rd ch from hook,
1 tr, 1 ch, miss 2 sts, * 1 tr, 1 picot (=
3 ch, 1 htr into first ch) and 1 tr worked into same st, 1 ch, miss 2 sts *.
Rep from * to * ending with 1 tr, 3
ch, turn.
Row 2: * (1 tr, 1 picot, 1 tr, 1 ch) into
1-ch loop. * Rep from * to * ending
with 1 tr into t-ch, 3 ch, turn.
Row 2 forms the pattern and is repeated as required.

Irish loop lace stitch

Make foundation ch in multiples of 7
plus 1.
Row 1: 1 dc into 2nd ch from hook, 5
ch, * miss 5 ch, 1 dc, 4 ch, 1 dc, 5 ch
*. Rep from * to * ending with 1 dc,
4 ch, 1 dc into last ch, 7 ch, turn.
Row 2: * (1 dc, 4 ch, 1 dc) into 5-ch
loop, 5 ch. * Rep from * to * ending
with 3 ch, 1 tr into last dc, 5 ch, turn.
Row 3: * (1 dc, 4 ch, 1 dc) into 5-ch
loop, 5 ch *. Rep from * to * ending
with (1 dc, 4 ch) into last 5-ch loop, 1
dc into 3rd ch, 7 ch, turn.
Rows 2 and 3 form the pattern and
are repeated as required.

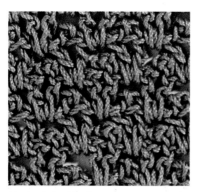

Mesh stitch with picots

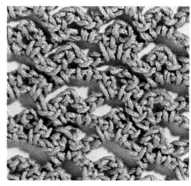

Irish loop lace stitch

Broken mesh stitch

Make foundation ch in multiples of 9 plus 5.

Row 1: 1 dc into 2nd ch from hook, ✻ 3 ch, miss 2 ch, 1 dc, 2 ch, miss 2 ch, 1 tr, 2 ch, miss 2 ch, 1 dc ✻. Rep from ✻ to ✻ ending with 3 ch, miss 2 ch, 1 dc, 3 ch, turn.

Row 2: ✻ 3 tr into 3-ch loop between first 2 dc, 2 ch, 1 dc into tr, 2 ch ✻. Rep from ✻ to ✻ ending with 3 tr into last 3-ch loop, 1 tr into dc, 3 ch, turn.

Row 3: ✻ 1 tr into 2nd of the 3-tr group, 2 ch, 1 dc into 2-ch loop, 3 ch, 1 dc into next 2-ch loop, 2 ch ✻. Rep from ✻ to ✻ ending with 1 tr into 2nd of last 3-tr group, 1 tr into t-ch, 1 ch, turn.

Row 4: 1 dc into first tr, 2 ch, 1 dc into next tr, 2 ch, ✻ 3 tr into 3-ch loop, 2 ch, 1 dc into tr, 2 ch ✻. Rep from ✻ to ✻ ending with 1 dc into t-ch, 1 ch, turn.

Row 5: 1 dc into first dc, ✻ 3 ch, miss 1 dc, 1 dc into 2-ch loop, 3 ch, 1 dc into next 2-ch loop ✻. Rep from ✻ to ✻ ending with 3 ch, 1 dc into last dc, 3 ch, turn.

Rows 2 to 5 form the pattern and are repeated as required.

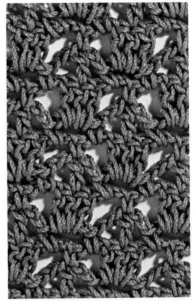

Broken mesh stitch

Double mesh stitch no. 1

Make foundation ch in multiples of 4 plus 2.

Row 1: Starting in 2nd ch from hook, ✻ 1 dc, 4 ch, miss 3 ch ✻. Rep from ✻ to ✻ ending with 1 dc into last ch, 1 ch, turn.

Row 2: ✻ 1 dc by inserting hook into same foundation ch as the dc in Row 1, 4 ch, miss 4 ch ✻. Rep from ✻ to ✻ ending with 1 dc into last ch, 2 ch, turn.

Row 3: 1 dc, 2 ch, ✻ 1 dc into ch loops of Rows 1 and 2, 4 ch ✻. Rep from ✻ to ✻ ending with 1 dc into both ch loops, 2 ch, 1 dc into dc, 1 ch, turn.

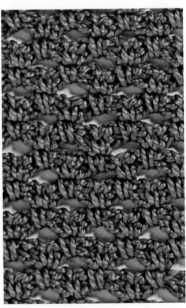

Double mesh stitch no. 1

Row 4: 1 dc, 2 ch, * 1 dc into dc of previous row, 4 ch *. Rep from * to * ending with 1 dc, 2 ch, 1 dc, 1 ch, turn.
Row 5: 1 dc into first dc, * 4 ch, miss 1 dc, 1 dc into ch loops of both Rows 3 and 4 *. Rep from * to * ending with 4 ch, 1 dc into dc, 1 ch, turn.
Rows 2 to 5 form the pattern and are repeated as required.

Double mesh stitch no. 2

Make foundation ch in multiples of 8 plus 2.
Row 1: Starting in 2nd ch from hook, * 1 dc, 3 ch, miss 3 ch *. Rep from * to * ending with 1 dc, 1 ch, turn.
Row 2: 1 dc into first dc, 1 dc into 3-ch loop, 4 ch, miss 1 dc, 1 dc into 3-ch loop, 1 dc into dc, 1 dc into next 3-ch loop *. Rep from * to * ending with 4 ch, 1 dc into 3-ch loop, 1 dc into dc, 1 ch turn.
Row 3: 1 dc into first dc, 3 ch, * 1 dc into 4-ch loop, 3 ch, 1 dc into 2nd of 3-dc group, 3 ch *. Rep from * to * ending with 1 dc into 4-ch loop, 3 ch, 1 dc into last dc, 4 ch, turn.
Row 4: * 1 dc into 3-ch loop, 1 dc into dc, 1 dc into next 3-ch loop, 4 ch. * Rep from * to * ending with 1 dc into 3-ch loop, 1 dc into dc, 1 dc into last 3-ch loop, 2 ch, 1 tr into last dc, 1 ch, turn.
Row 5: 1 dc into tr, * 3 ch, 1 dc into 2nd of 3-dc group, 3 ch, 1 dc into 4-ch loop *. Rep from * to * ending with 3 ch, 1 dc into 2nd of 3-dc group, 3 ch, 1 dc into turning ch, 1 ch, turn.
Rows 2 to 5 form the pattern and are repeated as required.

Hazelnuts on mesh

Make foundation ch in multiples of 8 plus 2.
Row 1: Starting in 4th ch from hook, * 1 htr, 1 ch, miss 1 ch *. Rep from * to * ending with 1 htr, 3 ch, turn.

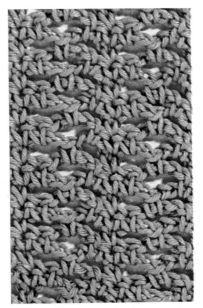

Double mesh stitch no. 2

Hazelnuts on mesh

Row 2: Miss last htr worked, * (1 htr into next htr, 1 ch) 3 times, into next htr work 1 hazelnut (= *** yoh, insert hook, draw yarn through to make a fairly long loop *** 3 times, yoh, draw yarn through all 7 loops on hook), 1 ch *. Rep from * to * ending with (1 htr into next htr, 1 ch) 3 times, 1 htr into 2nd of the 4 ch at start of previous row, 3 ch turn.

Row 3: Miss the last htr worked, * 1 htr into next htr, 1 ch *. Rep from * to * working over each hazelnut as though it were a htr and ending with 1 htr into 2nd of 3 t-ch, 3 ch, turn.

Row 4: Miss last htr worked, 1 htr into next htr, * 1 ch, 1 hazelnut into next htr, (1 ch, 1 htr into next htr) 3 times *. Rep from * to * ending with 1 ch, 1 hazelnut, 1 ch, 1 htr into next htr, 1 ch, 1 htr into 2nd of the 3 t-ch, 3 ch, turn.

Row 5: As Row 3.

Rows 2 to 5 form the pattern and are repeated as required.

Open lacy stitch

Make foundation ch in multiples of 10 plus 3.

Row 1: Miss first 6 ch from hook, * 1 unfin dtr into each of next 2 ch, yoh, draw yarn through all 3 loops on hook, 7 ch, miss 2 ch, 1 dc into next ch, miss 5 ch *. Rep from * to * ending with 2 unfin dtr finished together, 7 ch, miss 1 ch, 1 dc into last ch, 5 ch, turn.

Row 2: * (5 unfin dtr, yoh, draw yarn through all 6 loops on hook, 7 ch, 1 dc) into 7-ch loop, 1 ch, (2 unfin dtr finished together, 7 ch, 1 dc) into 1-ch loop, 1 ch. * Rep from * to * ending with 1 dc into t-ch, 5 ch, turn.

Row 3: * (2 unfin dtr finished together, 7 ch, 1 dc) into 7-ch loop, 1 ch *. Rep from * to * ending with 1 dc into t-ch, 5 ch, turn.

Row 4: * (5 unfin dtr finished together, 7 ch, 1 dc) into first 7-ch loop, 1 ch, (2 unfin dtr finished together, 7 ch, 1 dc) into next 7-ch loop, 1 ch. * Rep from * to * ending with 1 dc into t-ch, 5-ch, turn.

Rows 3 and 4 form the pattern and are repeated as required.

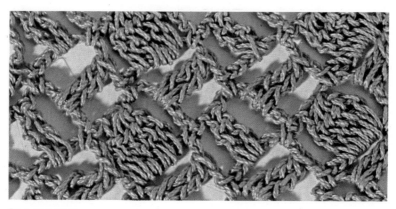

Open lacy stitch

Arabesque stitch

Make foundation ch in multiples of 4 plus 3.

Row 1: Starting in 3rd ch from hook, * work (1 tr, 1 ch, 1 tr into first st), miss 1 ch, 1 dc, miss 1 ch *. Rep from * to * ending with (1 tr, 1 ch, 1 tr) into last st, 2 ch turn.

Row 2: * 1 dc into 1-ch loop, (1 tr, 1 ch, 1 tr) into dc. * Rep from * to * ending with 2 ch, turn.

Row 2 forms the pattern and is repeated as required.

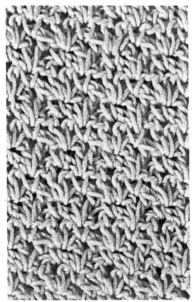

Arabesque stitch

Ridged double crochet with openwork

Make foundation ch in multiples of 3 plus 2.

Row 1: Starting in 2nd ch from hook, work in dc, ending with 1 ch, turn.

Row 2: 1 dc into each st, working through back loops only, ending with 1 ch, turn.

Rows 3, 4 and 5: As Row 2.

Row 6: 1 dc into first st (inserting hook into *both* threads of st), * 5 ch, miss 2 sts, 1 dc into next st *. Rep from * to *, 1 ch, turn.

Row 7: 3 dc into each 5-ch loop ending with 1 dc into t-ch, 1 ch, turn.

Rows 2 to 7 form the pattern and are repeated as required.

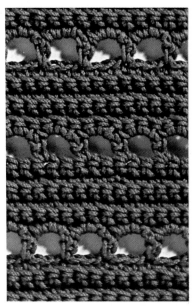

Ridged double crochet with openwork

Graziella's stitch

Make foundation ch in multiples of 6 plus 5.
Row 1: 2 tr into 4th ch from hook, * 2 ch, miss 2 ch, 2 tr into next ch *. Rep from * to * ending with 1 tr into last st, 3 ch, turn.
Row 2: * (1 dc, 2 ch) into 2-ch loop. * Rep from * to * ending with 1 dc into t-ch, 3 ch, turn.
Row 3: * 1 dc into first 2-ch loop of previous row, 6 tr into next 2-ch loop. * Rep from * to * ending with 1 dc into t-ch, 3 ch, turn.
Row 4: 2 tr into first dc, * 2 ch, 1 tr into 3rd tr, 1 tr into 4th tr of 6-tr group of previous row, 2 ch, 2 tr into dc *. Rep from * to * ending with 1 tr into t-ch, 3 ch, turn.
Rows 2 to 4 form the pattern and are repeated as required.

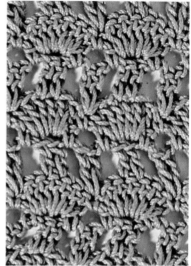

Graziella's stitch

Lella's stitch

Make foundation ch with an odd no. of sts.
Row 1: Starting in 2nd ch from hook, work in dc, ending with 2 ch, turn.
Row 2: 1 tr into first st, * 2 crossed tr (= miss 1 st, 1 tr into next st, 1 tr into missed st) *. Rep from * to * ending with 1 tr into last st, 1 ch, turn.
Row 3: 1 dc into each st, ending with 2 ch, turn.
Rows 2 and 3 form the pattern and are repeated as required.

Lella's stitch

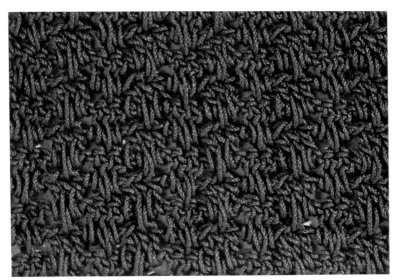

Martha's stitch

Martha's stitch

Row 1: 2 tr into 4th ch from hook, ✳ 3 ch, miss 3 ch, 3 tr into next ch ✳. Rep from ✳ to ✳ ending with 3 ch, turn.

Row 2: ✳ 1 tr into 3-ch loop of previous row, 1 tr into 2nd of ch missed in previous row, 1 tr into same loop as first tr, 3 ch. ✳ Rep from ✳ to ✳ ending with 1 sl st into t-ch, 3 ch, turn.

Row 3: 1 tr into 2nd of 3-tr group 2 rows below, 1 tr into 3-ch loop, ✳ 3 ch, 1 tr into next 3-ch loop, 1 tr into 2nd of 3-tr group 2 rows below, 1 tr into same 3-ch loop ✳. Rep from ✳ to ✳ ending with 3 ch, turn.

Row 4: ✳ 1 tr into 3-ch loop of previous row, 1 tr into 2nd of 3-tr group 2 rows below, 1 tr into same 3-ch loop, 3 ch ✳. Rep from ✳ to ✳ ending with 1 sl st into t-ch, 3 ch, turn.

Rows 3 and 4 form the pattern and are repeated as required.

Smocking stitch

Make foundation ch in multiples of 4 plus 3.
Row 1: Starting in 3rd ch from hook, * (1 tr, 2 ch, 1 tr) into ch (= V motif), miss 3 ch *. Rep from * to * ending with (1 tr, 2 ch, 1 tr) into last ch, 2 ch, turn.
Row 2: * 3 htr into 2-ch loop, 1 ch. * Rep from * to * ending with 1 htr into t-ch, 2 ch, turn.
Row 3: 1 tr into space before first V-motif 2 rows below, * miss 3 htr, (1 tr, 2 ch, 1 tr) into sp between next 2 V-motifs 2 rows below *. Rep from * to * ending with, miss 3 htr, 1 1 tr into t-ch 2 rows below, 1 ch, turn.
Row 4: 1 htr into first st, 1 ch, * 3 htr into 2-ch loop, 1 ch. * Rep from * to * ending with 1 htr into t-ch, 2 ch, turn.
Row 5: (1 tr, 2 ch, 1 tr) into first st, * miss 3 htr, (1 tr, 2 ch, 1 tr) into sp between next 2 V-motifs 2 rows below *. Rep from * to * ending with (1 tr, 2 ch, 1 tr) into t-ch, 2 ch, turn.
Rows 2 to 5 form the pattern and are repeated as required.

Smocking stitch

Ribbon insertion stitch

Make foundation ch in multiples of 2.
Row 1: Starting in 2nd ch from hook, work in dc, 1 ch, turn.
Rows 2 and 3: 1 dc into each st to end, 1 ch, turn.
Row 4: 3 ch, miss 2 st, * 1 tr, 1 ch, miss 1 st *. Rep from * to * ending with 1 tr, 1 ch, turn.
Row 5: * 1 dc into tr, 1 dc into ch. * Rep from * to * ending with 1 dc into 2nd t-ch, 1 ch, turn.
Rows 2 to 5 form the pattern and are repeated as required.

Ribbon insertion stitch

Sayonara stitch

Make foundation ch in multiples of 6 plus 2.
Row 1: * 1 dc into 2nd ch from hook, 2 ch, miss 2 ch, (1 tr, 1 ch, 1 tr) into next ch, 2 ch, miss 2 ch. * rep from * to * ending with 1 dc into last ch, 3 ch, turn.
Row 2: * (1 dc, 1 ch) 4 times into 1-ch sp between 2-tr of previous row, 2 ch. * Rep from * to * ending with 1 tr into last st, 3 ch, turn.
Row 3: * 1 tr into first 1-ch sp, 2 ch, 1 tr into 3rd 1-ch sp, 2 ch, 1 dc into 3-ch loop, 2 ch. * Rep from * to * ending with 1 tr into last dc, 3 ch, turn.
Rows 2 and 3 form the pattern and are repeated as required.

Sayonara stitch

Sara's stitch

Make foundation ch in multiples of 6 plus 5.
Row 1: Starting in 5th ch from hook, 4 dtr all into same ch, * 2 ch, miss 2 ch, 1 tr into 3rd ch, 2 ch, miss 2 ch, 4 dtr all into same ch. * Rep from * to * ending with 2 ch, turn.
Row 2: 1 dc between 2nd and 3rd dtr, 2 ch, * 4 dtr into tr, 2 ch, 1 dc between 2nd and 3rd dtr, 2 ch *. Rep from * to * ending with 1 dc between 2nd and 3rd dtr, 1 ch, 1 dc into t-ch, 4 ch, turn.
Row 3: 4 dtr into dc, * 2 ch, 1 dc between 2nd and 3rd dtr, 2 ch, 4 dtr into dc *. Rep from * to * ending with 2 ch, turn.
Rows 2 and 3 form the pattern and are repeated as required.

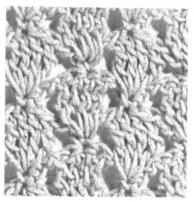

Sara's stitch

Sylvia's stitch

Make foundation ch in multiples of 6. (On Rows 2 to 5 turning ch of previous row counts as first tr of next row; last tr of row is always worked into turning ch).

Sylvia's stitch

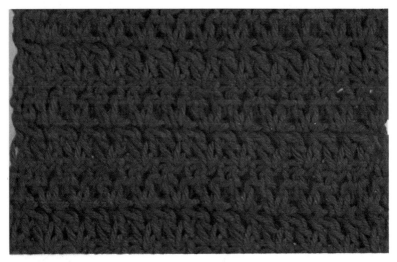

Wanda's stitch

Row 1: Starting in 4th ch from hook, 3 tr, * 2 ch, miss 2 ch, 4 tr *. Rep from * to * ending with 3 ch, turn.
Row 2: 4 tr, * 4 tr in 2-ch loop, 2 ch, 1 dc into sp between 2nd and 3rd tr of 4-tr group of previous row *. Rep from * to * ending with 4 tr into 2-ch loop, 4 tr, 3 ch, turn.
Row 3: 4 tr, * 4 tr above 4-tr group into 2-ch loop, 2 ch *. Rep from * to * ending with 8 tr as at beg of row, 3 ch, turn.
Row 4: 4 tr, * 2 ch, 1 dc into sp between 2nd and 3rd tr of 4-tr group of previous row, 2 ch, 4 tr into 2-ch loop *. Rep from * to * ending with 2 ch, 4 tr, 3 ch, turn.
Row 5: 4 tr, * 2 ch, 4 tr above 4-tr group into 2-ch loop *. Rep from * to * ending with 2 ch, 4 tr, 3 ch, turn.
Rows 2 to 5 form the pattern and are repeated as required.

Wanda's stitch

Make foundation ch with an even no. of sts.
Row 1: yoh, insert hook into 5th ch from hook, draw yarn through, * yoh, draw yarn through first 2 loops, yoh, miss 1 ch, insert hook into next ch, yoh, draw yarn through, yoh, draw yarn through 2 loops, yoh, draw yarn through all 3 loops on hook, 1 ch, yoh, insert hook into same st as last tr worked, insert hook into same st as last tr worked, draw yarn through *. Rep from * to * ending with 1 tr into last ch, 4 ch, turn.
Row 2: Yoh, insert hook into first 1-ch loop of previous row, draw yarn through, * yoh, draw yarn through 2 loops, yoh, miss 1 st, insert hook into next 1-ch loop, yoh, draw yarn through 2 loops, yoh, draw yarn through all 3 loops, 1 ch, yoh, insert hook into same 1-ch loop as last tr just worked, yoh, draw yarn through *. Rep from * to *, ending with 1 tr into 3rd ch of t-ch, 4 ch, turn.
Row 2 forms the pattern and is repeated as required.

Openwork stitch no. 1

Make foundation ch in multiples of 6 plus 3.
Row 1: 1 tr into 3rd ch from hook, ∗ miss 2 ch, (2 tr, 1 ch, 2 tr) into next ch, miss 2 ch, 1 tr ∗. Rep from ∗ to ∗ ending with 3 ch, turn.
Row 2: ∗ (2 tr, 1 ch, 2 tr) into 1-ch loop, 1 fwd tr on tr (see page 38). ∗ Rep from ∗ to ∗ ending with (2 tr, 1 ch, 2 tr) into last 1-ch loop, 1 tr into t-ch, 3 ch, turn.
Row 3: ∗ (2 tr, 1 ch, 2 tr) into 1-ch loop, 1 bk tr into tr (see page 38). ∗ Rep from ∗ to ∗ ending with (2 tr, 1 ch, 2 tr) into last 1-ch loop, 1 tr into t-ch, 3 ch, turn.
Rows 2 and 3 form the pattern and are repeated as required.

Openwork stitch no. 1

Openwork stitch no. 2

Make foundation ch in multiples of 8 plus 2.
Row 1: Starting in 2nd ch from hook, 4 dc, ∗ 1 ch, miss 1 ch, 7 dc ∗. Rep from ∗ to ∗ ending with 4 dc, 3 ch, turn.
Row 2: 1 motif into first st (= 1 tr, 1 ch, 1 tr) miss 3 sts, ∗ 3 open picots (∗∗ 1 dc, 3 ch ∗∗ 3 times, 1 dc) into 1-ch loop, 1 motif into 4th of 7-dc ∗. Rep from ∗ to ∗ ending with 1 motif into last dc, 1 ch, turn.
Row 3: 2 open picots into 1-ch loop of first motif, ∗ 1 motif into centre of 2nd of 3 open picots, 3 open picots into 1-ch loop of motif ∗. Rep from ∗ to ∗ ending with 2 open picots into last motif, 3 ch, turn.
Row 4: As Row 3, starting and ending with motif, 1 ch, turn.
Rows 3 and 4 form the pattern and are repeated as required.

Openwork stitch no. 2

Openwork stitch no. 3

Make foundation ch in multiples of 8 plus 4.

Row 1: 1 tr into 4th ch from hook, miss 3 ch, * (3 tr, 1 ch, 3 tr) into next ch, miss 3 ch, (1 tr, 3 ch, 1 tr) into next ch, miss 3 ch *. Rep from * to * ending with (3 tr, 1 ch, 3 tr) into next ch, miss 3 ch, 1 tr into last ch, 5 ch, turn.

Row 2: * (1 tr, 3 ch, 1 tr) into 1-ch sp, (3 tr, 1 ch, 3 tr) into 3-ch loop *. Rep from * to * ending with (1 tr, 3 ch, 1 tr) into 1-ch space, 2 ch, 1 tr into turning ch, 3 ch, turn.

Row 3: * (3 tr, 1 ch, 3 tr) into 3-ch loop, (1 tr, 3 ch, 1 tr) into 1-ch sp. Rep from * ending with (3 tr, 1 ch, 3 tr) into 3-ch loop, 1 tr into t-ch, 5 ch, turn.
Rows 2 and 3 form the pattern and are repeated as required.

Openwork stitch no. 3

Openwork stitch no. 4

Make foundation ch in multiples of 8 plus 6.

Row 1: Starting in 2nd ch from hook, * 5 dc, 2 ch, miss 1 ch, 1 tr, 2 ch, miss 1 ch *. Rep from * to * ending with 5 dc, 4 ch, turn.

Row 2: * 1 tr into 3rd dc, 2 ch, 2 dc into first 2-ch loop, 2 dc into 2nd 2-ch loop, 2 ch. * Rep from * to * ending with 1 tr into 3rd dc, 1 ch, 1 tr into last dc, 1 ch, turn.

Row 3: 1 dc into 1-ch loop (before the tr), 1 ch, 1 dc into 2-ch loop, * 6 ch, 1 dc into 2-ch loop (before the tr), 1 ch, 1 dc into 2-ch loop (after the tr) *. Rep from * to * ending with 6 ch, 1 dc, 1 ch, 1 dc into 3rd ch of t-ch, 3 ch, turn.

Row 4: * 1 tr into 1-ch loop between the 2 dc, 2 ch, 5 dc into 6-ch loop, 2 ch. * Rep from * to * ending with 1 tr, 1 ch, 1 tr into t-ch, 1 ch, turn.

Row 5: 1 dc into first tr, 1 ch, * 1 dc

Openwork stitch no. 4

into 2-ch loop, 2 ch, miss 2 dc, 1 tr into 3rd dc, 2 ch, miss 2 dc *. Rep from * to * ending with 1 dc into 2-ch loop, 1 ch, 1 dc into turning ch, 1 ch, turn.

Row 6: 1 dc into dc, 6 ch, * 1 dc into first 2-ch loop, 1 ch, 1 dc into 2nd 2-ch loop, 6 ch. Rep from * ending with 1 dc into dc, 1 ch, turn.

Row 7: 1 dc in first dc, * 5 dc in 6-ch loop, 2 ch, 1 tr into 1-ch loop, 2 ch. Rep from * ending with 5 dc into 6-ch loop, 1 dc into last dc, 4 ch, turn.

Rows 2 to 7 form the pattern and are repeated as required.

Openwork stitch no. 5

Make foundation ch in multiples of 6 plus 5.

Row 1: Starting in 2nd ch from hook, * 1 dc, 2 ch, miss 2 ch *. Rep from * to * ending with 1 dc, 3 ch, turn.

Row 2: * 1 tr into first 2-ch loop, 1 ch, (2 tr, 1 ch, 2 tr) into 2nd 2-ch loop, 1 ch *. Rep from * to * ending with 1 tr into last 2-ch loop, 1 tr into dc, 1 ch, turn.

Row 3: 1 dc between first 2 tr, * 2 ch, 1 dc into 1-ch loop after 1-tr, 2 ch, 1 dc into 1-ch loop between 4-tr, 2 ch, 1 dc into 1-ch loop before 1-tr *. Rep from * to * ending with 2 ch, 1 dc into t-ch, 3 ch, turn.

Row 4: * (2 tr, 1 ch, 2 tr) into 2-ch loop over 1-tr, 1 ch, 1 tr into dc over 4-tr group, 1 ch. * Rep from * to * ending with (2 tr, 1 ch, 2 tr) into last 2-ch loop, 1 tr into t-ch, 2 ch, turn.

Row 5: 1 dc into 1-ch loop between 4-tr, * 2 ch, 1 dc into 1-ch loop before 1-tr, 2 ch, 1 dc into 1-ch loop after 1-tr *. Rep from * to * ending with 2 ch, 1 dc into 1-ch loop between 4-tr, 2 ch, 1 dc into t-ch, 3 ch, turn.

Row 6: 1 tr into dc over 4-tr group, * 1 ch, (2 tr, 1 ch, 2 tr) into 2-ch loop over 1-tr, 1 ch, 1 tr into dc over 4-tr

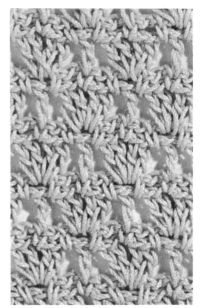

Openwork stitch no. 5

Openwork stitch no. 6

group *. Rep from * to * ending with 1 tr into t-ch, 1 ch, turn.
Rows 3 to 6 form the pattern and are repeated as required.

Openwork stitch no. 6

Make foundation ch in multiples of 4 plus 2. (Start with at least 14 ch.)
Row 1: Starting in 2nd ch from hook, * 1 dc, 4 ch, miss 3 ch *. Rep from * to * ending with 1 dc into last ch, 3 ch, turn.
Row 2: 5 tr into first 4-ch loop, * 6 tr into next 4-ch loop *. Rep from * to * ending with 5 tr into last 4-ch loop, 1 tr into last dc, 1 ch, turn.
Row 3: 1 dc into first tr, 2 ch, 1 dc between 3rd and 4th tr of 6-tr group (tr at beg of row and t-ch at end of row count as part of 6-tr groups), 4 ch *. Rep from * to * ending with 1 dc between 3rd and 4th tr of last 6-tr group, 2 ch, 1 dc into t-ch, 1 ch, turn.

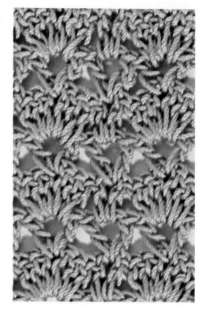

Openwork stitch no. 7

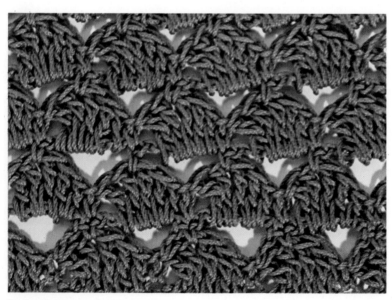

Openwork stitch no. 8

Row 4: 1 dc into dc, * 4 ch, 1 dc into next 4-ch loop *. Rep from * to * ending with 4 ch, 1 dc into last dc, 3 ch, turn.
Rows 2 to 4 form the pattern and are repeated as required.

Openwork stitch no. 7

Make foundation ch in multiples of 6 plus 3.
Row 1: Starting in 3rd ch from hook, * (1 tr, 2 ch, 1 tr) all into same ch, miss 2 ch *. Rep from * to * ending with (1 tr, 2 ch, 1 tr) into last ch, 2 ch, turn.
Row 2: * (1 tr, 2 ch, 1 tr) into first 2-ch loop, (3 tr, 1 ch, 3 tr) into 2nd 2-ch loop. * Rep from * to * ending with (1 tr, 2 ch, 1 tr) into last loop, 2 ch, turn.
Row 3: * (1 tr, 2 ch, 1 tr) into 2-ch loop, (1 tr, 2 ch, 1 tr) into 1-ch loop between the two 3-tr groups. * Rep

from * to * ending with (1 tr, 2 ch, 1 tr) into last 2-ch loop, 2 ch, turn.
Rows 2 and 3 form the pattern and are repeated as required.

Openwork stitch no. 8

Make foundation ch in multiples of 6 plus 2.
Row 1: Starting in 2nd ch from hook, * 1 dc, 1 tr, 4 dtr. Rep from * ending with 1 dc, 3 ch, turn.
Row 2: 1 tr into 1 dc, 3 ch, * 1 dc between 2nd and 3rd dtr, 6 ch *. Rep from * to * ending with 1 dc between 2nd and 3rd dtr, 3 ch, 1 tr into last dc, 4 ch, turn.
Row 3: 3 dtr into 3-ch loop, * 1 dc into dc, (1 tr, 4 dtr) into 6-ch loop. Rep from * ending with 1 dc into dc, (1 tr, 2 dtr) into 3-ch loop, 1 dtr into last tr, 1 ch, turn.
Row 4: 1 dc into first st, * 6 ch, 1 dc between 2nd and 3rd dtr, 1 dc into dc

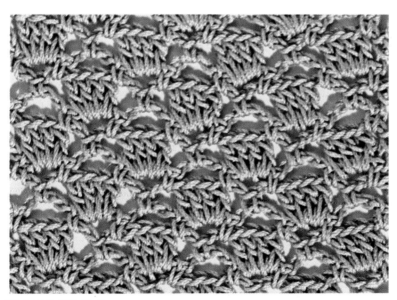

Openwork stitch no. 9

*. Rep from * to * ending with 1 dc into t-ch, 1 ch, turn.

Row 5: * 1 dc into dc, (1 tr, 4 dtr) into 6-ch loop. Rep from * ending with 1 dc into last dc, 2 ch, turn.

Rows 2 to 5 form the pattern and are repeated as required.

Openwork stitch no. 9

Make foundation ch in multiples of 7 plus 2.

Row 1: 1 tr into 4th ch from hook, * 2 ch, miss 1 ch, 1 dc into next ch, 2 ch, miss 1 ch, 1 tr into each of next 4 ch *. Rep from * to * ending with 2 tr (instead of 4) in last repeat, 5 ch, turn.

Row 2: 1 dc into first 2-ch loop, * 3 ch, 1 dc into 2nd 2-ch loop, 4 ch, 1 dc into next 2-ch loop *. Rep from * to * ending with 3 ch, 1 dc into last 2-ch loop, 2 ch, 1 tr into ch at beg of previous row, 1 ch, turn.

Row 3: 1 dc into first 2-ch loop, 2 ch, 1 fan (= 4 tr) into 3-ch loop, * 2 ch, 1 dc into 4-ch loop, 2 ch, 1 fan into 3-ch loop *. Rep from * to * ending with 2 ch, 1 dc into 3rd of 5 t-ch, 4 ch, turn.

Row 4: 1 dc into first 2-ch loop, * 4 ch, 1 dc into next 2-ch loop, 3 ch, 1 dc into next 2-ch loop *. Rep from * to * ending with 4 ch, 1 dc into next 2-ch loop, 2 ch, 1 htr into last st, 3 ch, turn.

Row 5: 1 tr into first 2-ch loop, * 2 ch, 1 dc into 4-ch loop, 2 ch, 1 fan into 3-ch loop *. Rep from * to * ending with 2 ch, 1 dc into 4-ch loop, 2 ch, 1 tr into 2nd of 4 t-ch of previous row, 5 ch, turn.

Rows 2 to 5 form the pattern and are repeated as required.

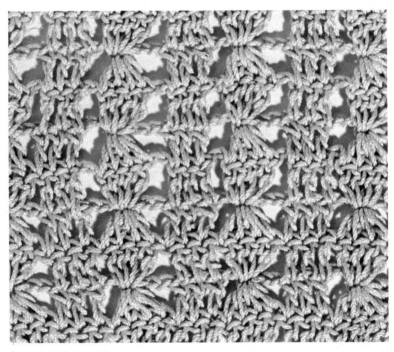

Openwork stitch no. 10

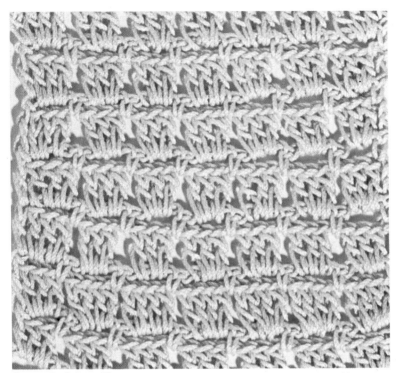

Openwork stitch no. 11

Openwork stitch no. 10

Make foundation ch in multiples of 6 plus 4.

Row 1: 4 tr into 4th ch from hook, ∗ miss 1 ch, 3 tr, miss 1 ch, 4 tr into next ch ∗. Rep from ∗ to ∗ ending with 3 ch, turn.

Row 2: ∗ Into 4-tr group of previous row work 4 unfin tr, yoh, draw yarn through all 5 loops on hook, 2 ch, 3 tr, 2 ch. ∗ Rep from ∗ to ∗ ending with 4 unfin tr finished tog on last 4-tr group, 1 tr into t-ch, 2 ch, turn.

Row 3: ∗ 4 tr into st finishing off the 4-tr group in previous row, 3 tr into 3 tr. ∗ Rep from ∗ to ∗, end with 4 tr into last group, 1 tr into t-ch, 2 ch, turn.

Rows 2 and 3 form the pattern and are repeated as required.

Openwork stitch no. 11

Make foundation ch in multiples of 4 plus 2.

Row 1: Starting in 2nd ch from hook, ∗ 1 dc, 3 ch, miss 3 ch ∗. Rep from ∗ to ∗ ending with 1 dc into last ch, 3 ch, turn.

Row 2: ∗ 3 tr into 3-ch loop, 1 ch. ∗ Rep from ∗ to ∗ ending with 1 tr into last dc, 2 ch, turn.

Row 3: 1 dc into first 1-ch loop, ∗ 3 ch, 1 dc into next 1-ch loop. Rep from ∗ ending with 3 ch, 1 dc into last t-ch.

3 ch, turn.
Rows 2 and 3 form the pattern and are repeated as required.

Openwork stitch no. 12

Make foundation ch in multiples of 8 plus 6.
Row 1: Starting in 2nd ch from hook, * 1 dc, 4 ch, miss 3 ch *. Rep from * to * ending with 1 dc, 3 ch, turn.
Row 2: * 4 tr into first 4-ch loop of previous row, 2 ch, 1 dc into 2nd 4-ch loop of previous row, 2 ch. * Rep from * to * ending with 4 tr into last 4-ch loop, 1 tr into dc, 5 ch, turn.

Row 3: * 1 dc into 2-ch loop after the 4-tr, 4 ch, 1 dc into 2-ch loop before next 4-tr, 4 ch. * Rep from * to * ending with 1 dc into t-ch, 4 ch, turn.
Row 4: * 1 dc into first 4-ch loop of previous row, 2 ch, 4 tr into 2nd 4-ch loop, 2 ch. * Rep from * to * ending with 1 dc into last 4-ch loop, 2 ch, 1 tr, 4 ch, turn.
Row 5: * 1 dc into 2-ch loop before next 4-tr, 4 ch, 1 dc into 2-ch loop after next 4-tr. * Rep from * to * ending with 2 ch, 1 tr into t-ch, 3 ch, turn.
Rows 2 to 5 form the pattern and are repeated as required.

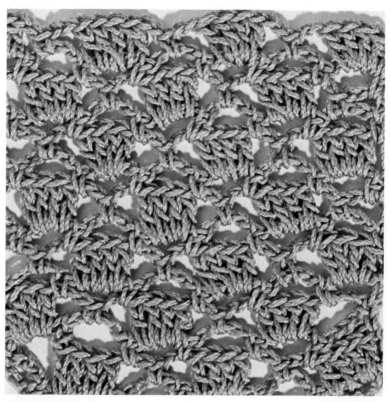

Openwork stitch no. 12

Motifs, Medallions and Patchwork

STRIPS AND GEOMETRIC SHAPES

Stitches for medallions to build up into afghans, curtains, bedspreads, tablecloths, etc.

The stitches covered in this chapter are designed for particular purposes. The basic stitches are simple and are used here to make small shapes – squares, circles, hexagons, and the like – and ornamental motifs of various kinds which, when joined together, may be made into highly individual and useful items.

The results are limited only by your imagination and all the shapes described can, of course, be made into anything you wish to make. For instance, in describing how certain medallions can be made into a bedspread, there is nothing to stop you from using the component parts for tablemats or even an evening shawl. The only distinction we have made is between work carried out in wool and manmade fibres, and in cotton: the former is usually bolder, modern and often in bright colours, while the latter is more elaborate and elegant.

Another consideration to bear in mind is the amount of time the work will take to complete. Whereas a cushion cover or a set of tablemats may be finished fairly quickly, undertaking a pair of full-length curtains or a double bedspread in a fine cotton requires determination and time. The rewards are great, however, for a beautifully crocheted bedspread, for instance, is a precious possession.

Stitches in wool for bedspreads, cot covers, etc.

Hazelnut stitch no. 1

Hazelnut stitch no. 1

This stitch makes a reversible fabric.
Make foundation with an odd no. of
sts.
Row 1: Starting in 3rd ch from hook.
∗ (yoh, draw yarn through) 3 times
into same st, yoh, draw yarn through
all 7 loops on hook (= 1 hazelnut), 1
ch, miss 1 ch ∗. Rep from ∗ to ∗
ending with 1 hazelnut into last ch, 4
ch, turn.
Row 2: ∗ 1 hazelnut into 1-ch loop, 1
ch ∗. Rep from ∗ to ∗ ending with 1
tr into t-ch, 3 ch, turn.
Row 3: ∗ 1 hazelnut into 1-ch loop, 1
ch ∗. Rep from ∗ to ∗ ending with 1
hazelnut into t-ch, 4 ch, turn.
Rows 2 and 3 form the pattern and
are repeated as required.

Hazelnut stitch no. 2

Hazelnut stitch no. 2

Make foundation ch in multiples of 3
plus 1.
Row 1: Starting in 2nd ch from hook,
work in dc, 1 ch, turn.
Row 2: 1 dc, ∗ 1 hazelnut (= 5 unfinished tr worked into same st, yoh,
draw yarn through all 6 loops on

91

Large star stitch

hook), 2 dc *. Rep from * to * ending with 1 hazel nut, 1 ch, turn.
Row 3: * Work dc into each dc, 1 dc into hazelnut. * Rep from * to * ending with 1 dc, 1 ch, turn.
Row 4: 2 dc, * 1 hazelnut, 2 dc *. Rep from * to * ending with 1 hazelnut, 1 ch, turn.
Rows 1 to 4 form the pattern and are repeated as required.

Large star stitch

Make foundation ch in multiples of 5 plus 2.
Row 1: In 5th ch from hook work 2 unfin dtr, yoh, draw yarn through all 3 loops on hook, * 4 ch, 5 unfin dtr into the loop at base of same ch, miss 4 foundation ch, 3 unfin dtr into next st, yoh, draw yarn through all 9 loops on hook *. Rep from * to * ending with 2 ch, turn.
Row 2: 2 unfin dtr into loop at base of ch, yoh, draw yarn through all 3 loops on hook, * 4 ch, 2 unfin dtr into loop at base of ch, 3 unfin dtr into same stitch as last 2 dtr, 3 unfin dtr into loop in centre of next star, yoh, draw yarn through all 9 loops on hook *. Rep from * to *, ending with 4 ch, turn.
Row 2 forms the pattern and is repeated as required.

Raised shell stitch

Make foundation ch in multiples of 4 plus 2.

Row 1: Starting in 2nd ch from hook, work in dc, ending with 1 ch, turn.

Row 2: 1 dc into first st, miss 3 sts *
(1 dc, 5 tr) into next st, miss 3 sts *.
Rep from * to * ending with missing
3 sts, 1 dc into last st, 3 ch, turn.

Row 3: 3 tr into first dc, * miss next shell (1 dc, 5 tr) into dc *. Rep from * to *, end with 1 dc into dc of last shell, 3 ch, turn.

Row 2 forms the pattern and is repeated as required.

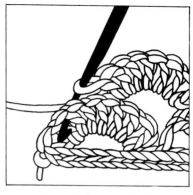

How to insert the hook in a shell

Raised shell stitch

Two-colour hexagon

Two-colour hexagon

Using first col, make 8 ch and join with a sl st to form ring.

Round 1: 18 dc into ring, ending with 1 sl st into first st.

Round 2: 1 ch, 1 dc into first dc of previous rnd, * 5 ch, miss 2 sts, 1 dc into next st *. Rep from * to * ending with 1 sl st into first dc (6 loops).

Round 3: 1 sl st into first loop, 5 ch, 7 tr tr into next loop, 8 tr tr into each foll loop, ending with 1 sl st into 5th ch, 1 ch.

Round 4: 1 dc into 5th ch and into each of the 7 tr tr of previous rnd, * 3 ch, 1 dc into each of the 8 tr tr *. Rep from * to * ending with 3 ch, 1 sl st into first dc. Fasten off first col.

Round 5: Join 2nd col in first 3-ch loop, 4 ch, [2 unfin dtr, yoh, draw yarn through all 3 loops (= 2-dtr cluster), 5 ch, 3 unfin dtr, yoh, draw yarn through all 4 loops (= 3-dtr cluster)] all into first 3-ch loop, * (3 ch, 1 3-dtr cluster into 3rd dc) twice, 3 ch, (1 3-dtr cluster, 5 ch, 1 3-dtr cluster) into next 3-ch loop *. Rep from * to * ending with (3 ch, 1 3-dtr cluster) twice into 3rd dc, 3 ch, 1 sl st into closing st of first cluster. Fasten off 2nd col.

Round 6: Using 1st col, (3 dc, 3 ch, 3 dc) into first 5-ch loop, * 3 dc into each of next 3 loops, (3 dc, 3 ch, 3 dc) into next space *. Rep from * to * ending with 3 dc into each of next 3 spaces, 1 sl st into first dc.

Round 7: 1 sl st into 2nd dc, 4 ch, 1 2-dtr cluster into same st as sl st just worked, * 3 ch, (1 3-dtr cluster, 5 ch, 1 3-dtr cluster) into next loop, 3 ch, 1 3-dtr cluster into 2nd dc, (3 ch, 1 3-dtr cluster) 3 times into 3rd dc *. Rep from * to * omitting 1 cluster at end of round and working 3 ch 1 sl st into closing st of first cluster.

Round 8: 3 dc into next 3-ch loop, * (3 dc, 3 ch, 3 dc) into next 5-ch loop, 3 dc into each of next five 3-ch loops *. Rep from * to * ending with 3 dc into each of last four 3-ch loops, 1 sl st into first dc. Fasten off first col.

Round 9: Using 2nd col, 3 dc into first 3-ch loop, * 1 dc into each of next 21 dc, 3 dc into next 3-ch loop *. Rep from * to * ending with 1 dc into each of next 21 dc, 1 sl st into first dc. Fasten off.

Diamond in double crochet

Diamond in double crochet

Make 3 ch.
Row 1: 1 dc into 2nd ch from hook, 1 dc into next ch, 1 ch, turn.
Row 2: 2 dc into first st, 1 dc into next st, 1 ch, turn.
Row 3: 2 dc into first st, 1 dc into each of next 2 sts, 1 ch, turn.
Row 4: 2 dc into first st, 1 dc into each of next 3 sts, 1 ch, turn.
Continue in dc, increasing 1 st at beg of every row until Row 15 has been worked, 1 ch, turn (16 sts).
Row 16: 1 decrease (= insert hook into first st, yoh, draw yarn through, insert hook into 2nd st, yoh, draw yarn through, yoh, draw yarn through all 3 loops on hook), 1 dc into each dc to end, 1 ch, turn.
Row 17: 1 dec, 1 dc into each of next 13 dc, 1 ch turn.
Continue in dc dec 1 st at beg of every row until Row 28 has been worked, 1 ch, turn.
Row 29: 1 dec, 1 dc, 1 ch, turn.
Row 30: 1 dec. Do not cut off yarn, but work a finishing row of dc around the edge of diamond, working 1 ch between dc at each corner and ending with a sl st into first edging dc. Fasten off.

Halved diamond

Make 2 ch.
Row 1: 1 dc into 2nd ch from hook, 1 ch, turn.
Row 2: 2 dc into 1 dc of previous row, 1 ch, turn.
Row 3: 2 dc, 1 ch, turn.
Row 4: 2 dc into first st, 1 dc, 1 ch, turn.
Row 5: 3 dc, 1 ch, turn.
Row 6: 2 dc into first dc, 2 dc, 1 ch, turn.
Continue in dc, inc 1 st on one side only on every alternate row until Row 15 has been worked. Starting with

Halved diamond (lengthwise)

97

Halved diamond (lower or upper part)

Row 16, dec 1 st at beg of next and every foll alternate row. Do not cut off yarn, but work the finishing dc only along the edge where the increases and decreases have been worked.

Halved diamond – lower or upper part

Begin work as for complete diamond, finishing after completion of Row 15. Complete by working the finishing dc along the two edges where the increases and decreases have been worked.

Square shape from circles

Note: The circles are double. Start at centre back and work to circumference (end of Round 3) then decrease on each round to centre front (end of Round 8).

Make 4 ch and join with a sl st to form ring. (1st circle)

Round 1: 3 ch, 14 tr into ring, closing the rnd with 1 sl st into top of starting 3-ch.

Round 2: 4 ch, miss 1 tr, ✳ 1 tr into tr, 1 ch, miss 1 tr ✳. Rep from ✳ to ✳ closing the rnd with 1 sl st into 3rd of starting 4-ch.

Round 3: 5 ch, ✳ 1 tr into tr, 2 ch ✳. Rep from ✳ to ✳ closing the rnd with 1 sl st into 3rd of starting 5-ch.

Round 4: As Round 3.

Round 5: As Round 2.

Round 6: 3 ch, (1 tr into tr,) 15 times, closing the rnd with 1 sl st into top of starting 3-ch, 3 ch.

Round 7: Turn the work round and work in opposite direction, * 1 dc into next tr, miss 1 tr *. Rep from * to * (8 dc will have been worked altogether). Close the rnd with 1 sl st into top of starting 3-ch.

Round 8: * 5 ch, 1 dc into 2nd ch from hook, 1 htr into 3rd ch, 1 tr into 4th ch, 1 tr into 5th ch, miss 1 dc of previous rnd, 1 sl st into next dc. * Rep from * to * (= 1 petal). When 4th petal has been worked, fasten off.

Work a 2nd circle, joining it to the first circle on Round 3 as follows: * 1 tr, 1 ch, take hook out of loop and insert it in one of the holes in Round 3 of the first circle. Pick up the working loop again and draw it back through hole

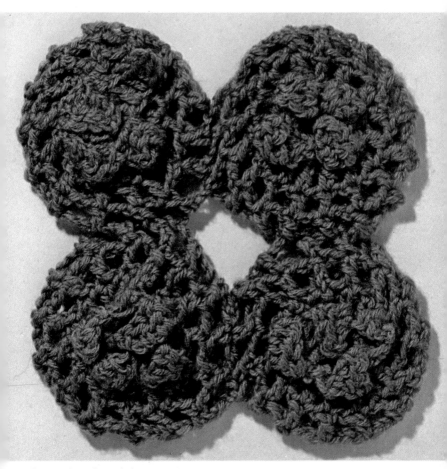

Square shape from circles

of first circle, 1 ch. ∗ Rep from ∗ to ∗ 3 times in all (linking up the 3 holes) and complete Round 3.

Now work Round 4, working tr into tr of previous rnd, as instructed for the previous circle; the joins do not hamper the trebles as they occur on the chains, as indicated. Both horizontally and vertically the joins are always on 3 holes, thus leaving 1 hole free between one join and the next. 4 circles are required to complete a square. Squares may also be made with 16 circles or more, depending upon whether you wish to make a cushion cover or a bedspread.

Square woollen medallion

Make 6 ch and join with a sl st to form ring.

Round 1: 8 dc into ring.

Round 2: 6 ch, ∗ 1 tr, 3 ch ∗. Rep from ∗ to ∗ 7 times. Complete this and every foll round with 1 sl st.

Round 3: 3 ch, 3 tr into 3-ch loop, ∗ 4 tr into 3-ch loop, 1 ch ∗. Rep from ∗ to ∗ 7 times.

Round 4: 6 ch, ∗ 1 dc into 1-ch loop, 5 ch ∗. Rep from ∗ to ∗ 7 times.

Round 5: (3 tr, 1 ch, 3 tr, 1 ch) into each 5-ch loop, working 3 ch, 2 tr at beg of rnd.

Square woollen medallion

Round 6: ∗ (3 tr, 2 ch, 3 tr) into first ch, ∗∗ miss 3 tr, 1 dc into next 1-ch loop, 3 ch ∗∗ working 3 ch, 2 tr at beg of rnd. Rep from ∗∗ to ∗∗ twice more, thus forming one side of square. ∗ Rep from ∗ to ∗ 4 times altogether.

Rounds 7 and 8: 1 ch, then work 1 dc into each st of previous row and 3 dc into 3-ch loops on each of 4 corners. Close rnd with 1 sl st. Fasten off.

Multicoloured zigzag strip

Make foundation ch with 20 sts. Change colour every 6 rows.

Row 1: Starting in 5th ch from hook, ∗ 3 tr all into same st (= 1 cluster), miss 2 ch ∗. Rep from ∗ to ∗ 4 times altogether, 3 tr into next ch, miss 2 ch, 1 tr into last ch (5 clusters), 3 ch, turn.

Row 2: Miss the 1 tr and last cluster worked, ∗ 1 cluster between 2 clusters of previous row ∗. Rep from ∗ to ∗ 4 times altogether, (1 cluster, 1 ch, 1 tr) into 4-ch loop at beg of Row 1, 4 ch, turn.

Row 3: 1 cluster into the ch next to the tr, (1 cluster between 2 clusters) 4 times, 1 tr into 3rd ch at beg of Row 2, 3 ch, turn. Rep Rows 2 and 3 until 11 rows have been worked.

Row 12: Miss 1 tr and last cluster worked, (1 cluster between 2 clusters) 4 times, 1 cluster into 4-ch loop at beg of previous row, 3 ch, turn.

Row 13: Miss last cluster worked, (1 cluster between 2 clusters) 4 times, (1 cluster, 1 ch, 1 tr) into 3-ch loop at beg of previous row, 4 ch, turn.

Row 14: 1 cluster into ch next to tr of previous row, (1 cluster between 2 clusters) 4 times, 1 tr into 3rd ch at beg of previous row, 3 ch, turn.

Row 15: Miss the tr and last cluster worked, (1 cluster between 2 clusters) 4 times, (1 cluster, 1 ch, 1 tr) into 4-ch loop at beg of previous row, 3 ch, turn.

Rep Rows 14 and 15 until Row 23 has been worked, 3 ch, turn.

Row 24: 1 cluster into ch next to tr, (1 cluster between 2 clusters) 4 times, 1 tr into 3rd ch at beg of previous row, 4 ch, turn.

Row 25: 1 cluster into space between last tr worked and 5th cluster of previous row, (1 cluster between 2 clusters) 4 times, 1 tr into 3rd ch at beg of previous row, 3 ch, turn. Repeat from 2nd row.

'Old America' medallion in three colours

'Old America' medallion in three colours

Make 4 ch in first col and join with a sl st to form ring.

Round 1: 3 ch, (2 tr, 2 ch) into ring, (3 tr, 2 ch) 3 times, ending with 1 sl st into top of starting 3-ch. Start each rnd with 3 ch to replace first tr.

Round 2 (2nd col): * (3 tr, 2 ch, 3 tr, 2 ch) into 2-ch loop. * Rep from * to * 4 times altogether, ending with 1 sl st into starting ch. Cut off yarn.

Round 3 (first col): * (3 tr, 2 ch, 3 tr) into corner, (2 ch, 3 tr, 2 ch) between one corner and the next. * Rep from * to * ending with 1 sl st into starting ch. Cut off yarn.

Round 4 (3rd col): * (3 tr, 2 ch, 3 tr) into corner, 2 ch, 3 tr into foll loop, 2 ch, 3 tr into loop just before the corner. * Rep from * to * 4 times altogether. Fasten off.

Multicoloured zigzag strip

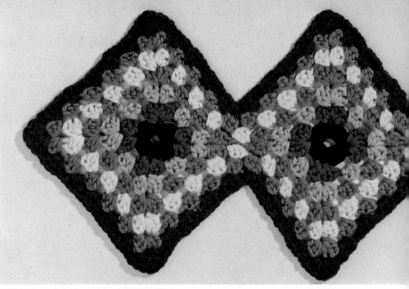

'Old America' design: (above) a strip for a rug
(below) four-colour medallion

'Old America' medallion in four colours

Make 6 ch in first col and join with a sl st to form ring.

Start each rnd with 2 ch to replace first tr.

Round 1: 4 tr and 1 ch into ring 4 times to form 4 leaves. Close this round and all foll rounds with a sl st into 2nd starting ch. Cut off yarn.

Round 2 (2nd col): (4 tr, 1 ch, 4 tr, 1 ch) into each of 4 1-ch loops dividing the tr groups. Cut off yarn.

Round 3 (3rd col): * (4 tr, 1 ch, 4 tr, 1 ch) into corner loop (4 tr, 1 ch) into each 1-ch loop between tr groups. * Rep from * to * 4 times altogether. Cut off yarn.

Round 4 (4th col): * (4 tr, 1 ch, 4 tr) into corner ch, 4 tr into ch before next 4-tr group of previous rnd, 4 tr into ch after same group 4-tr. * Rep from * to * 4 times altogether. Fasten off.

'Old America' design – strip for a rug

Make 5 ch in first col and join with a sl st to form ring.

Round 1: 2 ch, (3 htr, 1 ch) 4 times into ring . Close this rnd and all foll rnds with a sl st into top of starting 2-ch. Start each rnd with 2 ch to replace first htr. Cut off yarn.

Round 2 (2nd col): (3 htr, 1 ch, 3 htr, 1 ch) into each 1-ch loop. Cut off yarn. (4 corners worked)

Round 3 (3rd col): * (3 htr, 1 ch, 3 htr) into corner ch, 1 ch, (3 htr, 1 ch) into 1-ch loop between one corner and the next *. Rep from * to * 4 times altogether. Cut off yarn.

Round 4 (4th col): * (3 htr, 1 ch, 3 htr) into corner ch, (1 ch, 3 htr, 1 ch) on side between corners. * Rep from * to * 4 times altogether. Cut off yarn.

The medallion just completed is joined to next and following medallions on Round 4. Work 3 rnds but, on Round 4, after working 3 htr, 1 ch on the first corner, remove hook from work, insert it from back to front in one of the corner ch of previously completed medallion, pick up dropped stitch from medallion being worked, yoh, draw yarn through loop and stitch. (This will result in a strip of medallions which can be varied according to length or width of article being made.)

Rounds 5, 6 and 7 are worked around completed strip.

Round 5 (5th col): Starting from the top of strip, work * 1 corner, (3 htr, 1 ch, 3 htr), ** 1 ch, 3 htr ** 3 times, 1 ch, 1 corner, rep from ** to ** 3 times, (3 htr, 1 ch) once into 1-ch joining corner of first medallion *. Rep from ** to ** 3 times along side of 2nd medallion. Rep around entire strip working joinings as above. Cut off yarn.

Multicoloured strip of half-medallions for a rug

Round 6 (6th col): As Round 5, inc one 3-htr group on each side of medallion.

Round 7 (7th col): As Round 5, inc one 3-htr group on each side of medallion.

Multicoloured strip of half-medallions for a rug

Make 13 ch in first colour. Change col every 5 rows.

Row 1 (wrong side): 1 tr into 9th ch from hook, 4 ch, 1 dc into last ch, 3 ch, turn.

Row 2 (right side): 9 tr into first 4-ch loop, 1 tr into tr, 10 tr into 2nd 4-ch loop, 6 ch, turn.

Row 3: 1 tr into 3rd st, * 2 ch, miss 1 st, 1 tr into next st *. Rep from * to *, ending with 2 ch, 1 tr into 3rd ch of previous row (10 sp), 3 ch, turn.

Row 4: * 3 tr into 2-ch loop, 1 tr into tr. Rep from * ending with 3 tr into

t-ch of previous row, 6 ch, turn.

Row 5: Work as Row 3 (20 sp). This row completes the motif. Cut off yarn.

Row 6 (wrong side, i.e. working in same direction as Row 5): With 2nd col, 1 dc into 8th tr, 4 ch, miss 1 tr, 1 tr into middle tr of first motif, 4 ch, miss 1 tr, 1 dc into next tr. To start each foll row, work 2 ch and 1 sl st at the end of every row into the next tr of previous motif.

Row 7 (right side): 9 tr into first 4-ch loop, 1 tr into middle tr, 10 tr into 2nd ch loop. End this row and all foll rows with 1 sl st into next tr of previous motif.

Row 8: Miss 2 tr *, 1 tr, 2 ch, miss 1 tr *. Rep from * to * ending with 1 sl st into next tr of first motif (10 sp).

Row 9: * 3 tr into 2-ch loop, 1 tr into tr. * Rep from * to * ending with 1 sl st into next tr of previous motif.

Row 10: As Row 8 (20 sp).

Row 6 to 10 form the pattern and are repeated as required.

Medallion for four-leaf clover design

Make 12 ch. and join with a sl st to form ring.

Round 1: 2 ch, 27 htr into ring. Close this rnd and all foll rnds with a sl st into 2nd starting ch. Start each rnd with 2 ch to replace first htr.

Round 2: 2 htr into closing st of previous round, 1 htr into each of next 5 htr, 2 htr into next htr, * 2 htr into next st, 5 htr, 2 htr into next st *. Rep from * to *.

Round 3: 2 htr into closing st of previous rnd, 8 htr *, 2 htr into next st, 8 htr *. Rep from * to *.

Round 4: 11 htr, * 1 ch, 1 htr into same st as last htr, 10 htr *. Rep from * to * ending with 1 ch and 1 htr into 2nd ch at beg of round. There will now be 11 htr on each side.

Round 5: 12 htr, * 3 ch, 12 htr * (the first of these is worked into same st

Medallion for four-leaf clover design

as last htr and the 12th is worked after the last st of previous round). Rep from * to * ending with 3 ch, 1 htr into 2nd ch at beg of round.

Round 6: 13 htr, * 5 ch, 13 htr * (work first and 13th as described for first and 12th in Row 5). Rep from * to * ending with 5 ch, 1 htr into 2nd ch at beg of round.

Round 7: 14 htr, * 7 ch, 14 htr *. Rep from * to * ending with 7 ch, 1 htr into 2nd ch at beg of round.

Round 8: 14 htr, * 9 ch, 15 htr *. Rep from * to * ending with 9 ch, and 1 sl st into 2nd ch at beg of round.

Round and square medallions for curtains, coverlets and tablecloths

Once you have mastered the techniques for making different shaped medallions, there is no end to the possibilities available to you. While each medallion is a work of art in itself, with its delicate tracery reminiscent of fine lace, when the medallions are joined together to make such things as curtains, coverlets and tablecloths, they are a truly elegant and delightful sight to behold. This is where your real skills will be on display; there is nothing so original or beautiful as a handworked crocheted curtain or bedspread – and the fact that such things cannot be bought in shops makes them all the more unique.

Large circle

Start exactly as for small circle and work first 3 rounds.

Round 4: 3 ch, 6 tr into first 2-ch sp, 7 tr into each 2-ch sp to end of round.

Round 5: 4 sl st into first 4 of the 7-tr of previous round to reach centre of first motif, 8 ch (= 1 tr plus 5 ch), * 1 tr into 4th of the 7-tr of next motif, 5 ch *. Rep from * to * to end of round.

Round 6: * 7 tr into 5-ch loop (replacing first tr of round with 3 ch), 1 tr into tr. * Rep from * to * to end of round.

Round 7: 4 sl st into first 4 tr, 8 ch (= 1 tr plus 5 ch), * 1 tr, 5 ch, 1 tr into tr between the 7-tr of previous round, 5 ch *. Rep from * to * to end of round.

Round 8: Rep Round 3.

Round 9: Rep Round 4. Fasten off.

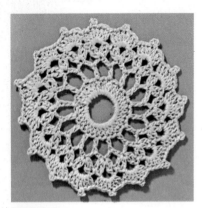

Small circle

Small circle

Make 14 ch and join with a sl st to form ring.

Round 1: 3 ch (= 1 tr), 31 tr into ring. Close this and foll rounds with 1 sl st into 3rd starting ch (32 tr).

Round 2: 8 ch (= 1 tr plus 5 ch), miss 1 tr (1 tr, 5 ch, miss 1 tr) 15 times (16 loops).

Round 3: 1 sl st into each of first 3 ch of the 5-ch loop in order to be in centre of loop, 3 ch (= 1 tr), (1 tr, 2 ch, 2 tr) into same st. Work (2 tr, 2 ch, 2 tr) into 3rd ch of each 5-ch loop to end of round. (16 looped motifs worked.)

Round 4: 2 sl st into first 2 tr of previous round to reach the first 2-ch loop, 3 ch (= 1 tr), 2 tr, 1 picot (= 3 ch, 1 sl st into 3rd ch), 3 tr into 2-ch loop, (3 tr, 1 picot, 3 tr) into each 2-ch loop to end of round. Close round with 1 sl st into 3rd starting ch (16 motifs). Fasten off.

Large circle

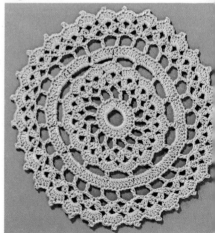

Medallion with lacy flowers

Medallion with lacy flowers

Make 6 ch and join with a sl st to form ring.

Round 1: 5 ch, (1 tr, 2 ch) 7 times into ring, ending with 1 sl st into 3rd starting ch.

Round 2: 3 ch (= 1 tr), then work 5 tr into each 2-ch loop, ending with 1 sl st into 3rd starting ch.

Round 3: 3 ch, * 1 tr into each tr of previous round, with 1 ch between every 5 tr, to correspond with the 5-tr groups in previous round *. Rep from * to * ending with 1 ch and 1 sl st into 3rd starting ch.

Round 4: 3 ch, 4 unfin tr, yoh, draw yarn through all 5 loops, * 2 ch, (1 tr, 1 ch, 1 tr) into 1-ch loop of previous round, 2 ch, 5 unfin tr, yoh, draw yarn through all 6 loops, 2 ch, (1 tr, 2 ch — these will form a corner — 1 tr) into 1-ch loop of previous round, 2 ch, 5 unfin tr, yoh, draw yarn through all 6 loops *, rep from * to * 3 times but instead of working the last 5 tr on the 3rd rep, work 1 sl st into closing st of first group of 5-tr.

Round 5: 1 sl st into first starting ch of previous round, 4 ch, * 1 tr into tr, 1 ch, 1 tr into tr, 1 ch, 1 tr into 2nd ch, 2 ch, (5 tr, 2 ch, 5 tr) into 2-corner-ch, 2 ch, miss closing st of 5-tr group, 1 tr into next ch, 1 ch *. Rep from * to *

111

3 times but instead of working the last tr and 1 ch on the 3rd rep, work 1 sl st into 2nd starting ch.

Round 6: 1 sl st into first ch, 3 ch, * 1 tr into tr, 1 ch *. Rep from * to * twice, ** 2 ch, 5 unfin tr, yoh, draw yarn through all 6 loops, 2 ch, 5 tr into corner, 2 ch, 5 unfin tr, yoh, draw yarn through all 6 loops, 2 ch, 1 tr into 2nd ch of previous round, * 1 ch, 1 tr into tr *. Rep from * to * 3 times more **, rep from ** to ** twice more, ending with 5 unfin tr, yoh, draw yarn through all 6 loops, 2 ch, 5 tr into corner, 2 ch, 5 unfin tr, yoh, draw yarn through all 6 loops, 2 ch, 1 tr into ch of previous row, 1 ch, 1 sl st into 2nd starting ch.

Round 7: 3 ch, 1 tr into tr, 1 ch, 1 tr, 1 ch, 1 tr, 1 ch, 1 tr into ch of previous round, * 6 ch, 5 unfin tr into 5-tr group, yoh, draw yarn through all 6 loops, 6 ch, miss next 5-tr group, 1 tr into next ch, ** 1 ch, 1 tr **, rep from ** to ** 4 times more, 1 ch, 1 tr into ch of previous round *. Rep from * to * twice more, ending with 6 ch, 5 unfin tr into 5-tr group, yoh, draw yarn through all 6 loops, 6 ch, 1 tr into ch of previous round, 1 tr, 1 ch, 1 sl st into 2nd starting ch.

Round 8: 3 ch, * 1 tr into tr, 1 ch *. Rep from * to * 4 times more, ** miss 1 ch, 1 tr into 2nd ch, 6 ch, 1 tr into corner st, 6 ch, miss 4 ch, 1 tr into 5th ch **. Rep from * to * along each side and from ** to ** round each corner ending with 1 sl st into 2nd starting ch. Substitute 3 ch for first tr on Rounds 9 to 12 and end each round with 1 sl st into 2nd starting ch.

Round 9: (9 tr over 9-tr of previous round with 1 ch between each) on all 4 sides of the square. Work 10 tr into every 6-ch loop and (1 tr, 2 ch, 1 tr) into each corner st.

Round 10: (1 tr, 2 ch, 1 tr) into each corner, (15 tr with 1 ch between each) on all 4 sides of the square (the 9 central sts will be on the 9 tr of previous round), the 6 side sts (3 each side) will be on the 10 tr of previous round, working in all sts.

Round 11: (2 tr, 2 ch, 2 tr) into each corner, (17 tr with 1 ch between each) on all 4 sides.

Round 12: (2 tr, 2 ch, 2 tr) into each corner, (21 tr with 1 ch between each) on all 4 sides. Fasten off.

Hexagons, flowers, squares and stars in cotton

In the following sections, the written instructions for certain patterns have been complemented by illustrations in chart form. The charts greatly simplify even the most complicated designs, as they are very easy to follow. They are built up of symbols representing the various stitches and are read in exactly the same way as the pattern is worked, i.e. a pattern worked in the round should be read anticlockwise, from the centre outwards; each circle represents one round, the beginning of which is indicated by the turning chain. Patterns worked in rows are read back and forth starting from the bottom left-hand corner. The pattern repeat is denoted by rows grouped together by a bracket. Where a border is added to the mainwork, an arrow indicates where the thread should be rejoined.

The key to the symbols is given below.

Key

o	chain (ch)
+	single crochet (sc)
T	half treble (htr)
⊤	double crochet (dc)
◘	treble (tr)
◘	double treble (dtr)
⋏	2 unfinished double crochet finished together

⋓	(yoh, drawn yarn through) 3 times, yoh, drawn yarn through all 7 loops on hook)
⋓	(yoh, draw yarn through) 5 times, yoh, draw yarn through all 11 loops on hook
⌒	slip stitch (sl st)
⌒⌒	picot (3 ch, sl st in first ch)
⋏	yoh twice, * insert hook into next ch loop, yoh draw yarn through, yoh, draw yarn through 2 loops on hook, * yoh, rep from * to * (yoh, draw yarn through 2 loops on hook) 3 times

113

Hexagon with star design

Hexagon with star design

Make 6 ch and join with a sl st to form ring.

Round 1: (1 tr, 2 ch) 6 times into ring. (Replace the first tr of a round with 3 ch but if the first st is a dc replace it with 1 ch only. Close each round with 1 sl st into last starting ch.)

Round 2: 3 dc into each 2-ch loop.

Round 3: * 1 hazelnut (= 5 tr into same st. Remove hook from work, insert it into first of 5 sts just worked, pick up working loop and draw it through), 1 ridged dc (= dc worked into *back* loop only instead of through both loops), 3 ridged dc into next st. * Rep from * to * to end of round.

Round 4: * 2 ridged dc, 3 ridged dc into same st, 2 ridged dc. * Rep from * to * to end of round.

Round 5: * 1 ridged dc, 1 hazelnut, 1 ridged dc, 3 ridged dc into next st (= 1 corner), 2 ridged dc, 1 hazelnut *. Rep from * to * to end of round.

Round 6: * 4 ridged dc, 1 corner, 4 ridged dc. * Rep from * to * to end of round.

Round 7: * 1 hazelnut, 1 ridged dc, 1 hazelnut, 2 ridged dc, 1 corner, 3 ridged dc, 1 hazelnut, 1 ridged dc. * Rep from * to * to end of round.

Round 8: * 6 ridged dc, 1 corner, 6 ridged dc. * Rep from * to * to end of round.

Round 9: * 1 ridged dc, 1 hazelnut, 5

ridged dc, 1 corner, 6 ridged dc, 1 hazelnut. * Rep from * to * to end of round.

Round 10: * 8 ridged dc, 1 corner, 8 ridged dc. * Rep from * to * to end of round.

Round 11: * 1 hazelnut, 8 ridged dc, 1 corner, 9 ridged dc. * Rep from * to * to end of round.

Round 12: * ** 1 ridged tr (worked into *back* loop), 1 ch, miss 1 st. **, rep from ** to ** 5 times, 1 ridged tr, 2 ch, 1 tr into same st, 1 ch, miss 2 sts, rep from ** to ** 4 times. * Rep from * to * to end of round.

Round 13: 1 ridged dc into each st, working 3 dc into 2-ch loop at each corner.

Round 14: * ** 3 ridged dc, 1 hazelnut, 1 ridged dc **, rep from ** to * twice, 2 ridged dc, 1 corner, rep from ** to ** twice. * Rep from * to * to end of round.

Round 15: * ** 2 ridged dc, 1 hazelnut, 1 ridged dc, 1 hazelnut **, rep from ** to ** twice, 3 ridged dc, 1

Stylized flower

corner, 1 ridged dc, rep from ** to ** twice more. * Rep from * to * to end of round.

Round 16: * ** 1 ridged dc, 1 hazelnut, 3 ridged dc **, rep from ** to ** twice. 1 ridged dc, 1 hazelnut, 2 ridged dc, 1 corner, 2 ridged dc, rep from ** to ** twice more. * Rep from * to * to end of round.

Round 17: * 1 ridged tr, 1 ch, miss 1 st * along each side. * 1 tr, 3 ch, 1 tr * at each corner.

Round 18: 1 ridged dc into each st, 3 ridged dc into same stitch at each corner. Fasten off.

Stylized flower

(Replace first st of round as follows: tr tr by 5 ch, dtr by 4 ch, tr by 3 ch, dc by 1 ch. Close each round with 1 sl st in top of starting ch.)

Make 16 ch and join with a sl st to form ring.

Round 1: 34 tr tr into ring.

Round 2: 1 tr into each tr tr.

Round 3: * 3 dtr, 3 ch, 1 picot (= 3 ch, 1 sl st into first ch), 3 ch, miss 1 st. * Rep from * to * 8 times.

6 sl st into first 6 sts in order to reach first picot. The 4 corners of the

Chart for Stylized flower

Small square medallion

square are now worked separately, as follows:

Round 4: (1 dc, 6 ch, 1 dtr, 7 ch, 1 dtr, 7 ch, 1 dtr, 6 ch, 1 dc) into picot. Turn work and work 10 tr into each ch loop. Turn work again and work 1 tr into each st (40 tr).

Turn work, 2 ch, 1 sl st into ch foll the 3-dtr of Round 3, 1 tr into each tr ending with 1 sl st into ch loop of Round 3.

Having completed the 4 corners, finish the square by working all around it as follows:

Round 5: * 1 tr into the 5th corner tr, 2 ch, miss 1 st, (1 tr, 2 ch, miss 1 st) until 5th corner is reached. * Rep from * to * 4 times.

Round 6: (1 dc, 1 picot, 1 dc) into each 2-ch sp of previous row. Fasten off.

Small square medallion

Make 18 ch and join with sl st to form ring.

Round 1: 1 ch, 36 dc into ring, ending with 1 sl st into first st, 4 ch.

Round 2: 1 unfin dtr into each of next 2 sts, yoh, draw yarn through all loops on hook (first petal), * 5 ch, (1 petal = 3 unfin dtr into next 3 sts, yoh, draw yarn through all loops on hook). Rep from * to end of round, ending with 5 ch and 1 sl st into closing st of first petal, 1 ch.

Round 3: 1 dc into next st, * 5 ch, miss next 5-ch loop, ([1 tr tr, 2 ch] 9 times, 1 tr tr]) into foll 5-ch loop, 5 ch, miss next 5-ch loop, 1 dc into closing st of next petal *. Rep from * to * 3 more times, ending with 2 ch and 1 tr

Three-colour medallion

worked into first dc (instead of 5 ch and 1 dc).

Round 4: 3 ch, ✳ 1 tr into next 5-ch loop, (5 ch, miss next 2-ch sp, 1 dc into next 2-ch sp) twice, (5 ch, 1 dc into next space) twice, 5 ch, miss next space, 1 dc into next space, 5 ch, miss next last 2-ch sp, 1 tr into 5-ch loop ✳. Rep from ✳ to ✳ 3 more times, replacing last tr in final rep with 1 sl st into 3rd starting ch, 1 ch.

Round 5: 3 dc, 3 ch, 3 dc (= 1 scallop) into each 5-ch loop of previous row, ending with 1 sl st into first dc. Fasten off.

To join the first square to the 2nd and so on, work 2nd square in the same way until Round 4 has been completed.

Round 5: 1 scallop into each of the first 3 loops, (3 dc, 1 ch, 1 dc inserting hook into 3-ch loop of corresponding scallop of first square, 1 ch, 3 dc) 6 times altogether, then continue as for first square.

Three-colour medallion

(Replace first tr of round with 3 ch, first htr with 2 ch. Close each round with sl st into top of starting ch.)

Medallion with interwoven centre

Make 3 ch in first col and join with a sl st to form ring.

Round 1: 14 tr into ring.

Round 2: 2 tr into each tr (28 tr).

Round 3: * 1 tr into sp between 2 tr of previous round, 2 ch, (4 unfinished htr, yoh, draw yarn through all loops on hook) into sp between next 2-tr, 1 ch. * Rep from * to *. Cut off first col. Join in 2nd col.

Round 4 (2nd col): * (1 tr, 1 ch, 1 tr, 1 ch, 1 tr, 1 ch) into 2-ch sp. * Rep from * to *.

Round 5: 5 ch, * (4 unfin tr, yoh, draw yarn through all loops on hook) into middle tr of previous round, 1 ch, 1 tr between the foll 2 tr of previous row *. Rep from * to *.

Round 6: 3 tr into each ch of previous round. Cut off 2nd col. Join in 3rd col.

Round 7: (3rd col): * 10 dc, 1 htr, 2 tr, miss 2 sts, 5 tr into next st, miss 2 sts, 2 tr, 1 htr. * Rep from * to *.

Round 8: * 16 htr, 2 tr, (2 tr, 1 ch, 2 tr) into corner st, 2 tr. * Rep from * to *.

Round 9: * 1 tr, 1 ch, miss 1 st. * Rep from * to * along sides, working (2 tr, 1 ch, 2 tr).

Medallion with interwoven centre

(Replace first st of round as follows: dtr by 4 ch, tr by 3 ch, dc by 1 ch. Close each round with a sl st.)

Make 18 ch and join with a sl st to form ring.

Round 1: 36 tr into ring.

Cut off yarn. Work 7 more identical rings, interweaving them as the work progresses. The interweaving is done before closing the foundation ch into a ring. Slip the length of ch through the previous ring and join with sl st into first ch. Then work the 36 tr into it by turning the new ring gradually and making sure that all the stitches are worked in the same direction.

On starting the 8th ring, slip the length of ch into the last ring worked and into the first, thus linking all the rings into a circle, and complete as before.

Rejoin yarn to point of attachment of 2 of the rings, insert hook through tr of front and back rings simultaneously, * 1 dc, 9 ch, miss 6 sts of 2nd ring, 1 dc into next st of same ring, 9 ch, insert hook through tr of 2nd and 3rd ring, at point of attachment *. Rep from * to * 7 times more.

Round 1: 14 dc into each 6-ch loop.

Round 2: * (2-tr-cluster = 2 unfin tr, yoh, draw yarn through all 3 loops, 2 ch) 7 times, miss 5 sts, 3 tr, 2 ch, miss 6 sts. * Rep from * to *.

Round 3: * (2-tr-cluster, 2 ch) into 6 2-ch loops above 2-tr-clusters of previous round, 1 tr into 2-ch loop on right of the 3 tr of previous row (= 1 right increase), 1 tr into each of 3-tr, 1 tr into 2-ch loop on left of the same 3 tr (= 1 left increase), 2 ch. * Rep from * to *.

Round 4: * (2-tr-cluster, 2 ch) into 5 2-ch loops above 2-tr-clusters of previous round, 1 right inc, 5 tr, 1 left inc, 2 ch. * Rep from * to *.

Round 5: (2-tr-cluster, 2 ch) into 4 2-ch loops above 2-tr-clusters in previous round, 1 right inc, 7 tr, 1 left inc, 2 ch. * Rep from * to *.

Rounds 6 to 8: As Round 5, inc the no. of tr in each tr-group to 15 and reducing the no. of 2-tr-clusters in each 2-tr-cluster group to 1. At the same time, make 1 inc each round in the ch loops on each side of the tr.

Round 9: * 7 dc into first 2-ch loop, 1 dc into each of the 15 tr, 7 dc into next 2-ch loop. * Rep from * to *.

Round 10: * 1 dc into dc over last 2-tr-cluster, 5 ch, 1 dc into first of 15 dc, 14 ch, 1 dc into last of 15 dc, 5 ch, (1 tr, 3 ch, 1 tr) into dc over last 2-tr-cluster (corner), 5 ch, 1 dc into first of next 15 dc, 14 ch, 1 dc into last of 15 dc, 5 ch. * Rep from * to *.

Round 11: * 7 dc into 5-ch loop, 15 dc into 14-ch loop, 7 dc into 5-ch loop, (2 tr, 2 ch, 2 tr) into 3-ch loop (corner), 7 dc into 5-ch loop, 15 dc into 14-ch loop, 7 dc into 5-ch loop. * Rep from * to *.

Round 12: 1 tr into each st but on the 4 sts at each corner work (1 tr, 2 ch) twice, (1 tr, 3 ch, 1 tr) into 2-ch loop, (2 ch, 1 tr) twice.

Round 13: * 1 tr, 2 ch, miss 2 sts. * Rep from * to * along each side, working each corner as follows: (1 tr, 2 ch into each tr) 3 times, 1 tr, 3 ch, 1 tr into 3-ch corner loop, (1 tr, 2 ch into each tr) 3 times, 2 ch.

Round 14: As Round 13. Fasten off.

Medallion with central flower

Medallion with central flower

In starting from the middle of the flower, care must be taken always to work with the right side facing you, without ever turning the work (not normally done, in any case, when working rounds). The petals of the flower should always be towards you.

Where a very small centre is required, an alternative method is to wind the yarn 2 or 3 times round a pencil leaving a short end free. Slip this ring off the pencil and hold it firmly between thumb and forefinger of left hand, keeping yarn away from you. Insert crochet hook through ring from front to back and draw loop through. Work 1 ch. Continue working as many dc as required in ring, joining last dc to beginning 1-ch with a sl st. When a few rounds of pattern have been worked, the free end of yarn may be drawn up tightly and fastened off.

Make 6 ch and join with a sl st to form ring.

Round 1: 6 ch (= 1 tr plus 3 ch), (1 tr, 3 ch) 7 times in ring. Complete round with 1 sl st into 3rd of 6 starting ch (8 loops).

Round 2: 1 ch (1 dc, 3 tr, 1 dc) into each 3-ch loop of previous round. (First round of 8 petals.)

Round 3: 1 ch, 1 dc in sl st of Round 1 (between 2 petals), 4 ch (1 dc in next tr of Round 1 (between 2 petals), 4 ch 7 times. Complete round with 1 sl st in dc of previous round. (8 loops).

Round 4: 1 ch, (1 dc, 1 tr, 3 dtr, 1 tr, 1 dc) in each 4-ch loop of previous round. (2nd round of 8 petals).

Round 5: 1 ch 1 dc in sl st of Round 3 (between 2 petals), 5 ch, (1 dc in next dc of Round 3, between 2 petals, 5 ch) 7 times. Complete round with 1 dc in first dc of previous round (8 loops).

Round 6: 1 ch (1 dc, 1 tr, 5 dtr, 1 tr, 1 dc) in each 5-ch loop of previous row. (3rd round of 8 petals).

Round 7: 1 ch 1 dc in sl st of Round 5 (between 2 petals), 6 ch (1 dc in next dc of Round 5, between 2 petals, 6 ch) 7 times. Complete round with 1 sl st in first dc of previous round. (8 loops).

Round 8: 1 ch, (1 dc, 1 tr, 3 dtr, 1 ch, 3 dtr, 1 tr, 1 dc) in each 6-ch loop of previous round. (4th round of 8 petals).

The flower is now complete.

Round 9: 1 sl st in first 5 sts of first petal in order to reach central ch of petal, 4 ch (= 1 dtr), (3 dtr, 2 ch, 4 dtr, 2 ch) in 1-ch loop, 2 tr between 2 petals, 3 ch, 1 dc in central 1-ch) loop of next petal, 3 ch, 2 tr between next 2 petals, 2 ch, (4 dtr, 2 ch, 4 dtr, 2 ch.) in central 1-ch ch loop of next petal, 2 tr between the 2 petals, 3 ch, 1 dc in central 1-ch loop of next petal, 3 ch, 2 tr between the 2 petals, 2 ch. Complete round with 1 sl st in 4th starting ch.

Round 10: 1 sl st in 4 dtr in order to reach corner 2-ch loop. (4 ch [= 1 dtr], 4 dtr, 2 ch, 5 dtr, 2 ch) in corner 2-ch loop *, (2 tr, 2 ch) in 2-ch loop of previous round, (2 tr, 2 ch) in next 3-ch loop, (2 tr, 2 ch) in central dc of petal, (2 tr, 2 ch) in 3-ch loop, (2 tr, 2 ch) in next 2-ch loop, 2 ch (5 dtr, 2 ch, 5 dtr, 2 ch) in corner 2-ch loop *. Rep from * to *. Complete round with 1 sl st in 4th starting ch.

Round 11: 1 sl st in 5 dtr in order to reach corner 2-ch loop, (4 ch [= 1 dtr], 4 dtr, 2 ch, 5 dtr, 2 ch) in corner 2-ch loop, * (2 tr, 2 ch) in next two 2-ch loops of previous round, miss next 2 ch, (2 tr, 2 ch) between 2-tr of previous round, miss next 2 ch, (2 tr, 2 ch) in next two 2-ch loop, (5 dtr, 2 ch, 5 dtr, 2 ch) in corner 2-ch loop *. Rep from * to *. Complete round with 1 sl st in 4th starting ch.

Round 12: Rep Round 11.

Round 13: Rep round 11, working 3 ch (instead of 2) between the 2-tr groups.

Round 14: 3 ch (= 1 tr), 1 tr in every ch, tr and dtr of previous row, except on the corners. On each 2-ch loop at corner work 2 tr, 2 ch, 2 tr. Complete round with 1 sl st in 3rd starting ch. Fasten off.

Medallion with eight-petal flower

Make 12 ch and join with a sl st to form ring.

The first tr of each round must be replaced by 3 ch and the first dtr by 4 ch; all rounds are completed by working sl st in beg ch.

Round 1: Work 24 dtr in ring.

Round 2: 1 tr, 3 ch, (3 tr, 3 ch) 7 times, ending with 3 ch, 2 tr.

Round 3: (3 tr, 3 ch, 3 tr) in each 3-ch loop.

Round 4: Sl st in each of first 3 tr of previous row to bring work to first loop. (3 tr, 3 ch, 3 tr, 3 ch) in each 3-ch loop to end of round.

Round 5: Sl st in first 3 tr to bring work to first loop *, (3 tr, 1 ch, 3 tr) in first loop, 2 ch, 1 dc in 1-ch loop of round 3, 2 ch *. Rep from * to * 7 more times.

Round 6: Sl st to centre of first group, *1 dc in 1-ch loop, 5 ch, 1 cluster (cluster = **yoh, insert hook under ch-loops of 3rd and 4th rounds between the 2 groups, **3 times, yoh, draw yarn through all 7 loops on hook), 5 ch*. Rep from * to * 7 more times.

Round 7: 8 tr in each 5-ch loop of previous round.

Round 8: 1 ch*, 1 dc in st corresponding with the dc of Round 6, 5 ch, 2 tr to correspond with cluster between next 2 groups, 5 ch, 1 dc in st corresponding with the dc of Round 6, 5 ch, (2 dtr, 3 ch, 2 dtr) to correspond with next cluster (corner), 5 ch*. Rep from * to * 3 more times.

Round 9: 1 ch, * 1 dc in dc, 5 dc in 5-ch loop, 1 dc in each of 2 tr, 5 dc in 5-ch loop, 1 dc in dc, (2 dc, 1 htr, 3 tr) in 5-ch loop, 1 tr between 2 dtr, (3 tr, 3 ch, 3 tr) in corner 4-ch loop, 1 tr between 2 dtr, (3 tr, 1 htr, 2 dc) in next 5-ch loop *. Rep from * to * 3 more times.

Round 10: 1 tr in each st of previous row on all 4 sides, working (2 tr, 3 ch, 2 tr) in each of the 3-ch corner loops.

Round 11: 5 ch, * (miss 2 sts, 2 tr, 2 ch) 6 times, miss 2 sts, (3 tr, 3 ch, 3 tr) in corner 3-ch loop, 2 ch, miss 2 sts, (2 tr, 2 ch, miss 2 sts) twice 2 tr *. Rep from * to * 3 more times.

Round 12: * (2 tr in 2-ch loop, 1 tr in each tr) 7 times (2 tr, 3 ch, 2 tr) in corner 3-ch loop, (1 tr in each tr, 2 tr in 2-ch loop) 3 times, 1 tr in tr, sl st to join. Fasten off.

Medallion with star design

(The first tr of Rounds 5 to 13 are replaced by 3 ch).

Make 10 ch and join with a sl st to form ring.

Round 1: 1 ch*, 1 dc, 1 htr, 3 tr, 1 htr. Rep from * to * 4 more times. Complete this and every following round with 1 sl st in beg st.

Round 2: 1 ch, *, insert hook from *back to front* in dc of petal and work 1 dc, 4 ch *. Rep from * to * 4 more times. (Petals will lie forward with ch loops behind).

Round 3: 1 ch, * (1 dc, 1 htr, 5 tr, 1 htr, 1 dc) in 4-ch loop *. Rep from * to * 4 more times (5 petals).

Round 4: 1 ch, 1 dc in first dc of Round 2, 6 ch, 1 dc between 2 dc. Rep from * to * 3 more times, 6 ch.

Round 5: * 1 tr in dc, 2 ch (1 tr, 2 ch) twice in 6-ch loop *. Rep from * to * 4 more times.

Round 6: * 1 tr in tr, 2 ch, 1 hazelnut (= ** yoh, insert hook in next st, yoh, draw yarn through ** 5 times, yoh, draw yarn through all 11 loops on hook, 1 ch), 1 ch, 1 tr in tr, 2 ch *. Rep from * to * 6 more times, 1 tr on tr, 2 ch, 1 hazelnut, 1 ch, 1 tr in base of beg 3-ch, 2 ch, sl st in top of 3-ch.

Round 7: * 1 tr in tr, 2 ch, 1 hazelnut to the right and 1 hazelnut to the left of hazelnut in previous row, 1 ch, 1 tr in tr, 2 ch *. Rep from * to * 7 more times.

Round 8: 1 tr in tr, 2 ch, 3 hazelnuts (1 to the right, 1 in between and 1 to the left of hazelnuts in previous row), 1 ch, 1 tr in tr, 2 ch *. Rep from * to * 7 more times.

Round 9: * 1 tr in tr, 2 ch, 1 hazelnut in 2-ch loop, 1 hazelnut between each of next 2 hazelnuts, 1 hazelnut in 2-ch loop, 1 ch, 1 tr in tr, 2 ch *. Rep from * to * 7 more times.

Round 10: * 1 tr in tr, 2 ch, 1 tr in closing st of next hazelnut, 2 ch, 3 hazelnuts, 1 ch, 1 tr in closing st of 4th hazelnut, 2 ch, 1 tr in tr, 2 ch *. Rep from * to * 7 more times.

Round 11: * 1 tr in tr, 2 ch, 1 tr, 2 ch, 1 tr in closing st of next hazelnut, 2 ch, 2 hazelnuts, 1 ch, 1 tr in closing st of 3rd hazelnut, (2 ch, 1 tr in tr) twice, 2 ch*. Rep from * to * 7 more times.

Medallion with eight-petal flower

Round 12: ✳ (1 tr in tr, 2 ch) 3 times, 1 tr in closing st of next hazelnut, 2 ch, 1 hazelnut, 1 ch, 1 tr in closing st of 2nd hazelnut, 2 ch, (1 tr in tr, 2 ch) 3 times ✳. Rep from ✳ to ✳ 7 more times.

Round 13: ✳, (1 tr in tr, 2 ch) 4 times, 1 tr in closing st of hazelnut, 2 ch, (1 tr in tr, 2 ch) 4 times ✳. Rep from ✳ to ✳ 7 more times.

Round 14: 1 ch, ✳, (1 ridged dc – formed by working in back loop only instead of through both loops – in tr, 2 ridged dc in 2-ch loop) 4 times, 4 ch; miss one 2-ch loop, (1 dc, 1 picot [= 3 ch and 1 sl st in last st worked] 1 dc, 4 ch) in next ch loop, 5 times, miss one 2-ch loop, (2 dc in 2-ch loop, 1 dc in tr) twice 2 dc in 2-ch loop). Rep from ✳ to ✳ 3 more times.

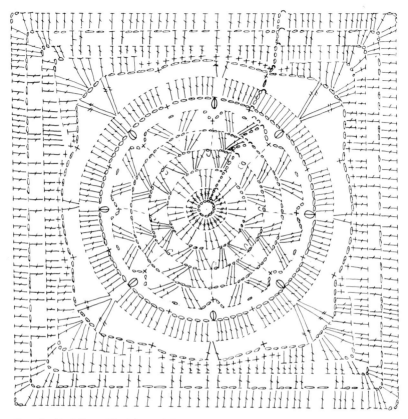

Chart for Medallion with eight-petal flower

Round 15: 1 ch, 12 ridged dc in ridged dec of previous round, *, 2 ridged dc into next 2 ch, 5 ch, (1 dc, 1 picot, 1 dc, 4 ch) in each of next four 4-ch loops, 1 ch, 2 ridged dc in last 2 ch, 20 ridged dc, *. Rep from * to * 3 more times, ending last rep 8 ridged dc.

Round 16: 1 ch, 14 ridged dc in ridged dc, *, 2 ridged dc in next 2 ch, 6 ch, (1 dc, 1 picot, 1 dc, 4 ch) 3 times, 2 ch, 2 ridged dc in next 2 ch, 24 ridged dc *. Rep from * to * 3 more times ending last rep 10 ridged dc.

Round 17: 1 ch, 16 ridged dc in ridged dc, *, 2 ridged dc in next 2 ch 6 ch, (1 dc, 1 picot, 1 dc, 4 ch) twice, 2 ch, 2 ridged dc in next 2 ch, 28 ridged dc, *. Rep from * to * 3 more times ending last rep 12 ridged dc.

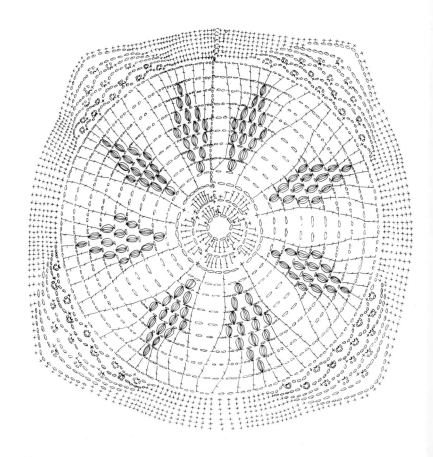

Chart for Medallion with star design

Round 18: 1 ch, 18 ridged dc in ridged dc, *, 2 ridged dc in next 2 ch, 7 ch, 1 dc, 1 picot, 1 dc, 7 ch, 2 ridged dc in next 2 ch, 32 ridged dc, *. Rep from * to * 3 more times, ending last rep 14 ridged, dc.

Round 19: 1 ch, 20 ridged dc in ridged dc, *, 2 ridged dc in next 2 ch 15 ch (= corner), 2 ridged dc in last 2 ch of 7-ch loop worked after picot, 36 ridged dc, *. Rep from * to * 3 more times, ending last rep 16 ridged dc.

Round 20: 1 ridged dc in every st to end of round. Fasten off.

Medallion with four-pointed star and four rays

Make 6 ch and join with a sl st to form ring.

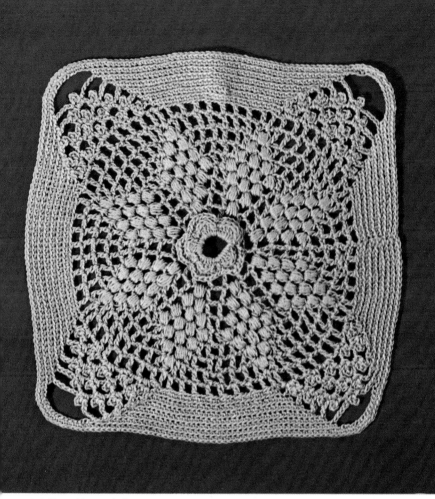

Medallion with star design

Round 1: 16 dc in ring, ending with 1 sl st in first st.

Round 2: In dc, increasing 4 sts (20 sts).

Round 3: (Each point is worked back and forth by turning the work at the end of each row) 20 ch, starting in 6th ch from hook, * 1 tr, miss 1 st *. Rep from * to * 3 times more, 3 tr, 4 dc, 1 dc in next dc (of Round 3).

Round 4: Turn the work, 15 ridged dc (work into *back* loop only of sts just worked including 4 turning ch, 5 dc in next ch at tip of point), 15 ridged dc along the other side, 1 dc into next dc.

Round 5: Turn work, 1 ch, 1 dc in first 7 sts, 5 ch, 1 dc in last st worked (= 1 picot), (3 dc, 1 picot) twice, 5 dc, 1 picot (tip of star), 5 dc, 1 picot (3 dc, 1

Medallion with four-pointed star and four rays

picot) twice, 6 dc, 1 dc in next dc of Round 3. This completes work on first point of star.

Round 6: (Start first ray) 11 ch, 1 sl st in 6th ch from hook. Work in ring just made: 1 dc, 3 ch, remove hook from working loop and insert it in the first picot of the first point, pick up working loop again, yoh, draw yarn through, 2 ch, * 1 dc in ring (the first link has been completed), 5 ch *, rep from * to * 4 times, 1 dc in each of 5 ch (at start of first ray), 1 dc in base of 11-ch (this completes the ray), miss 1 st of Round 3. Rep Rounds 3, 4 and 5 to make a 2nd point. On the last round, link first picot with 5th picot of ray, as already described. Work 4 points alternating with 4 rays altogether.

Cast off and put completed star on one side. Now work the frame in rows, back and forth, in ridged tr. Starting from one corner, make 21 ch.

Row 1: 1 tr in 4th ch from hook, 17 tr, 3 ch, turn.

Row 2: 18 tr.

Row 3: 1 sl st in first 6 tr (in order to reach middle sts), 3 ch, 6 tr, turn, 3 ch 6 tr. Cut off yarn.

Row 4: Turn the work, insert hook in last foundation ch (on the right), work 9 ch.

Row 5: 1 tr in 4th ch from hook, 1 tr in each of next 5 ch, 6 tr worked opposite the tr of Row 1 (they will therefore be worked on the other side of the foundation ch), turn.

Row 6: 3 ch, 1 tr in 12 tr of previous row, 9 ch.

Row 7: 1 tr in 4th ch from hook, 1 tr in

each of next 5 ch, 1 tr in each of 6 tr of previous row, turn. (6 tr remain.)

Row 8: As Row 6.

Rep Rows 6 and 7 until 6 rectangles of 2 rows of 12 tr, 3 ch, have been worked (1 side of frame).

To make the 2nd corner: Work as for Row 7, then return to beg of row with sl sts, rep Row 6 (the rectangle for the 2nd corner is now complete), continue to make the other sides as before and alternate the corners (1st and 2nd). In the last rep of Row 6 (before the 3rd corner), work 15 ch instead of 9.

To complete the frame, on the final row of the 4th corner, link up with the 6 tr of the first side (6 central sts will remain unworked).

Now work 2 rounds around the in-side of the frame which will link it to the star already made:

Round 1: 1 dc in inside corner of first rectangle, * 9 ch, 1 dc in corner of 2nd rectangle, * rep from * to * 4 times, 5 ch, 1 dc in first rectangle of 2nd side. Continue the round in this way, ending with 1 sl st in starting st.

Round 2: (5 dc, 1 picot, 5 dc) in each 9-ch loop. At each corner, work 5 dc in the 5-ch loops. As you work this round, link the central star with the 4 picots of the 4 rays.

On the outside edges of the frame work 2 finishing rounds as worked inside except that the corners are worked as follows:

Round 1 – 9 ch, and on Round 2 – 5 dc, 1 picot, 5 dc.

Medallion with triangular design

(Replace first tr of round by 3 ch. Close each round with a sl st).
Make 6 ch and join with a sl st to form ring.
Round 1: (3 tr, 2 ch) 4 times in ring.
Round 2: ∗ 1 tr in each tr of previous round, (2 tr, 3 ch, 2 tr) in each 2-ch loop. ∗ Rep from ∗ to ∗ to end of round.
Rounds 3, 4, 5, and 6: Rep Round 2, thus increasing 4 tr on each side. (At completion of Round 6, there will be 23 tr on each side).
Round 7: ∗ 3 ch, 1 sl st in next tr, 3 ch, miss next tr, 1 sl st in next tr. ∗ Rep from ∗ to ∗ to end of round but at each corner work 5 ch instead of 3. There will now be 8 loops close together and 7 loops spaced by 1 tr on each side of square.
Round 8: 1 sl st in first loop (one of those spaced by a tr). ∗ 5 ch, miss 1 close loop, 1 sl st in next spaced loop. ∗ Rep from ∗ to ∗ to end of round, working 5 ch, 1 sl st, 5 ch, 1 sl st, 5 ch in each corner loop.
There will now be 8 loops on each side and 1 loop on each corner.
Round 9: ∗ (1 sl st [5 ch, 1 sl st] 3 times) in next loop ∗. Rep from ∗ to ∗ along each side, working in all 4 corner loops as follows: 1 sl st (6 ch, 1 sl st) 4 times.
There will now be 3 small loops on each of the loops on all 4 sides and 4 on each corner loop. Fasten off.

Medallion with star

(Replace first st of round as follows: tr tr by 5 ch, dc by 1 ch. Close each round with sl st).
Make 8 ch and join with a sl st to form ring.
Round 1: 12 dc in ring.
Round 2: (2 dc, 2 dc in next st) 4 times.
Round 3: ∗ 1 tr tr, 2 ch ∗. Rep from ∗ to ∗ 15 more times.
Round 4: 1 dc in each tr and ch (48 sts).
Round 5: (7 dc, 2 dc in next st) 6 times (54 sts).
Round 6: (8 dc, 2 dc in next st) 6 times (60 sts).
Round 7: (9 dc, 2 dc in next st) 6 times (66 sts).
Round 8: ∗ 11 dc, turn; 3 ch, miss 1 dc, 9 dc, turn; 3 ch, miss 1 dc, 7 dc,

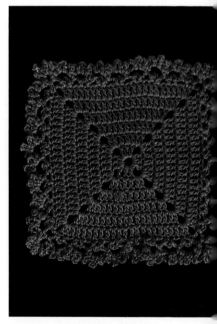

Medallion with triangular design

turn; continue in this way, decreasing 1 dc at each end of every row until 1 dc remains. Return to base of point by working sl sts along left side *. Rep from * to * 5 more times, but omit sl sts after last point has been worked.

Round 9: * 1 dc in tip of point, 16 ch *. Rep from * to * 5 more times.

Round 10: 1 dc in each ch, 3 dc in dc at each point. Fasten off.

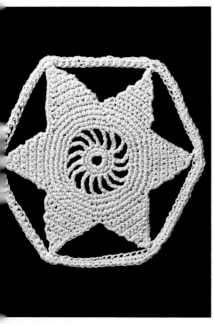

Medallion with star

BORDERS, EDGINGS AND INSERTIONS

Crochet for the finishing touches

Borders are simply strips of crochet made to finish and embellish a garment or an object (tablecloths, handkerchiefs, and so on). They may be worked separately and then attached to the edge of the fabric or they may be worked directly onto the fabric itself. Instructions for a few smaller borders (which we have called 'trimmings') have also been included. These have only a few rows and are extremely useful for finishing the edges of knitted or crocheted jackets, cardigans, and so on (in wool), or of handkerchiefs, guest towels, etc. (in varying thicknesses of cotton, according to the texture of the fabric).

Edgings, on the other hand, are usually more elegant and elaborate. They are always worked separately and only attached to the item for which they may be intended on completion.

Insertions are also decorative but are placed – as the name implies – into or on the body of the fabric and attached to it on both sides. The fabric may remain underneath (ie as with appliqué crochet) or it may be cut away. Insertions are useful, too, for joining two pieces of fabric together, for lengthening a skirt or decorating sleeves.

Borders

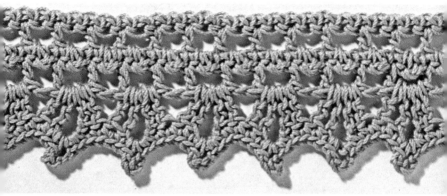

Border no. 1

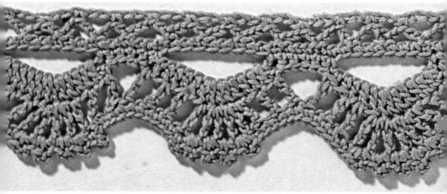

Border no. 2

Border no. 1

Make foundation ch in multiples of 4 plus 3.

Row 1: 1 dc in 2nd ch from hook, 1 dc in each ch ending with 3 ch, turn.
Row 2: Miss 2 sts, * 1 tr in next st, 1 ch, miss 1 st, *.
Rep from * to *, ending with 1 tr, 1 ch, turn.
Row 3: * 1 dc in tr, 1 tr in 1-ch space *. Rep from * to *, ending with 1 dc, 3 ch, turn.

Row 4: Miss 2 sts, * 1 tr in next st, 1 ch, miss 1 st *. Rep from * to *, ending with 1 tr.
Row 5: 1 sl st in first 1-ch space, 4 ch (1 dtr, 2 ch, 2 dtr) in same 1-ch space, * miss one 1-ch space, (2 dtr, 2 ch, 2 dtr) in next space *. Rep from * to * ending with 1 ch, turn.
Row 6: 1 dc in each of first 2 dtr, * (2 dc, 4 ch, 2 dc) in 2-ch space, 1 dc in each of next 4 dtr. *.
Rep from * to *, ending with 2 dc. Fasten off.

Border no. 2

Make foundation ch in multiples of 42 plus 29.
Row 1: 1 dc into 2nd ch from hook, ∗ 5 ch, miss 2 ch, 1 dc into next ch ∗. Rep from ∗ to ∗, 3 ch, turn.
Row 2: Sl st into 3rd ch of 5-ch loop, ∗ 3 ch, sl st into 3rd ch of next 5-ch loop ∗. Rep from ∗ to ∗ ending with 1 ch, 1 tr into last dc, 1 ch, turn.
Row 3: 1 dc into tr, 1 dc into 1-ch loop, ∗ 3 dc into 3-ch loop ∗. Rep from ∗ to ∗ ending with 2 dc into last 3-ch loop, 1 ch, turn.
Row 4: ∗ 3 dc, 12 ch, miss 8 sts, 3 dc ∗. Rep from ∗ to ∗ to end.
Row 5: ∗ Sl st over 3 dc, 1 tr into each of next 5 ch, (2 tr into next ch) twice, 1 tr into each of next 5 ch, sl st over 3 dc ∗. Rep from ∗ to ∗, 4 ch, turn.
Row 6: ∗ 1 dtr into tr, 1 ch, miss 2 sts, 1 dtr, 1 ch, miss 1 st, 1 dtr, (1 ch, 2 dtr into next st) twice, 1 ch, 1 dtr, 1 ch, miss 1 st, 1 dtr, 1 ch, miss 2 sts, 1 dtr ∗. Rep from ∗ to ∗ ending with 1 dtr into 3rd sl st, 1 ch, turn.
Row 7: 1 dc into first tr, ∗ (1 dc into tr, 1 dc into 1-ch loop) twice, 1 dc into tr, (3 ch, 1 dc into 1-ch loop, 3 ch, 1 dc between 2-tr) twice, 3 ch, 1 dc into 1-ch loop, miss 1 tr, 1 dc into 1-ch loop, 1 dc into tr ∗. Rep from ∗ to ∗ ending with 1 dc into t-ch. Fasten off.

Border no. 3

Make foundation ch in multiples of 4 plus 3.
Row 1: In 5th ch from hook work ∗ 1 tr, 1 ch, miss 1 st. Rep from 1, ending with 1 tr in last ch, 1 ch, turn.
Row 2: 1 dc in first tr, ∗ 7 ch, miss 1 tr, 1 dc in next tr. Rep from ∗ ending with 1 dc in 2nd ch, 1 ch, turn.
Row 3: Work 10 dc in each 7-ch loop.
Row 4: 1 sl st in first 5 dc, to bring working st to top of loop, ∗ 7 ch, 1 sl st in centre top of next loop. Rep

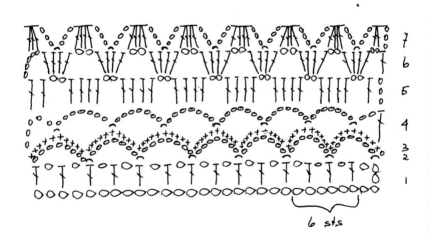

Chart for Border no. 3

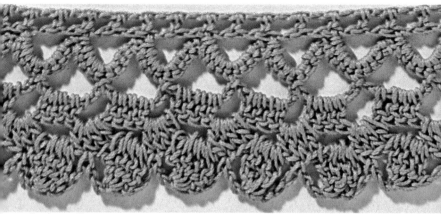

Border no. 3

from * ending with 1 sl st in centre top of last loop of previous row, 3 ch, turn.

Row 5: 3 tr in 7-ch loop of previous row, * 2 ch, 4 tr in next 7-ch loop. Rep from * to end, 5 ch, turn.

Row 6: 3 tr in first 2-ch loop of previous row, * 2 ch, 4 tr into next 2 ch loop *. Rep from * to *, ending with 3 ch, turn.

Row 7: * 3 unfin dtr in next 2-ch loop, yoh, draw loop through all 4 loops on hook, 3 ch, 1 sl st in middle of the 4-tr of previous row, 3 ch *. Rep from * to * but making 4 unfin dtr instead of 3. Fasten off.

Border no. 4

Make a foundation ch in multiples of 22 plus 6.

Row 1: 1 dc in 2nd ch from hook, 1 dc in each ch to end, 3 ch, turn.

Row 2: Miss 1 st, * 1 tr, 1 ch, miss 1 st *. Rep from * to * ending with 2 tr, 3 ch, turn.

Row 3: Miss 2 tr, (1 tr in 1-ch loop, 1 ch) 4 times, * 1 tr in 1-ch loop, 5 ch, miss two 1-ch loops, (1 tr in 1-ch loop, 1 ch) 8 times *. Rep from * to * ending with (1 tr in 1-ch loop, 1 ch) 5 times, 1 tr in turning ch, 3 ch, turn.

Row 4: (1 tr in 1-ch loop, 1 ch) 5 times, * (2 tr, 1 ch, 2 tr, 1 ch, 2 tr, 1 ch) in 5-ch loop, (1 tr in 1-ch loop, 1 ch) 8 times *. Rep from * to * ending with (1 tr in 1-ch loop, 1 ch) 4 times, 1 tr in turning ch, 3 ch, turn.

Row 5: (1 tr in 1-ch loop, 1 ch) 4 times, * 1 tr in 1-ch loop ch, 1 tr in each of next 2 tr, 1 ch, 1 tr in tr, 2 tr in next tr, 1 ch, 1 tr in each of next 2 tr, 1 tr in 1-ch loop, 1 ch, (1 tr in 1-ch loop, 1 ch) 7 times *. Rep from * to * ending with (1 tr in 1-ch loop, 1 ch) 4 times, 1 tr in turning ch, 3 ch, turn.

Row 6: (1 tr in 1-ch loop, 1 ch) 4 times, * (1 tr in each of next 2 tr, 2 tr in 3rd tr, 1 ch) 3 times, (1 tr in 1-ch loop, 1 ch) 6 times *. Rep from * to * ending with (1 tr in 1-ch loop, 1 ch) 3 times, 1 tr in turning ch, 3 ch, turn.

Row 7: (1 tr in 1-ch loop, 1 ch) 3 times, * (1 tr in each of next 3 tr, 2 tr in 4th tr, 1 ch) 3 times, (1 tr in 1-ch loop, 1 ch) 5 times *. Rep from * to * ending with (1 tr in 1-ch loop, 1 ch) 3 times, 1 tr in turning ch, 3 ch, turn.

Row 8: (1 tr in 1-ch loop, 1 ch) 3

times, * (1 tr in each of next 4 tr, 2 tr in 5th tr, 1 ch) 3 times, (1 tr in 1-ch loop, 1 ch) 4 times *. Rep from * to * ending with (1 tr in 1-ch loop, 1 ch) twice, 1 tr in turning ch, 3 ch, turn.
Row 9: (1 tr in 1-ch loop, 1 ch) twice, * (1 tr in each of next 6 tr, 1 ch) 3 times, (1 tr in 1-ch loop, 1 ch) 3 times *. Rep from * to * ending with (1 tr in 1-ch loop, 1 ch) twice, 1 tr in turning ch, 1 ch, turn.
Row 10: * (1 dc in tr, 1 dc in 1-ch loop) twice, 1 dc in tr, miss 1 ch, (1 tr in each of next 6 tr, 1 tr in 1-ch loop) twice, 1 tr in each of next 6 tr, miss 1 ch *. Rep from * to * ending with 1 dc in tr, 1 dc in 1-ch loop, 1 dc in tr, 1 dc in each of next 2 ch (of turning ch), 1 ch, turn.
Row 11: * 1 dc in each of next 2 dc, 4 ch, miss 1 dc, 1 dc in each of next 2 dc, 1 dc in tr, (1 dc in tr, 4 ch, miss 1 tr) 9 times, 1 dc in last tr of group *. Rep from * to * ending with 1 dc in next 2 dc, 4 ch, miss 1 dc, 1 dc in next 2 dc. Fasten off.

Border no. 5

Make foundation ch in multiples of 6 plus 3.
Row 1: 1 dc in 2nd ch from hook, 1 dc into ch to end 3 ch, turn.
Row 2: 1 tr in 2nd st, * 1 ch, miss 1 st, 2 tr *. Rep from * to * ending with 1 ch, turn.
Row 3: 1 dc in tr, 1 tr in next tr (1 tr, 1 dtr) in 1-ch loop miss 2 tr and 1 ch, 1 dc in tr, 1 dtr in next tr *. Rep from * to * ending with 1 dc in tr, 1 dtr in following ch, 4 ch, turn.
Row 4: * dc in dtr, 6 ch, *. Rep from * to * ending with 2 ch, 1 tr in dc, 4 ch, turn.
Row 5: (3 dtr, 1 tr), in 2-ch loop. * (1 tr, 6 dtr, 1 tr) in each 6-ch loop *. Rep from * to * ending with 1 tr, 4 dtr in 4-ch loop, 1 ch, turn.
Row 6: * 1 dc, 4 ch in each st. * Rep from * to * to end of row. Fasten off.

Border no. 6

Make foundation ch in multiples of 16 plus 5.
Row 1: 1 tr in 5th ch from hook, * 1 ch, miss 1 ch, 1 tr * Rep from * to * ending with 3 ch, turn.
Row 2: * (1 tr, 2 ch, 1 tr) in first 1-ch loop of previous row, 3 ch, miss three 1-ch loops, (1 dtr, 5 ch, 1 dtr) in next 1-ch loop, miss three 1-ch loops *. Rep from * to * ending with (1 tr, 2 ch, 1 tr) in turning ch, 3 ch, turn.
Row 3: * (1 tr, 2 ch, 1 tr) in 2-ch loop, (4 dtr, 5 ch, 4 dtr) in 5-ch loop *. Rep from * to * ending with (1 tr, 2 ch 1 tr) in 2-ch loop, 3 ch, turn.
Row 4: * (1 tr, 3 ch, 1 tr) in 2-ch loop, (4 dtr, 5 ch, 4 dtr) in 5-ch loop *. Rep from * to * ending with 1 tr 2 ch, 1 tr in 2-ch loop. Fasten off.

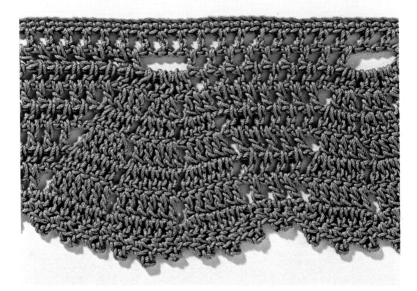

Border no. 4

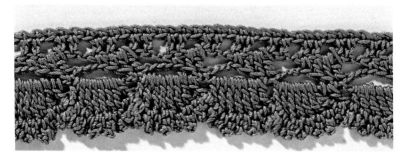

Border no. 5

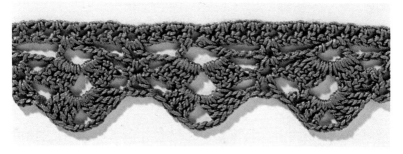

Border no. 6

Border no. 7

Border no. 8

Border no. 9

138

Border no. 7

Make foundation ch in multiples of 12 plus 10.

Row 1: 1 dc in 2nd ch from hook, 1 dc into each ch ending with 3 ch, turn.

Row 2: 2 tr, * 3 ch, miss 3 sts, 3 tr, *. Rep from * to * ending with 5 ch, turn.

Row 3: Miss 3 tr, * 1 dc in first 3-ch loop, 3 ch, (3 tr, 2 ch 3 tr) in 2nd 3-ch loop, 3 ch. *. Rep from * to * ending with 1 dc in last 3-ch loop, 3 ch, 1 tr in turning ch, 4 ch, turn.

Row 4: * 1 dc in dc of previous row, 4 ch, (3 tr, 2 ch, 3 tr) in 2-ch loop, 4 ch. * Rep from * to * ending with 1 dc in dc of previous row, 1 dc in 2nd ch, 4 ch, turn.

Row 5: * (2 tr, 2 ch, 2 tr) in dc of previous row, 3 ch, (1 tr, 1 ch) 6 times in 2-ch loop, 2 ch *. Rep from * to * ending with 1 tr, 4 ch, turn.

Row 6: * (1 tr, 2 ch, 1 tr) in 2-ch loop of previous row, 1 ch (1 tr in tr, 1 tr in ch) 5 times, 1 tr in tr, 1 ch *. Rep from * to 1 * ending with 1 tr in 2nd ch, 3 ch, turn.

Row 7: * 1 dc in 2-ch loop, 1 dc in each of 10 tr *. Rep from * to * ending 1 dc in 2-ch loop, 2 ch, 1 dc in turning ch. Fasten off.

Border no. 8

Make foundation ch in multiples of 7 plus 3.

Row 1: 1 dc in 2nd ch from hook, 1 dc in each ch ending with 4 ch, turn.

Row 2: Miss 1 st, 1 dtr, miss 2 sts, * (1 dtr, 3 ch, 1 dtr) in next st, miss 2 sts, 2 dtr *. Rep from * to * ending with 6 ch, turn.

Row 3: 1 dtr in space between 2 dtr, * 2 dtr in 3-ch loop, (1 dtr, 3 ch, 1 dtr) in space between 2 dtr *. Rep from * to * ending with (1 dtr, 3 ch, 1 dtr) in turning ch, 5 ch, turn.

Row 4: (1 dtr, 1 ch in 3-ch loop) twice, 1 dtr in same loop, * 1 dc in space between next 2 dtr, (1 dtr, 1 ch in 3-ch loop) 3 times, 1 dtr in same loop *. Rep from * to * ending with (1 dtr, 1 ch in turning ch) 3 times, 1 dtr in turning ch, 1 ch, turn.

Row 5: 3 dc, * 3 ch, 1 dc in next 9 dc *. Rep from * to *. Fasten off.

Border no. 9

Make foundation ch in multiples of 12 plus 2.

Row 1: 1 dc in 2nd ch from hook, 1 dc in each ch ending with 1 ch, turn.

Row 2: * 1 dc, 5 ch, miss 5, sts *. Rep from * to * ending with 1 dc, 4 ch, turn.

Row 3: * 3 tr in 5-ch loop, 3 tr in next 5-ch loop, 4 ch *. Rep from * to * ending with 2 ch, 1 tr in last st, 3 ch, turn.

Row 4: 2 tr in 2-ch loop, * 3 ch, 7 tr in 4-ch loop *. Rep from * to * ending with 3 ch, 3 tr in turning ch, 3 ch, turn.

Row 5: * 3 ch, 7 tr in 3-ch loop *. Rep from * to * ending with 1 tr in last tr, 1 tr in turning ch, 1 tr in 2nd tr. Fasten off.

Border no. 10

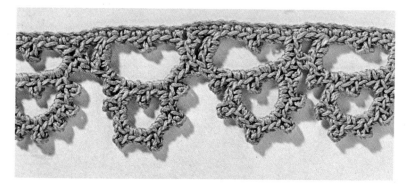

Border no. 11

Border no. 10

Make foundation ch in multiples of 6 plus 2.

Row 1: 1 dc in 2nd ch from hook, 1 dc in each ch ending with 1 ch, turn.

Row 2: * 1 dc, 5 ch, miss 5 sts *. Rep from * to * ending with 1 dc 4 ch, turn.

Row 3: * 1 dc in 5-ch loop, 5 ch *. Rep from * to * ending with 1 dc in 5-ch loop, 2 ch, tr in last dc, 3 ch turn.

Row 4: (1 tr, 1 picot [= 3 ch, 1 sl st in top of tr just worked], 3 tr) in 2-ch loop, 1 dc in dc *, (5 tr, 1 picot 4 tr) in 5-ch loop, 1 dc in dc *. Rep from * to * ending with (3 tr 1 picot, 2 tr) in last loop. Fasten off.

Border no. 11

Make a foundation ch in multiples of 9 plus 6.

Row 1: Starting in 2nd ch from hook, work 3 dc, 1 picot (3 ch and 1 sl st in first ch), 3 dc, 12 ch. Remove hook from work, insert it in the 3rd st to the right of picot, replace working st (of 12th ch) on hook and work 1 sl st (3 dc, 1 picot, 3 dc, 1 picot, 4 dc, 1 picot, 2 dc). In the loop thus formed work 10 ch, remove hook and insert it in the middle of 4 dc just worked, replace working st (of 10th ch) on hook and work 1 sl st (3 dc, 1 picot) 5 times in the new loop. This will bring work back to the 12-ch loop underneath. In this work 2 dc, 1 picot 3 dc, 1 picot, 3 dc. This will bring work back to the foundation ch.

In this work 6 dc (1 in next 6 ch) 1 picot, 3 dc, 12 ch, insert hook in 3rd st to the right of the picot, 1 sl st (3 dc, 2 ch). In the new loop formed make a link with the picot on nearby loop, 1 ch, 3 dc, 1 picot, 4 dc, 1 picot, 2 dc. Work 10 ch, insert hook in the middle of 4 dc just worked, 1 sl st (3 dc, 1 picot) 5 times. In the new loop formed 12-ch loop with 2 dc, 1 picot, 3 dc, 1 picot, 3 dc. Work will now be back to the foundation ch *. Rep from * to * until all foundation ch has been worked. Fasten off.

Border no. 12

Make foundation ch in multiples of 15 plus 12.

Row 1: 1 dc in 2nd ch from hook, 1 dc in each ch, ending 3 ch, turn.

Row 2: Miss 2 sts, 1 tr, 1 tr in 2nd missed st (yoh, insert hook into st just passed over, yoh at back of work, draw yarn through to front and complete as for normal tr), 1 ch, miss 1 st, 1 tr, 1 tr in missed st *. Rep from * to * ending with 3 ch turn.

Row 3: * 1 tr in 1-ch loop, 1 tr in preceding tr (ie 2nd tr missed of previous row) *. Rep from * to * ending with 2-ch turn.

Row 4: * 1 dc between first and 2nd groups of 2 crossed tr, 7 ch, miss 8 tr *. Rep from * to * ending with dc in turning ch, 4 ch, turn.

Row 5: * (1 dtr, 1 ch, 1 dtr) in 7-ch loop, 2 ch, 1 dtr, 1 ch, 1 dtr, 3 ch, 1 dtr, 1 ch, 1 dtr) in next 7-ch loop, 2 ch *. Rep from * to * ending with 1 dtr in turning ch 4 ch, turn.

Row 6: 1 dtr in first st, 2 ch, * 1 dc in ch between 2 dtr, 2 ch, (1 dtr, 1 ch, 1 dtr) in next 1-ch loop, (1 ch, 1 dtr) 5 times in next 3-ch loop (1 dtr, 1 ch, 1 dtr, in next 1-ch loop) 2 ch. * Rep from * to * ending with (1 dtr, 1 ch, 1 dtr) in turning ch, 1 ch, turn.

Row 7: * 1 dc and 1 picot (3 ch, 1 dc in first ch) in each 1-ch loop, miss 2 ch 1 dc and 2 ch *. Rep from * to *. Fasten off.

Border no. 12

141

Border no. 13 with corners

Make foundation ch in multiples of 8 plus 5 for each side, 1 ch for each corner and 1 t ch.

Row 1: 1 dc in 2nd ch from hook, 1 dc in each remaining ch, working 3 dc in 1 dc where corners are to be made and ending with 5 ch, turn.

Row 2: Miss 2 dc * 1 tr, 3 ch, miss 1 dc *. Rep from * to * ending with 2 ch, turn.

Row 3: * 1 dc in 3-ch loop of previous row, 2 ch, 7 dtr in next 3-ch loop of previous row, 2 ch, 7 dtr next 3-ch loop, 2 ch *. Rep from * to * working 9 dtr in corners and ending with 1 dc in t ch, 1 ch, 1 dc in 3rd t ch, 3 ch, turn.

Row 4: * 1 dc in dc of previous row, 3 ch, (1 dtr, 1 ch) 7 times * 2 ch. Rep from * to * onsides, working (1 dtr, 1 ch) 9 times in each corner and ending with 1 dc in dc, 1 ch, 1 dc in t ch, 4 ch turn.

Row 5: * 1 tr tr in dtr, 3 ch *. Rep from * to * including corners and ending with 1 dc in 3 t ch.

Row 6: 4 dc, 1 picot (= 3 ch, 1 dc in first ch) in every 3-ch loop. Fasten off.

Border no. 13 with corner

TRIMMINGS

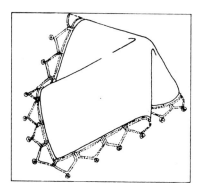

Trimming no. 1 with corner

Trimming no. 1 with corners

Make a foundation ch in multiples of 4 plus 3 for each side, 1 ch for each corner and 1 t-ch.
Row 1: 1 dc into 2nd ch from hook, 1 dc into each remaining ch, 1 ch, turn.
Row 2: dc, working 3 dc into st where corners are to be made.
Row 3: 1 dc, * 5 ch, miss 3 dc, 1 dc into next dc *. Rep from * to * on sides, working (1 dc, 5 ch, miss 2 sp, 1 dc into central dc on corner, 5 ch, miss 2 sts, 1 dc) on each corner.
Row 4: (3 dc, 1 picot, 3 dc) into each 5-ch loop (picot = 3 ch and 1 sl st into first ch). Fasten off.

Trimming no. 2 with corners

Make a foundation ch in multiples of 5 plus 1 for each side, 1 ch for each corner and 1 t-ch.
Row 1: 1 dc into 2nd ch from hook, 1 dc into each remaining ch, 1 ch turn.
Row 2: In dc, working 3 dc into st where corners are to be made.
Row 3: 7 ch, * miss 3 sts, 1 dtr, 4 ch, (3 unfin dtr, yoh, draw yarn through all 4 loops on hook) into next st *.

Trimming no. 2 with corner

Rep from * to * on sides but on central st of each corner work 4 ch, 3 unfin dtr, yoh, draw yarn through all 4 loops on hook.
Row 4: * (1 dc, 3 ch, 1 dc 3 ch) into each 4-ch loop, 1 sl st between dtr and dtr cluster. *. Rep from * to *. Fasten off.

Trimming no. 3 with corners

Make a foundation ch in multiples of 6 plus 2 for each side, 1 ch for each corner and 1 t-ch.
Row 1: 1 dc into 2nd ch from hook, 1 dc into remaining ch, 1 ch, turn.
Row 2: In dc, working 3 dc into st where corners are to be made.
Row 3: 1 dc * 4 ch, miss 2 sts, 1 dc into next st. *. Rep * from * on sides but for each corner work 1 dc into st preceding central corner st, 4 ch, 1 dc into st immediately following corner st.
Row 4: Sl st to centre of 4-ch loop, *, 1 dc in 4-ch loop (3 tr, 1 picot, 3 tr) in next 4-ch loop, (picot = 3 ch 1 dc in last tr of 3-tr group). Rep from * to * along sides working (3 tr 1 picot, 3 tr) in 4-ch loop on each side of corner (2 tr, 1 picot, 2 tr) in corner 4-ch loop.

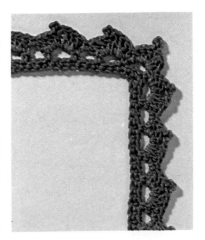

Trimming no. 3 with corner

Trimming no. 4 with corners

Make a foundation ch in multiples of 4 plus 3 for each side, 1 ch for each corner and 1 t ch.
Row 1: 1 dc into 2nd ch from hook, 1 dc into each remaining ch, 1 ch, turn.
Row 2: In dc, working 3 dc into st where corners are to be made.
Row 3: 3 ch, *, miss 2 sts, 1 scallop (1 tr, 2 ch, 1 tr) into next st. *. Rep from * to * on all sides but work (1 scallop, 2 ch and 1 scallop) on central dc at each corner.
Row 4: 3 ch, *, 1 scallop between 1 scallop and the next of previous row *. Rep from * to * on the sides. At each corner work (2 ch, 1 scallop) twice into central 2-ch loop, 2 ch.
Row 5: * 2 tr, 1 picot (3 ch and 1 sl st into last tr worked) *. Rep from * to * in each 2-ch loop. Fasten off.

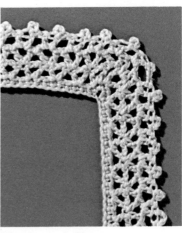

Trimming no. 4 with corner

Trimming no. 5 with corners

Make a foundation ch in multiples of 4 plus 2 for each side, 1 for each corner and 1 t ch.

Row 1: 1 dc into 2nd ch from hook, 1 dc into each remaining ch, 1 ch, turn.

Row 2: 9 ch, ∗ miss 2 sts, (1 tr tr, 2 ch, 1 tr tr) into next st. ∗. Rep from ∗ to ∗ on each side. Where corners are to be made, work ([1 tr tr, 2 ch] 3 times, 1 tr tr) into same st.

Row 3: 4 ch, ∗ (4 unfin tr tr, yoh, draw yarn through all loops on hook, 2 ch) into each 2 ch loop. ∗. Rep from ∗ to ∗.

Row 4: ∗ 3 dc into 2 ch loop, 1 dc into top of tr tr cluster, 1 picot (= 3 ch and 1 sl st into first ch) ∗. Rep from ∗ to ∗.

Trimming no. 5 with corner

Trimming no. 6 with corners

Make a foundation ch in multiples of 9 plus 2 for each side, 1 for each corner and 1 t ch.

Row 1: 1 dc into 2nd ch from hook, 1 dc into each remaining ch, 1 ch, turn.

Row 2: In dc, working 3 dc into st where corners are to be made.

Row 3: ∗ 5 ch, miss 4 sts, 1 dc into next st, 5 ch, miss 4 sts, (1 tr, 3 ch, 1 tr) into next st, ∗. Rep from ∗ to ∗ on each side but work (1 tr, 3 ch, 1 tr) on either side of 3-dc at each corner.

Row 4: ∗ 6 dc into 5-ch loop, 1 sl st into next dc, 6 dc into next 5-ch loop (1 htr, 1 picot, 1 htr, 1 picot, 1 htr, 1 picot, 1 htr) into 3-ch loop ∗ (picot = 3 ch, 1 dc into first ch). Rep from ∗ to ∗.

Trimming no. 6 with corner

Trimming no. 7 with corners

Make a foundation ch in multiples of 3 for each side, 1 ch for each corner and 1 t-ch.

Row 1: 1 dc into 2nd ch from hook, 1 dc into each remaining ch, 1 ch, turn.

Row 2: In dc, working 3 dc into st where corners are required.

Row 3: 6 ch, miss 2 sts, * 1 tr, 2 ch, miss 2 sts. *. Rep from * to * along each side, working (1 tr, 2 ch, 1 tr) into centre st at each corner.

Row 4: * 7 ch, 1 dc into 4th ch from hook, 5 ch, 1 dc into same 4th ch, 4 ch, 1 dc into same 4th ch (3 picots made), 3 ch, miss 1 tr of previous row, 1 dc into next tr. *. Rep from * to * to end of row. Fasten off.

Trimming no. 7 with corner

Trimming no. 8 with corners

Make a foundation ch in multiples of 4 plus 2 for each side, 1 ch for each corner and 1 t ch.

Row 1: 1 dc in 2nd ch from hook, 1 dc in each remaining ch, 1 ch, turn.

Row 2: In dc, working 3 dc in st where corners are to be made, ending with 3 ch, turn.

Row 3: 1 tr in second st, 1 picot (= 3 ch, 1 sl st in first ch), * 3 ch, miss 2 sts, 2 unfin tr, yoh, draw yarn through all 3 loops on hook, 1 picot *. Rep from * to * on sides but turn corners as follows:

Trimming no. 8 with corner

On first of 3 dc work 1 tr 2 ch, on central dc work 2 unfin tr, yoh, draw yarn through, 1 picot, 2 ch, 1 tr on 3rd dc, then continue from * to *. Fasten off.

Trimming no. 9 with corners

Make a foundation ch in multiples of 9 plus 7 for each side, 1 ch for each corner and 1 t ch.

Row 1: 1 dc into 2nd ch from hook, 1 dc in each remaining ch, 1 ch, turn.

Row 2: ** 9 dc, 3 ch *. Rep from ** to * along sides to within 4 sts of corner, 4 dc, (1 dc, 3 ch, 1 dc) in corner, 4 dc, 3 ch, then rep from **.

Trimming no. 10 with corners

Make a foundation ch in multiples of 4 plus 3 for each side, 1 ch for each corner and 1 t ch.

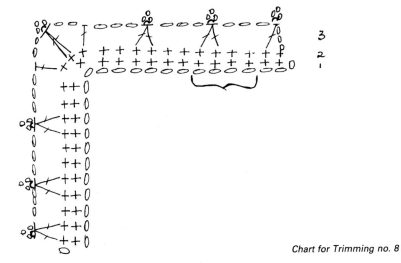

3
2
1

Chart for Trimming no. 8

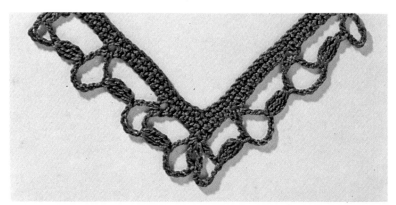

Trimming no. 9 with corner

Trimming no. 10 with corner

147

EDGINGS

Edging no. 1

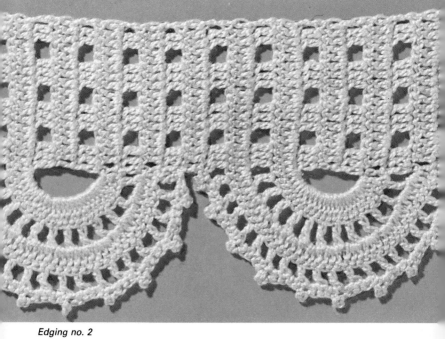

Edging no. 2

Row 1: 1 dc into 2nd ch from hook, 1 ch into each remaining ch, 1 ch, turn.
Row 2: In dc, working 3 dc into st where corners are to be made.
Row 3: * 1 dc, (3 ch, 3 tr) into next st, miss 2 sts *. Rep from * to * on sides but turn corners missing dc (3 ch, 6 tr) into corner st missing 1 st. Fasten off.

Edging no. 1

Make 7 ch.
Row 1: 1 tr in 4th ch from hook (2 ch, 2 tr) in same st, turn, 3 ch, 5 ch, turn.
Row 2: (2 tr, 2 ch, 2 tr) into 2-ch loop of previous row, 5 ch.
Row 3: (2 tr, 2 ch, 2 tr, 2 ch) into 2-ch loop of previous row, 1 tr into last of 4-tr of previous row, 3 tr into 5-ch loop, 10 ch.
Row 4: 1 tr into 4 tr of previous row, 2 ch, 1 tr into next tr. 2 ch, (2 tr, 2 ch, 2 tr) into 2-ch loop, 5 ch.
Row 5: (2 tr, 2 ch, 2 tr) into 2-ch loop of previous row, 2 ch, 1 tr into 4th of 2 tr, 2 ch, 1 tr into next tr, 2 ch, 3 tr into next 2-ch loop, 1 tr into first of 4-tr of previous row, 2 ch, 16 tr into 10-ch loop (made at the end of Row 3), 5 ch, 1 tr into 5-ch loop made in Row 1, 2 ch.
Row 6: 1 tr into 3rd of 5-ch, 1 tr into first of 16-tr, * 1 picot (= 5 ch, 1 dc into first ch), miss 1 st, 1 tr into next st) *. Rep from * to * into the 16 tr, 4 tr into 2-ch loop, 2 ch, 1 tr into next tr, 2 ch, 1 tr into next tr, 2 ch, 1 tr into next tr of previous row, 2 ch, 2 tr, 2 ch, 2 tr into next 2-ch loop, 5 ch.
Row 7: As Row 2.
Rows 2 to 7 form the pattern and are repeated as required.
When the edging is complete work 1 row on the side which will be attached to the fabric as follows: 1 dc into centre of 5-ch loop, 5 ch. * Rep from * to *. Fasten off.

Edging no. 2

Make 20 ch (Replace 1st tr of each row with 3 ch)
Row 1: 1 tr in 4th ch from hook, 1 tr in each ch to end.
Row 2: * 3 tr, 2 ch, miss 2 sts *. Rep from * to * twice more, 3 tr.
Rows 3, 5, 7: As Row 1.
Rows 4, 6: As Row 2.
Row 8: As Row 2, continuing with 14 ch, 1 sl st into 3rd starting ch of Row 5, 2 ch, 1 dc into first starting ch of Row 5, turn.
Row 9: 24 tr into 14-ch loop, 18 tr.
Row 10: (3 tr, 2 ch, miss 2 sts) 3 times, 3 tr, (2 ch miss 1 tr, 1 tr into next st), 2 ch, 1 sl st into 3rd starting ch of Row 3, 1 ch, 1 dc into first ch of Row 3, turn.
Row 11: 2 tr into each 2-ch loop and 1 tr into each tr.
Row 12: (3 tr, 2 ch, miss 2 sts) 3 times, 3 tr, (2 ch, miss 1 tr, 1 tr into next st) 19 times, 1 ch, 1 sl st into 3rd starting ch of Row 1, turn.
Row 13: 1 ch, 1 dc into first 1-ch loop * 1 picot (= 3 ch, 1 sl st into first ch), 1 dc in 2-ch loop, 1 dc in tr, 1 dc in 2-ch loop *. Rep from * to * ending with 1 picot in last 2-ch loop.
Rows 2 to 13 form the pattern and are repeated as required.

Edging no. 3

Make 14 ch.
Row 1: 1 dtr in 9th ch from hook, 8 ch, 1 dc in last ch, 1 ch, turn.
Row 2: 1 ch, 11 dc in 8-ch loop, 1 dc in dtr, 1 ch, 1 dc in 2nd ch, 4 ch, turn.
Row 3: 1 tr in dc of previous row, (2 ch, miss 1 st, 1 dc in next st) 4 times, 4 ch, miss 4 sts, 1 dc, in last st, 6 ch, turn.
Row 4: 1 dc in 4-ch loop (5 ch, 1 dc) in each 2-ch loop, 1 ch, 1 dc in tr of previous row, 1 ch, 1 dc in 2nd ch, 6 ch, turn.
Row 5: 1 dtr in 2nd dc of previous row, 8 ch, miss 1 loop, 1 dc in next 5-ch loop.
Rows 2 to 5 form the pattern and are repeated as required.

Edging no. 4

Make 17 ch
Row 1: 1 tr in 4th ch from hook, 10 tr, 1 ch, miss 1 ch, 2 tr, 3 ch, turn.
Row 2: Miss first st, 1 tr, 1 ch, miss 1 ch, 2 tr, 8 ch, miss 9 sts, 1 scallop into last st (=[1 tr, 2 ch, 3 times, 1 tr] all into the same st), 1 ch, turn.

Row 3: 1 petal (= 1 dc, 1 htr, 3 tr, 1 htr, 1 dc all into 2-ch loop into each of 3 loops on scallop, 6 ch, 1 tr into 7th ch, 1 tr into 8th ch, 1 tr into next 2 tr, 1 ch, miss 1 ch, 2 tr, 3 ch, turn.
Row 4: Miss 1 st, 1 tr, 1 ch, miss 1 ch, 4 tr, 1 tr into first ch, 1 tr into 2nd ch, 8 ch, 1 scallop into 2nd tr in centre of 2nd petal, 1 ch, turn.
Row 5: 1 petal into each of the three 2-ch loops, 6 ch, 1 tr, into 7th ch, 1 tr into 8th ch, 6 tr, 1 ch, miss 1 ch, 2 tr, 3 ch, turn.
Row 6: Miss 1 st, 1 tr, 1 ch, miss 1 ch, 8 tr, 1 tr into first ch, 1 tr into 2nd ch, 8 ch, 1 scallop into 2nd tr of 2nd petal, 1 ch, turn.
Row 7: 1 petal into each of the three 2-ch loops, 6 ch, 1 tr, 7th ch, 1 tr into 8th ch, 10 tr (12 tr in all), 1 ch, miss 1 ch, 2 tr, 3 ch, turn.
Rows 2 to 7 form the pattern and are repeated as required.

Edging no. 3

Edging no. 4

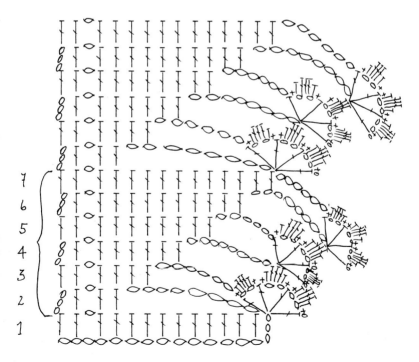

7
6
5
4
3
2
1

Chart for Edging no. 4

Edging no. 5

Edging no. 6

Edging no. 5

Make 12 ch.

Row 1: 1 dc into 8th ch from hook, 5 ch, miss 3 ch, (1 tr, 3 ch, 1 tr) into 1 st ch, 3 ch, turn.

Row 2: 9 tr into first 3-ch loop of previous row, 1 dc into 5-ch loop, 5 ch, 1 dc into last loop, 7 ch, turn.

Row 3: 7 ch, 1 dc into 5-ch loop, 5 ch, 1 tr into 5th of 9 tr of previous row, 3 ch, 1 tr in t-ch, 3 ch, turn.

Rows 2 and 3 form the pattern and are repeated as required.

Edging no. 6

Make 11 ch.

Row 1: 1 tr into 5th ch from hook, 2 ch, (1 tr, 2 ch, 1 tr) into same st (3 loops), turn.

Row 2: 1 ch, (1 dc, 3 tr, 1 dc) into each of the three 2-ch loops, 3 ch, 1 tr into 3rd foundation ch, turn.

Row 3: 7 ch, 1 tr into 2nd tr of middle group (2 ch, 1 tr) 3 times into same st, turn.

Rows 2 and 3 form the pattern and are repeated as required.

Edging with fan design

Make 20 ch.
Row 1: 1 tr into 8th ch from hook, 2 tr, 2 ch, miss 2 ch, 3 tr, 5 ch, turn.
Row 2: 3 tr into 2-ch loop, 2 ch, miss 3·tr, 3 tr into starting ch of previous row, 5 ch, turn.
Row 3: Miss 3 tr, 3 tr into 2-ch loop, 2 ch, miss 3 tr, 3 tr into 5-t-ch, 10 ch, 1 dc into first of the 20 foundation ch, 2 t-ch, turn.
(When working subsequent fans, link the 10 ch with a dc into the 4th picot of the previous fan.)
Row 4: 14 tr into 10-ch loop, 2 ch, miss 3 tr, 3 tr into 2-ch loop, 2 ch, miss 3 tr, 3 tr into 5-t-ch, 5 ch, turn.
Row 5: Miss 3 tr, 3 tr into 2-ch loop, 2 ch, miss 3 tr, 3 tr into 2-ch loop, 14 tr worked between 14-tr of previous row, 2 ch, turn.
(When working subsequent fans, af-ter the 14 tr work 1 dc into the 7th picot of previous fan.)
Row 6: (1 tr, 1 ch) 14 times, worked between 14-tr of previous row, 2 ch, miss 3 tr, 3 tr into next 2-ch loop, 2 ch, 3 tr into 5-t-ch, 5 ch, turn.
Row 7: Miss 3 tr of previous row, 3 tr into 2-ch loop, 2 ch, miss 3 tr, 3 tr into next 2-ch loop, 1 ch, (1 dtr into 1 ch loop, 1 ch) 14 times, 2 ch, turn.
(When working subsequent fans, af-ter the 14 tr work 1 dc into the 9th picot of previous fan.)
Row 8: * 4 ch, 1 dc into 1-ch loop, 1 dc into next dtr of previous row *. Rep from * to * 15 times more work-ing picots on the last 3 sts; 2 ch, 3 tr into 1-ch loop, 2 ch, miss 3 tr, 3 tr into next 5-t-ch, 5 t-ch, turn.
Row 9: Miss 3 tr, 3 tr into 2-ch loop, 2 ch, miss 3 tr, 3 tr into 2 ch loop, 5 ch, turn.
Rows 2 to 9 form the pattern and are repeated as required.

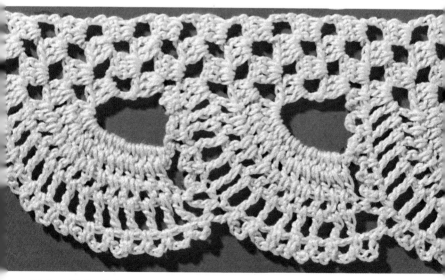

Edging with fan design

Edging with chain lace crochet

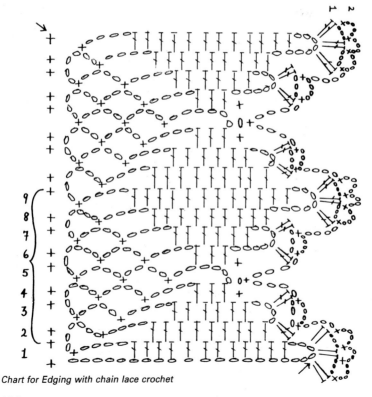

Chart for Edging with chain lace crochet

Edging with chain lace crochet

Make 23 ch.

Row 1: (Right side) 1 tr in 7th ch from hook, 11 tr, 4 ch, miss 4 ch, 1 dc, 6 t-ch.

Row 2: 1 dc into first ch loop, 4 ch, miss 2 tr, 9 tr in between tr of previous row, miss 2 tr, 4 t-ch.

Row 3: Miss 2 tr, 6 tr between tr of previous row, 4 ch, miss 2 tr, 1 dc into 4-ch loop, 4 ch, 1 dc into t-ch-loop, 6 tch.

Row 4: 1 dc into first 4-ch loop of previous row, 4 ch, 1 dc into next 4-ch loop, 4 ch, miss 2 tr, 3 tr in between tr of previous row, miss 2 tr, 6 tch.

Row 5: Miss 3 tr, 1 dc into first 4-ch loop of previous row, 4 ch 1 dc into next 4-ch loop, 4 ch, 1 dc into tch, 6 t-ch.

Row 6: 1 dc into first 4-ch loop, 4 ch, 1 dc into next 4-ch loop, 4 ch, 3 tr into t-ch.

Row 7: 8 ch, 1 tr into 7th ch from hook, 1 tr into next ch, 2 tr between tr of previous row, 2 tr into 4-ch loop, 4 ch, 1 dc into next 4-ch loop 6 t-ch.

Row 8: 1 dc into 4-ch loop, 4 ch, 2 tr into next 4-ch loop, 5 tr between tr of previous row, 2 tr into starting ch of previous row.

Row 9: 8 ch, 1 tr into 7th ch from hook, 1 tr into next ch, 8 tr in between tr of previous row, 2 tr into 4-ch loop, 4 ch, 1 dc into t-ch, 6 t-ch.

Rows 2 to 9 form the pattern and are repeated as required.

To complete the scalloped edge, work as follows:

∗ (2 tr, 3 ch, 2 tr, 3 ch, 2 tr) into 6-ch loop at point of scallop; (2 tr, 3 ch, 2 tr) into 4-ch loop at side on 6 tr row (Row 3); 1 dc into tr at side on 3-tr row (Row 6); (2 tr, 3 ch, 2 tr) into 6-ch loop on 6 tr row (Row 7) ∗. Rep from ∗ to ∗ for entire length.

Row 2: (1 dc 3 ch) twice in next three 3-ch loops, ∗ 1 dc in 1-ch loop (3 ch, 1 dc) twice in next four 3-ch loops ∗. Rep from ∗ to ∗. With right side facing, rejoin yarn to right hand corner of straight edge and work 1 row of dc along entire length.

INSERTIONS

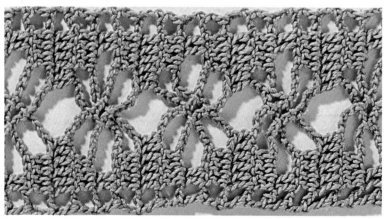

Insertion no. 1

Insertion no. 1

Make 26 ch.

Row 1: 1 tr in 8th ch from hook, 5 tr, 9 ch, miss 4 ch, 6 tr, 2 ch, miss 2 ch, 1 tr into last ch, turn.

Row 2: 5 ch (= 1 tr plus 2 ch), 6 ch, miss 2 tr, 1 sl st into 5th of 9-ch loop, 6 ch, miss 2 tr, 4 tr, 2 ch, 1 tr into 3rd starting ch of previous row, turn.

Row 3: 5 ch (= 1 tr plus 2 ch), 2 tr, 6 ch, miss 2 tr, 1 sl st into 5th ch of 6-ch loop, 3 ch, 1 sl st into 2nd ch of next 6-ch loop, 6 ch, miss 2 tr, 2 tr, 2 ch, 1 tr into 3rd starting ch of previous row, turn.

Row 4: 5 ch, 2 tr, 2 tr in first 2 ch of 6-ch loop, 6 ch, 1 sl st into 2nd ch of 3-ch loop, 6 ch, 2 tr into last 2 ch of 6-ch loop, 2 tr, 2 ch, 1 tr into 3rd starting ch of previous row, turn.

Row 5: 5 ch, 4 tr, 2 tr in first 2 ch of 6-ch loop, 9 ch, 2 tr in last 2 ch of 6-ch loop, 4 tr, 2 ch, 1 tr into 3rd starting ch of previous row, turn.

Rows 2 to 5 form the pattern and are repeated as required.

Insertion no. 2

Make 12 ch.

Row 1: 1 tr in 4th ch from hook, 3 tr, 4 ch, miss 4 ch, 1 tr in last ch, 3 ch, turn.

Row 2: 4 tr in 4-ch loop, 4 ch, miss 4 tr, 1 tr in running ch, 3 ch, turn.

Row 2 forms the pattern and is repeated as required. Finish edges as follows:

Join yarn to 2nd ch of 3-turning loop, work along length, 4 ch, (1 dtr, 4 ch, 1 dtr) in each space between the dtr blocks, which will be at right-angles to this row, and ending with 1 dtr in last ch. Fasten off and work the other side in the same way.

Chart for Insertion no. 2

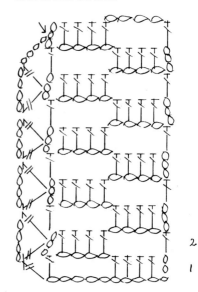

2

1

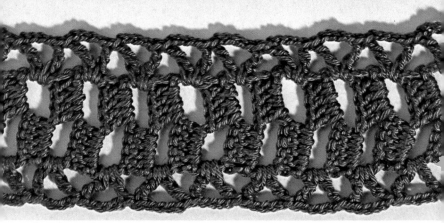

Insertion no. 2

Insertion no. 3

Make 20 ch.
Row 1: 1 tr in 8th ch from hook, 2 ch, miss 2 ch, 4 tr, 2 ch, miss 2 ch, 1 tr, 2 ch, miss 2 ch, 1 tr in last ch, 5 ch, turn.
Row 2: 1 tr in 2nd tr, 2 ch, 1 tr in 4 tr, 1 tr in 2-ch loop, 1 tr in next tr, 2 ch, 1 tr in 3rd starting ch of previous row, 10 ch, turn.
Row 3: Starting in 8th ch from hook work 1 tr, 2 ch, miss 2 ch, 1 tr in next tr, 2 tr in 2-ch loop, 1 tr in first of next 7 tr, 2 ch, miss 2 sts, 1 tr, 2 ch, miss 2 sts, 1 tr, 5 ch, turn.
Rows 2 and 3 form the pattern and are repeated as required.

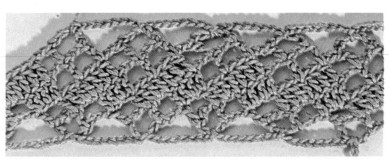

Insertion no. 3

157

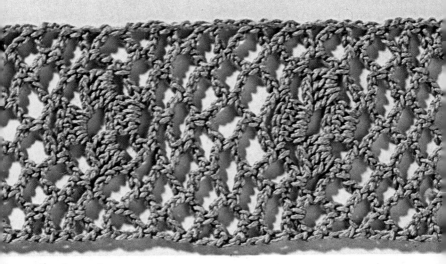

Insertion no. 4

Insertion no. 5

Insertion no. 4

Make 30 ch.

Row 1: 1 dc 6th ch from hook, ✳ 5 ch, miss 5 ch, 1 dc ✳. Rep from ✳ to ✳, ending with 1 dc, 5 ch, turn.

Row 2: ✳ 1 dc into 3rd of 5-ch loop, 5 ch ✳. Rep from ✳ to ✳ ending with 1 dc in 3rd tch, 5 ch, turn.

Rows 3-7: As Row 2.

Row 8: Work loops as in Row 2 but when 2nd loop has been completed work 3 ch, 4 tr into next 5-ch loop, 3 ch, 1 dc into next loop, 5 ch 1 dc in 3rd t-ch, 5 ch, turn.

Row 9: 1 dc in 5 ch loop, 3 ch, 4 tr in 3-ch loop, 3 ch, miss 4 tr, 4 tr in 3-ch loop, 3 ch, 1 dc in 5-ch loop, 5 ch, 1 dc in 3rd tch, 5 ch, turn.

Row 10: 1 dc in 5-ch loop 5 ch, 1 dc in 3-ch loop, 3 ch, miss 4 tr, 4 tr in 3-ch loop, 3 ch miss 4 tr, 1 dc in 3-ch loop, 5 ch, 1 dc in 3rd t-ch, 5 ch, turn.

Row 11: 1 dc in 5-ch loop, 5 ch, 1 dc

in 3-ch loop, 5 ch, miss 4 tr, 1 dc in 3-ch loop, 5 ch, 1 dc in 5-ch loop, 5 ch, 1 dc in 3rd t-ch, 5 ch, turn.
Rows 2 to 11 form the pattern and are repeated as required.

Insertion no. 5

Make 18 ch.
Row 1: 1 tr in 6th ch from hook, 1 tr, 3 ch, miss 3 ch, (1 tr, 2 ch, 1 tr) into next ch, 3 ch, miss 3 ch, 2 tr, 1 ch, miss 1 ch, 1 tr, 4 ch, turn.
Row 2: Miss 1 tr and 1 ch, 2 tr, 3 ch, (2 tr, 2 ch, 2 tr) into 2-ch loop, 3 ch, 2 tr, 1 ch, 1 tr into 3rd starting ch of previous row, 4 ch, turn.
Row 3: Miss 1 tr and 2 tr 1 ch, 3 ch, (1 tr, 2 ch, 1 tr) into 2-ch loop, 3 ch, 2 tr, 1 ch, 1 tr into 3rd starting ch of previous row, 4 ch, turn.

Rows 2 and 3 form the pattern and are repeated as required.

Insertion no. 6

Make 30 ch.
Row 1: 1 tr in 5th ch from hook, 2 ch, miss 2 ch, 8 tr, 2 ch, miss 1 ch, 8 tr, 2 ch, miss 2 ch, 1 tr, 2 ch miss 2 ch, 1 tr, miss 2 ch, turn.
Row 2: 1 tr in 2nd tr, 2 ch, 4 tr, miss 4 tr, 5 ch, 1 tr into 2-ch loop, 5 ch miss 4 tr, 4 tr, 2 ch, 1 tr, 2 ch, 1 tr in 3rd of 5 starting ch, 5 ch, turn.
Row 3: 1 tr in 2nd tr, 2 ch, 2 tr, 5 ch, miss 2 tr, 1 dc into 3rd ch of 5-ch loop, 5 ch, 1 dc 3rd ch of next 5-ch loop, 5 ch, miss 2 tr, 2 tr, 2 ch, 1 tr, 2 ch, 1 tr into 3rd of 5 starting ch, 5 ch, turn.
Row 4: 1 tr in 2nd tr, 2 ch, 2 tr, 2 tr in first 2 ch of 5-ch loop, 5 ch, 1 tr into

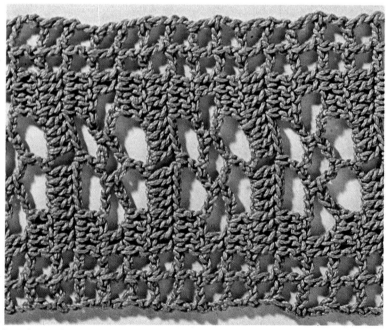

Insertion no. 6

3rd ch of 2nd 5-ch loop, 5 ch, 4 tr (working 2 on 4th and 5th ch and 2 on next 2 tr), 2 ch, 1 tr, 2 ch, 1 tr into 3rd of 5 starting ch of previous row. Rows 1 to 4 form the pattern and are repeated as required.

Insertion no. 7

Make 15 ch.
Row 1: 1 tr in 4th ch from hook, 1 tr, 5 ch, miss 3 ch, 1 dc in next ch, miss 3 ch, 5 ch, 3 tr, 2 ch, turn.

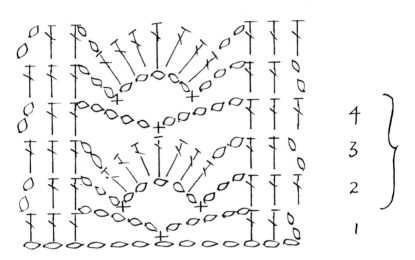

Chart for Insertion no. 7

Insertion no. 7

160

Insertion no. 8

Row 2: 2 tr, 3 ch, 1 dc in first ch loop, 5 ch, 1 dc in 2nd ch loop, 3 ch, 3 tr, 2 ch, turn.
Row 3: 2 tr, 2 ch, 7 tr in 5-ch loop, 2 ch, 3 tr, 2 ch, turn.
Row 4: 2 tr, 5 ch, 1 dc in 4th of 7 tr, 5 ch, 3 tr, 2 ch, turn.
Rows 2 to 4 form the pattern and are repeated as required.

Insertion no. 8

Make a chain of 12 sts and join with a sl st to form ring.
Row 1: 1 ch (= 1 dc), 11 dc into ring, keeping these sts on one half of ring, turn.
Row 2: 4 ch (= 1 tr, 1 ch) miss 1 dc, 1 tr, 1 ch into each dc, ending with 1 tr into starting ch of previous row, turn.
Row 3: 5 ch (= 1 tr, 2 ch) miss 1 tr, (1 tr, 2 ch) into each tr, ending with 1 tr into 3rd starting ch.
Without breaking the yarn, continue as follows:

∗ Make 12 ch and join with sl st into first ch to form another ring.
Row 1: Working into only half the ring, on the opposite side to previous ring, 1 ch, 11 dc, turn.
Row 2: 4 ch miss 1 dc, (1 tr, 1 ch) into each tr, ending with 1 tr into starting ch. Work 1 sl st into last tr of Row 2 of previous motif, do not turn.
Row 3: 1 sl st into last dc of Row 1 of first motif, turn. (No turning ch required as work is now level with top of tr), 2 ch, 1 tr into each of foll 12 tr ∗.
Rep from ∗ to ∗ for entire length of insertion, each motif being made on alternate sides of ch rings.
Complete both sides of insertion by working 9 dc into each unworked half ring and 3 dc into each 2-ch loop.

Insertion no. 9 in fillet crochet

Make 41 ch.
Row 1: 1 tr in 8th ch from hook (= 1 square), (2 ch miss 2 ch, 1 tr) 3 times,

161

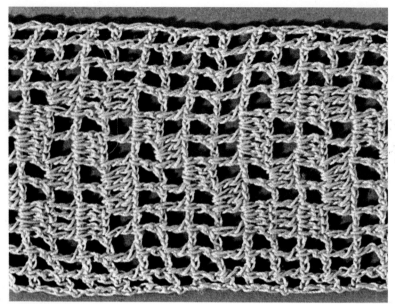

Insertion in filet crochet

3 tr, (2 ch, miss 2 ch, 1 tr) 7 times, 5 ch, turn.
Row 2: Miss 1 tr and 2 ch, (1 tr in tr, 2 ch) 3 times, (1 tr in tr 2 tr in 2-ch loop) twice, 1 tr in tr, 2 ch, 1 tr in tr, 2 ch, miss 2 tr, 1 tr in tr, 2 tr in 2-ch loop (1 tr in tr, 2 ch), 3 times, 1 tr in 3rd tch, 5 ch, turn.

Continue in pattern as set, reading odd rows of chart from right to left and even rows from left to right.
1 square = 2 ch, miss 2 ch or 2 tr, 1 tr in next ch or tr.
1 cross = 4 tr plus 3 tr for each additional cross in group.

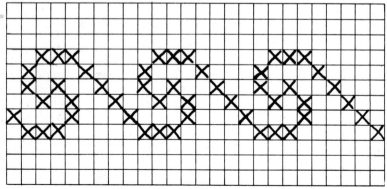

Diagram for filet insertion

Patterns

COMPLETE PATTERNS FOR

GARMENTS AND ACCESSORIES

Creating things to wear

In this chapter we have combined instructions for patterns with some of the stitches described in previous sections. Exactly the same techniques apply, whether you are making a square for a patchwork rug, a coat or a baby's garment. The items we have selected should only be regarded as samples of the unlimited variations an enthusiastic crocheter may devise. It is hoped that the suggestions offered will encourage you to design articles not only for yourself but for your family and friends, for your home and as gifts.

With practice you will become more skilled and, as your skill develops, your work will become more self-expressive, giving useful objects that special touch of individualism that sets them apart from the mass-produced things which surround us today. Included are examples of garments for men, women and children, with ideas for accessories over a wide range including belts, collars, shopping bags, caps, and so on.

Blue and white bib no. 1

Materials: 1 ball each crochet cotton no. 5 in white and blue; 2.00 mm (1½) crochet hook.
Stitches used: Double crochet, treble.
With white cotton make 30 ch.
Row 1: 1 dc in 2nd ch from hook, 27 dc, 3 dc into next ch, work 28 dc back on opposite side of ch, 1 ch, turn.
Row 2: 28 dc, 2 dc into next st, 1 dc, 2 dc into next st, 28 dc, 1 ch, turn.
Row 3: 28 dc, 2 dc into next st, 1 dc, 3 dc into next st, 1 dc, 2 dc into next st, 28 dc, 1 ch, turn. Continue in dc for 7 more rows, increasing as in Row 3 into the same sts on each row.
Still increasing 4 sts on each row as in Row 3, make neckband:
Next row: In dc to end, 11 ch, turn.
Next row: Starting in 2nd ch from hook, work in dc, end with 11 ch, turn.

White and blue bib no. 2   *Blue and white bib no. 1*

Next row: Starting in 2nd ch from hook, work in dc.
Break white, join in blue.
Row 1: * (1 dc, 1 ch, 2 tr) into 1 st, miss 2 sts *. Rep from * to * ending with (1 dc, 1 ch, 2 tr) into last st.
Row 2: * (1 dc, 1 ch, 2 tr) into the dc of previous row. * Rep from * to *.
Rep Row 2 for 8 more rows.
Finish as follows: * 4 dc, 1 picot (= 3 ch, 1 dc into dc preceding the ch) * Rep from * to * to end of row. Fasten off.
Make two cords in white as follows: 60 ch, 1 dc into each st. Fasten off and sew neatly to ends of neckband.

White and blue bib no. 2

Materials: 1 ball crochet cotton no. 5 in white, oddment of blue cotton; 2.00 mm (1½) crochet hook.
Stitches used: Double crochet, treble, crab.

Bib is worked backwards and forwards lengthwise.
With white cotton make 76 ch.
Row 1: 1 dc in 2nd ch from hook, 1 dc in each ch to end, 1 ch (75 sts).
Rows 2 to 16: Work in dc.
Continue in dc for 26 more rows working only on 55 sts. At the end of last row make 20 ch and work on all 75 sts for 16 more rows. Finish the bib as follows:
Row 1: dc, working 3 dc into each corner st.
Row 2: With blue cotton work * 3 tr into 1 st, miss 2 sts. * Rep from * to *.
Continue all round outside bib edge from * to *, working 5 tr into 1 st on each corner.
Rows 3 and 4: With white cotton, as Row 1.
Row 5: As Row 1, but continuing round inside neck edge.
Row 6: Work in crab st.
Make 2 cords in white as follows: 60 ch, 1 dc into each st.

White and red bib

White and red bib

Materials: 1 ball crochet cotton no. 5 in white; oddment of red colour; 2.00 mm (1½) crochet hook.
Stitches used: Double crochet, half treble, treble, crab.
With white cotton make 67 ch.
Row 1: 1 htr in 3rd ch from hook, 8 htr, * 3 htr into 1 ch, 1 htr into each of next 10 ch *. Rep from * to * 4 more times, giving 5 points in all. Continue working in htr for another 11 rows, turning with 2 ch and increasing on the central st of each increase in previous row. Work only between the 3 central points, still increasing on each central increase in previous row as follows:
Next row: Work in dc to 4th point, increasing at centre as before, turn without increasing.
Next row: Work in dc back to 2nd point, increasing at centre as before, turn without increasing.
Work 8 more rows between 2nd and 4th points increasing at centre on every row.
Next row: Work to 4th point, then continue to end of row.
Finish as follows:
Join in red cotton.
Row 1: * 3 tr into 1 st, miss 1 st, 1 dc, miss 1 st *. Rep from * to *. Break red cotton.
Row 2: (white cotton) Work in dc.
Row 3: Work in crab st.
Make 2 cords in white as follows: 60 ch, 1 dc into each st. Fasten off and sew neatly to each inside corner of neck opening.

Child's collar no. 1

Materials: 1 ball crochet cotton no. 5. 2.50 mm (0) crochet hook
Stitches used: Double crochet, treble, crab.
Make 101 ch.
Row 1: Miss 1 ch, * 1 tr, 1 ch, miss 1 ch *. Rep from * to * 3 ch, (50 tr).
Row 2: * (2 tr, 2 ch, 2 tr) into 1-ch loop, 4 ch, miss 2 loops *. Rep from * to * 3 ch, (17 motifs).
Row 3: * (2 tr, 2 ch, 2 tr) into 2-ch loop, 4 ch. *. Rep from * to *, 3 ch.
Row 4: * (2 tr, 2 ch, 2 tr) into 2-ch loop, 2 ch, 1 dc worked under ch-loops of Rows 2 and 3, 2 ch *. Rep from * to *.
Row 5: As Row 2,
Row 6: As Row 3.

Child's collar no. 1

Row 7: As Row 4.
Row 8: * (1 dc, 3 ch) 3 times into first loop, 1 dc into 2nd loop, 2 ch, 1 dc into 3rd loop, 3 ch *. Rep from * to *.
Finish collar by working along both sides and inside neck edge as follows: 1 row in dc and 1 row in crab st. Fasten off.
Work two cords of 50 ch and sew neatly to each inside corner of neck.

Child's collar no. 2

Materials: 1 ball crochet cotton no, 5; 2.50 mm (0) crochet hook.
Stitches used: Double crochet, treble, unfin double treble, crab.
Make 94 ch.
Row 1: Starting into 2nd ch from hook, work in dc to end (93 sts).
Row 2: 3 ch, 1 tr in first st, * 4 ch, miss 3 sts, 2 tr into 1 st 4. Rep from * to * 23 times, 1 ch.
Row 3: * 1 dc into first tr of previous row, 3 ch, 1 dc into next tr, 4 dc into 4-ch loop *. Rep from * to * ending with 1 dc in tr, 3 ch, 1 dc in tch, 5 ch.

Child's collar no. 3

Row 4: * (3 unfin dtr, yoh, draw yarn through all 4 loops on hook, 3 ch) 3 times into 3-ch loop, 3 ch, 1 dc into next 3-ch loop, 3 ch *. Rep from * to * ending with (3 unfin dtr fin tog) 3 times into last 3-ch loop, 3 ch.
Row 5: * (5 tr, 1 ch, 1 picot, 1 ch) into first 3-ch loop of previous row, 5 tr into 2nd 3-ch loop, 4 ch *. Rep from * to * ending with (5 tr, 1 ch, 1 picot, 1 ch) into last 3-ch loop, (Picot = 4 ch sl st into first ch).
Finish the collar by working along both sides and inside neck edge as follows: 1 row in dc and 1 row in crab st. Make 2 cords of 50 ch each and sew them neatly to inside corners of neck opening.

Child's collar no. 3

Materials: 1 ball crochet cotton no. 5; 2.50 mm (0) crochet hook
Stitches used: Double crochet, treble, crab.
Make 92 ch.
Row 1: Starting into 2nd ch from hook, work in dc to end, 3 ch.
Row 2: * 1 tr, 5 ch, miss 4 sts, (2 tr, 3 ch, 2 tr) into next st, 5 ch, miss 4 sts *. Rep from * to *, 1 ch.
Row 3: 1 dc into tr, * 1 dc into 5-ch loop, 4 ch, 8 tr into 3-ch loop, 4 ch, 1

Child's collar no. 2

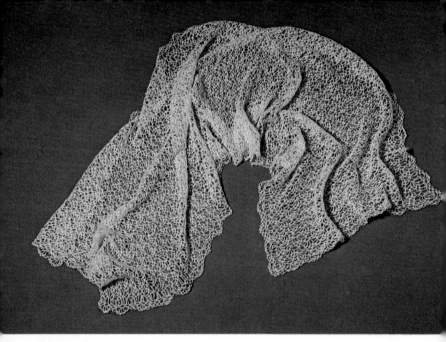

Cream stole

dc into next 5-ch loop ∗. Rep from ∗ to ∗ ending with 1 dc in last tr.

Row 4: 3 ch, ∗ 4 ch, (1 tr, 1 ch) 8 times into tr, 3 ch, 1 tr between 2-dc of previous row. ∗. Rep from ∗ to ∗.

Row 5: 1 dc into tr, ∗ 1 dc into next loop, 1 ch, (1 tr, 1 picot of 3 ch closed with sl st into tr just worked, 1 ch) 8 times, 1 ch, 1 dc into next loop. ∗. Rep from ∗ to ∗.

Work both ends of the collar in dc to link up with start of trebles and picots. Finish off inside neck edge and both ends with 1 row of crab st. Make 2 cords of 50 ch each and sew them neatly to inside corners of neck opening.

Cream stole

Materials: 300 g 2-ply mohair, 2.00 mm (0) crochet hook

Stitches used: Double crochet, tre-ble, double treble.

Make a loose ch about 50 cm (20 in) long in multiples of 28 ch plus 9 ch.

Row 1: Starting in 2nd ch from hook, ∗ 1 dc, 6 ch, miss 6 ch ∗. Rep from ∗ to ∗ to end of row, finishing with 1 dc.

Row 2: 5 ch, 1 dc in first loop, ∗ 6 ch, miss 1 loop, (1 dtr, 4 ch) 4 times into next loop, miss 1 loop 2 ch, 1 dc into next loop ∗. Rep from ∗ to ∗ ending with 2 ch, 1 tr into last dc.

Row 3: 5 ch, ∗ 1 dc into dc, 6 ch, 1 dc into 4-ch loop between first and 2nd dtr, 6 ch, 1 dc into 4-ch loop between 2nd and 3rd dtr, 6 ch, 1 dc into 4-ch loop between 3rd and 4th dtr, 6 ch ∗. Rep from ∗ to ∗ ending with 2 ch, 1 tr into 3rd t-ch.

Row 4: 1 ch, 1 dc in tr, ∗ 1 dc, 6 ch. ∗. Rep from ∗ to ∗ into each 6-ch loop of previous row.

Row 5: 8 ch, 1 dtr into first 6-ch loop, 6 ch, miss 1 loop, ∗ 1 dc into next

Mohair scarf

6-ch loop, 6 ch, miss 1 loop, (1 dtr, 4 ch) 4 times into next 6-ch loop, 2 ch, miss 1 loop *. Rep from * to * ending with 1 dc in next 6-ch loop, 6 ch, miss 1 loop, 1 dtr into last 6-ch loop, 4 ch, 1 dtr into dc.

Row 6: 5 ch, 1 dc into 4-ch loop, * 6 ch, 1 dc into dc, 6 ch, 1 dc into 4-ch loop between first and 2nd dtr, 6 ch, 1 dc into 4-ch loop between 2nd and 3rd dtr, 6 ch, 1 dc into 4-ch loop between 3rd and 4th dtr *. Rep from * to * ending with 6 ch, 1 dc into dc, 6 ch, 1 dc into last 4-ch loop, 2 ch, 1 tr into 5th t-ch.

Row 7: 1 ch, 1 dc into tr, * 6 ch, 1 dc *. Rep from * to * into each ch-loop to end of row.

Continue repeating Rows 2 to 7 until the stole measures about 180 cm (72 in).

Complete by working an edging as follows:

Round 1: * 1 dc, 6 ch *. Rep from * to * on all 4 sides, sl st to join.

Round 2: Sl st to central st of first loop, * 1 dc into first loop, 6 ch, 1 dc into next loop, 6 ch, 1 dc into next loop, 6 ch, (1 dtr, 4 ch) twice 1 dtr, 6 ch *. Rep from * to * working (1 dtr, 4 ch) 4 times, 1 dtr into each corner loop instead of repeating the dtr twice, sl st to join.

Round 3: sl st to central st of first loop, * 1 dc, 6 ch *. Rep from * to * into each loop of previous round. Fasten off.

Mohair scarf

Materials: 320 g 2-ply mohair; 5.00 mm (6) crochet hook.
Stitches used: Double crochet, double treble, fancy.
Instructions for fancy stitch:
Row 1: * (1 dtr, 2 ch, 1 dtr) into 1 ch, miss 3 ch, 1 ch, 1 dc, 1 ch, miss 3 ch *. Rep from * to * ending with (1 dtr, 2 ch, 1 dtr) in last ch.

Row 2: ✳ 1 dc into 2-ch loop, 1 ch, (1 dtr, 2 ch, 1 dtr) into 1 dc, 1 ch ✳. Rep from ✳ to ✳ ending with 1 dc in 2-ch loop, 3 ch.
Row 3: ✳ (1 dtr, 2 ch, 1 dtr) into 1 dc, 1 ch, 1 dc, 1 ch into 2-ch loop ✳. Rep from ✳ to ✳.
Rows 2 and 3 form the pattern.
Instructions for scarf: Make 60 ch and starting in 4th ch from hook and work in fancy stitch for about 130 cm (52 in).
To complete scarf, make a fringe of about 25 cm (10 in) on each short side.
To make fringe: Cut a number of strands of yarn approximately 50 cm (20 in) long and place them in groups of 3 or 4 strands according to thickness required. With wrong side of edge to be fringed uppermost, insert a crochet hook (several sizes larger than the one used for main work) as near the edge as possible, fold strands in half to form a loop, put loop on hook, pull through edge of work, place hook behind all strands of yarn and draw through loop. Continue in this way along both edges, spacing the groups at regular intervals. If required, each cluster of strands can be divided in half and knotted so that half of one cluster is knotted to half of the next.

Cream triangular shawl

Materials: 500 g 2-ply mohair; 5.00 mm (6) crochet hook.
Stitches used: Double, treble crochet, lattice.
Centre: This consists of 2 equal traingles which are joined with 2 tr into the loops down one side of each triangle. The 2 triangles are placed so that the ch loops of each go in opposite directions.
Triangle: Make one loop to start, increasing one loop on each row until 23 loops have been made. Work a

Cream triangular shawl

second triangle in the same way and join it to the first.
Flower: Make 6 ch and join with a sl st to form ring. Continue in rounds replacing first st of first and 2nd rounds by 1 ch; first st of 3rd round by 3 tr. Close each round with a sl st into beg ch.
Round 1: Work 12 dc into ring.
Round 2: ✳ 3 dc, 6 ch ✳. Rep from ✳ to ✳.
Round 3: ✳ 10 tr into 6-ch loop, 1 tr into 2nd of 3 dc ✳. Rep from ✳ to ✳. Fasten off.
Work 12 flowers and sew them invis-

Detail of fringing

Black shawl in filet crochet

ibly along the 2 equal sides of the large triangle made by joining the 2 small triangles.

Picking up the stitches from the outside edges of the flowers, work a border 12 cm (4¾ in) in depth in lattice st along the lower edge, working twice into 'corner' loop on every alternate now.

To finsish border, make a 15 cm (6 in) knotted fringe (see illustration page 171 and instructions for mohair scarf). On the 3rd side work 1 row of dc and 2 rows as follows:

Row 1: ∗ 1 dc, 3 ch and 1 dc. ∗. Rep from ∗ to ∗.

Row 2: ∗ 1 dc into dc of previous row, 3 ch and 1 dc into dc of previous row. ∗. Rep from ∗ to ∗. Fasten off.

Black shawl in filet crochet

Materials: 400 g 3-ply wool in black; 3.00 mm (10) crochet hook.
Stitches used: Mesh with blocks and spaces.

Make 3 ch and then, working in mesh st, increase 1 st on each side as follows: On first and last tr of each row work 1 tr, 1 ch and 1 tr.

Begin to work the first butterfly in the centre of Row 14, following the diagram (1 cross = 3 tr plus 2 tr for each additional cross in black).

When the first butterfly has been worked, continue with 6 rows of mesh st.

Now work 11 mesh sts and begin the

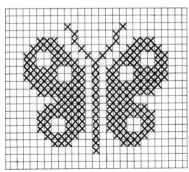

Diagram for butterfly

172

Poncho

next butterfly on the 12th. The 3rd butterfly is then worked, keeping it symmetrical with the 2nd by counting 10 mesh sts back from the end of the row. When these 2 butterflies have been worked, continue with 6 more rows of mesh st.

On next row work another 2 butterflies each side and another in the middle. The 4th should start on the 12th mesh st and the 6th on the 11th st from end of row (t-ch makes the 12th bar).

The 5th butterfly should be lined up with the first central one. When these 3 butterflies have been worked, continue with 6 more rows of mesh st.

On the next row work another 2 butterflies each side, as before, and 2 in between, lined up with the 2nd and 3rd butterflies. There will now be 10 butterflies in all.

Work 13 rows in mesh st.

Work on row of dc and one row of crab st on the long side. To finish make a 30 cm (12 in) fringe.

Poncho

Materials: 700 g double knitting in equal amounts of different colours; 4.00 mm (8) crochet hook.

Stitches used: Double crochet, half treble, treble.

Make 84 ch and join with a sl st to form ring.

Round 1: 3 ch (= 1 htr, 1 ch) ∗ 1 htr, 1 ch, miss 1 ch ∗. Rep from ∗ to ∗. Continue for another 9 rounds, working the htr into the 1-ch loops of previous round. At the same time, inc at shoulder until there are 60 htr with 1 ch between each. To increase, work (1 htr, 1 ch) 9 times, (1 htr, 1 ch) twice in next 1-ch loop (1 htr, 1 ch) 20 times (1 htr, 1 ch) twice in next 1-ch loop, work to end of round. Keep subsequent increases in line.

Round 1: ∗ (2 tr, 2 ch, 2 tr) into same st (= 1 corner), (miss 2 sts, 1 ch, 2 tr into next st) 9 times, 1 ch, miss 2 sts ∗. Rep from ∗ to ∗.

Round 2: ∗ 1 corner, (2 tr into 1-ch loop, 1 ch) 10 times ∗. Rep from ∗ to

*. Continue in this way, changing colour every 2 rounds, until the required length is reached.
Complete by working 1 row of dc around entire outside edge and by making a fringe about 5 cm (2 in) long.

Woman's coat

Materials: 1500 g double knitting yarn; 3 buttons; 5.00 mm (6) crochet hook.
Stitches used: Double crochet, shell, crab.
Back: Make a ch 50 cm (20 in) long and work in shell st for 110 cm (43½ in).
Half front: Make a ch 30 cm (12 in) long and work in shell st for 95 cm (37½ in). Now dec gradually, for neck, until shoulder edge measures 18 cm (7 in). Work another half front in the same way reversing shaping for neck.
Sleeves: Make a ch 40 cm (15½ in) long and work in shell st for 52 cm (20½ in). Sew side and shoulder seams and insert sleeves.
Collar: Place a marker on each side of neck 25 cm (10 in) from centre back. Work 15 cm (6 in) in shell st between markers.
Work 1 row dc and 1 row crab st all round collar, cuffs, both fronts and lower edge.
Sew buttons on left side, evenly spaced and button through on right front. Turn cuffs back.

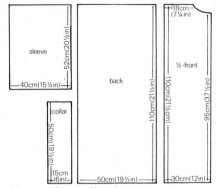

Diagram of woman's coat

Woman's jacket

Materials: 600 g 4-ply yarn in white; few grammes each red and black; 5.00 mm (6) crochet hook.
Stitches used: Treble, crab.
Back: With white wool make 50 ch and work in treble for 30 rows. Fasten off.
Right front: (This is worked sideways, the foundation ch constituting the centre front edge) with white wool make 50 ch and work in tr changing the colours as follows: 2 rows white, 1 row red, 3 rows white, 1 row black, 3 rows white, 1 row red, 2 rows white. Fasten off.
Work the left side in the same way.
Sleeves: With white wool make 22 ch and work in tr for 24 rows, increasing 1 st at each end of 8th and following 6th row twice so that there are 28 sts.
Shape top by decreasing 2 sts at each end of next row, 1 st at each end of next 7 rows. Then 2 sts at each end of following row to make 6 sts. Fasten off.
Sew side, shoulder and sleeve seams. Insert sleeves.
Collar: Work 9 rows round neck edge in tr. Fasten off. Complete jacket by working a row of crab st in black or red wool all round edge of jacket, including the collar, and round the edge of the sleeves which may be turned back to form cuffs.
Belt: Make 2 ch loops about 2.5 cm (1 in) and sew them to each side of jacket. To make the belt, plait several long strands of all 3 colours, finishing ends by knotting and fraying out the cut strands to form tassels.

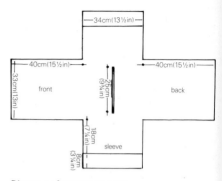

Diagram of mauve sweater

Mauve sweater

Materials: 300 g 4-ply wool in mauve; 30 g in white; 5.00 mm (6) crochet hook
Stitches used: Double, crochet, treble, ridge.
Welt: (worked sideways) Make 14 ch and work 47 rows in ridge st (work into *back* loop only instead of through both loops).
Back and half sleeves: Crocheting first row along 1 side of welt, work 20 rows in treble. Now make 24 ch on each side of work for sleeves and continue on all sts in tr for 10 rows. Work 1 row in white wool, 1 row in mauve, 1 row in white.
Make the front and half sleeves in the same way, including the welt. Join side and underarm seams. Join shoulder seams leaving an opening of 25 cm (10 in) for neck.

Woman's jacket

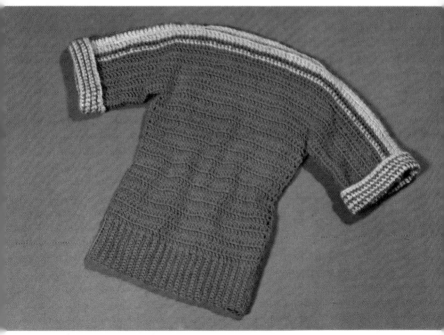

Mauve sweater

177

Hat

Hat

Materials: 100 g fluffy wool in different colours; 3.00 mm (10) crochet hook.
Stitches used: Double crochet, half treble, ridged half treble (worked into *back* loop only instead of through both loops), crab.
(The hat is worked from the wrong side.)
Make 3 ch and join with a sl st to form ring.
Work in rounds of htr, increasing regularly, until there is a flat disc 10 cm (4 in) in diameter. Continue for 10 more rounds without shaping.
Next round: Inc 1 st every 2 sts. Continue for another 4 rounds, increasing to ensure that shaping is correct. Complete with 1 round of crab st.
Decorate the hat with a flower: Make 4 ch and join with a sl st to form ring.
Round 1: Work 10 htr into ring.
Rounds 2, 3 & 4: 3 htr into 1 htr, miss 2 sts *. Rep from * to *. Make one or more leaves as follows: Continuing from last st worked, make 7 ch and work 1 dc into each. When enough leaves have been made, fasten off.

White and gold skirt

Materials: 500 g 4-ply white wool; 250 g gold lurex; 1 round button mould; 15 cm (6 in) zip fastener; 4.50 mm (7) crochet hook.
Stitches used: Treble, double crochet, crab.
The skirt is worked with the two threads (1 wool, 1 Lurex) tog and is made up of 4 equal pieces sewn tog.
Make 45 ch and work for 65 cm (25½ in) in tr, decreasing 1 st on each side every 6.5 cm (3 in) until there are 27 sts left.
Make another 3 pieces in the same way. Sew all seams, leaving 15 cm (6 in) open on one side for fastening. Work 8 rows in dc and 1 row in crab st at waist. On Row 4 make a horizontal buttonhole of 3 sts, 4 sts from front edge of opening. Cover the button by working a small disc in the same yarns as the skirt and gathering it in underneath the base. Sew to back edge of opening to correspond with buttonhole. Insert zip.

White and gold sleeveless slipover

Materials: 200 g 4-ply white wool, 100 g gold Lurex; 4.50 mm (7) crochet hook.
Stitches used: Double crochet, openwork no. 11, crab.
Back: Make a ch 40 cm (15½ in) in length and work in openwork st no. 11 for 27 cm (11 in), decreasing 1 st at each side when work measures 2 cm (¾ in) and again when it measures 6 cm (2½ in).
When work measures 23 cm (9 in), inc 1 st on each side and again when it measures 26 cm (10½ in).
Shape armhole by decreasing 2 sts in

White and gold skirt with sleeveless slipover and Lurex cap

the first row and another st in the 2nd (increases and decreases to be worked always on the treble row).

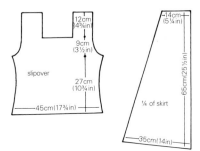

Diagram of slipover and skirt

Continue for 9 cm (3½ in) then shape neck by decreasing 12 sts at centre of work. Work right side for 14 cm (5½ in) without shaping and fasten off.

Rejoin yarn to left side and finish to match.

Front: Work as for back.

Join side and shoulder seams and complete by working 1 row in dc and 1 row in crab stitch around the edge of both armholes, neck and lower edge of slipover.

Lurex cap

Materials: 6 reels of Lurex (all 6 strands are worked tog); 5.00 mm (6) crochet hook.

Stitches used: Double crochet, treble, slip.

Make 4 ch and join with a sl st to form ring.

Round 1: Work 10 dc into ring.

Round 2: 20 tr worked between dc of previous row beg with 3 ch (= 1 tr), sl st to join.

Continue for another 4 rounds, always working between sts of pre-vious row and increasing 7 sts regularly spaced on each round.

8th round: Work in tr increasing 5 sts regularly to make 60 sts.

Continue without increasing for a further 9 rounds, closing the final round as before with 1 sl st.

Cut the strands, fasten off and neaten by weaving the ends invisibly into work.

Silver evening top

Materials: 200 g silver Lurex (work-ed 6 strands at a time); 5.00 mm (5) crochet hook.

Stitches used: Treble, double treble, four-leaf clover, crab.

Lower part: Make 100 ch and work 22 rows in four-leaf clover stitch.

Fasten off but leave a long end of Lurex to sew seam. Make sure this seam comes at centre back.

Upper part: To make one cup, make 15 ch and work in tr, ending with (1 tr, 1 ch, 1 tr) into last ch. Work back in tr along the unworked side of base ch. Work another 4 rows on both sides, with (1 tr, 1 ch, 1 tr) into the 1-ch loop of previous row.

Work last row as follows: ∗ 2 tr into 1 st, miss next st. Rep from ∗ to ∗ to last st, 2 tr.

Make another cup to match and sew them to the front of the lower part of garment, slightly overlapping the cups at centre front.

Halter ties: At the top of each cup work on 5 centre sts in tr for 60cm (24 in). Work 1 row in dc and 1 row in crab st around the lower and top edges, excluding halter ties.

Bikini swimsuit

Materials: 100 g crochet cotton no. 5 each in yellow and brown; 2.00 mm (14) crochet hook.

Bikini swimsuit

Silver evening top

Stitches used: Double crochet, treble, crab.

Bra: 19 ch in yellow cotton.

Row 1: 18 dc.

Row 2: 17 dc.

Row 3: 3 dc into end dc and then work 17 dc along unworked side of base ch.

Row 4 (brown cotton): 19 tr, 3 tr into centre dc, 19 tr on 2nd side.

Row 5: Work in dc, with 3 dc into centre tr at turning point.

Rows 6 & 7 (yellow cotton): As Rows 4 & 5, working 3 sts into centre st on each row.

Rows 8 & 9 ((Brown cotton): As Rows 4 & 5.

Rows 10 & 11 (yellow cotton): As Rows 4 & 5.

Row 12 (brown cotton): * 1 tr, 2 ch, miss 1 st, 3 tr into next st. *. Rep from * to *.

Waistcoat

Row 13: Work in dc, with 2 dc into each 2-ch loop and 5 dc into the 3 centre tr.

Row 14: Work in tr, with 3 tr into centre dc.

Row 15 (yellow cotton): Work in dc.

Row 16: As Row 11.

Row 17: As Row 12.

Row 18: * 1 dc, 5 ch, miss 3 sts. *. Rep from * to *.

Row 19 (brown cotton): * 1 dc into same st as used by dc in Row 18, 4 tr into next 5-ch loop. *. Rep from * to *.

Fasten off.

Work 2nd cup in the same way.

Complete bra by working in yellow cotton on lower edge of one cup as follows: * 1 dc into each st, 4 dc into tr, 3 ch *. Rep from * to * and continue along lower edge of 2nd cup. The two cups are now joined. Do not cut yarn.

Back ties: Make 120 ch and work 1 row of dc. Fasten off. Rejoin yarn to the first st worked and make 120 ch. Work 1 dc into each ch. Fasten off. Halter ties: Join yellow cotton at top of one cup and make a ch of 60 cm (24 in). Work 1 dc into each ch. Fasten off. Make a similar strap on the other cup.

Complete the bra with 1 row of crab st in brown cotton.

Pants: Starting at the back, make 86 ch in yellow cotton. Working one row in tr and one row in dc, change colour every 2 rows. Work 12 rows in this way. Continue for a further 28 rows, alternating the colours as before and decreasing as follows: (2 sts at each end of next row, 1 st at each end of following 4 rows) 5 times, then 1 st at each end of next 3 rows.

Work in dc for 32 rows on remaining 20 sts.

Still working in dc, increase 2 sts at each end of Row 33 (4 sts) and continue to increase 4 sts on each row for 11 more rows.

Continue in dc increasing 1 st at each end of next 3 rows. Work row. Rep last 4 rows twice more to make 86 sts. Fasten off.

Make 2 insertions in brown cotton for the sides as follows: 12 ch, work 16 rows in dc.

Sew insertions to side edges of back and front of pants and complete by working 1 row of dc and 1 row of crab st around leg openings and top edge.

Waistcoat

Materials: 500 g grey double knitting wool; 5 buttons; 6.00 mm (4) crochet hook.
Stitches used: Double crochet, alternating no. 1.
Back: Make ch 42 cm (16¾ in) long. Work in alternating st no. 1 for 42 cm (16¾ in).
Decrease 4 sts at each end of next row for armholes and continue in alternating st no. 1 for another 22 cm (8¾ in).
Half Front: Make ch 20 cm (8 in) long.
Work in alternating st no. 1 for 12 cm (4¾ in). Decrease 1 st at beg of every alternate row for V-neck. When 42 cm (16¾ in) have been worked from the beginning, dec 4 sts for armhole on the side opposite the front shaping and continue for another 22 cm (8¾ in) in alternating st no. 1.
Work the 2nd half front to match, reversing shapings.
Join side and shoulder seams.
Complete the armholes, V-neck, front edgings and lower edge by working 5 rows dc increasing 1 st on every row at lower edge of fronts to form mitred corners. On the right front, make 5 vertial buttonholes, spaced evenly between lower edge and start of V-neck.
Sew buttons on other side to correspond with buttonholes.

Man's jacket

Materials: 1500 g double knitting wool; 6 buttons; 5.50 mm (5) crochet hook.

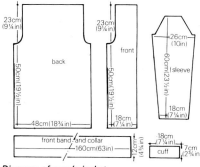

Diagram of man's jacket

Stitches used: Double crochet, basketweave.
To make the jacket a little lighter, the basketweave stitch has been modified as follows: Row 1: tr Row 2: ✳ 2 raised tr (yoh, insert hook from front to back of vertical bar of first tr, bring forward between 2nd and 3rd tr, yoh and complete as for normal tr), 2 reverse raised tr (worked in same way except that hook is inserted from back to front and brought to back of work between 2nd and 3rd tr) ✳. On following rows, alternate the pattern every 2 rows so that ordinary raised tr are worked over reverse raised tr.
Back: Make 54 ch and work in basketweave for 50 cm (19½ in).
Shape armholes by dec 3 sts at each end of first row, 2 ch each end of 2nd and 1 at each end of 3rd. Continue in basketweave for 23 cm (9 in) more. Fasten off.
Half front: Make 20 ch and work in basketweave for 50 cm (19½ in). Shape only for armhole at one side as for back. Finish as for back. Work 2nd half front, reversing for shaping for armhole.
Sleeves: Make 30 ch and work in basketweave for 40 cm (15½ in) increasing 1 st on each side every 10 rows and taking inc sts into pattern. Shape top by decreasing as for back

Man's jacket

and continue decreasing regularly for 20 cm (8 in) more until 3 sts remain. Sew sides, shoulder and sleeve seams. Insert sleeves.

Collar and front borders: Make a ch the same length as the 2 fronts and back neck edge. Work in dc for 12 cm (4¾ in). When 3 cm (1¼ in) have been worked of left border, make the first set of 3 buttonholes, equally spaced. After a further 6 cm (2½ in) have been worked, make 3 more buttonholes to correspond with the first three. Sew border to front edges and back neck edge. Complete each sleeve with a 7 cm

(2¾ in) cuff of dc, worked separately. Join seam, set in line with sleeve seam and sew on to *right* side of work. Turn cuffs back. Sew buttons on right front to correspond with buttonholes.

Blue matinée coat

Materials: 100 g 3-ply blue wool; small quantity in white; length of narrow baby ribbon (optional); 3.00 mm (10) crochet hook.
Stitches used: Double crochet, treble, open work no. 5, crab.
Back and fronts (worked in one piece

184

to armholes): Make 130 ch and work in openwork st no 5 for 16 cm (6½ in). Remove hook from working loop but do not fasten off.

Sleeves (both alike): Make 40 ch and work in openwork st no. 5 for 15 cm (6 in). Remove hook from working loop but do not fasten off.

Yoke: Pick up working loop on front and work in white wool in openwork st no. 5 across half-front, (34 sts) top of one sleeve, back, (62 sts) top of 2nd sleeve and 2nd half-front (34 sts) for 4 rows. Now work 5 rows in dc in blue wool, 2 rows in white, 6 rows in blue, decreasing 12 sts regularly on each row. (54 sts remain on completion of yoke). Join side and sleeve seams.

Round neck and wrist edges work * 1 tr, 1 ch, miss 1 st. * Rep from * to * for insertion of cords. (Most manufactured garments for babys do not include cords for safety reasons: the inclusion in this work is optional.)

Finish neck, wrists, front and lower

Blue matinée coat

White matinée coat

edges with 1 row of dc and 1 row of crab st.

If not using ribbon, make a fairly long ch and work 1 row dc for neck tie and 2 shorter ones for wrists. Thread through insertion holes.

White matinée coat

Materials: 100 g 3-ply white wool; length of narrow baby ribbon (optional); 3.00 mm (10) crochet hook.

Stitches used: Double crochet, treble, arabesque stitch, crab stitch.

Back: Make 54 ch and work in arabesque st for 15 cm (6 in) ending with Row 1 (1 tr, 1 ch, 1 tr). Now work 1 row in dc working only into each 1-ch loop of previous row, thus gathering the work for beg of yoke. Remove hook from working loop but do not fasten off.

Half fronts (both alike): Make 27 ch and work as for back to yoke. Remove hook from working loop but do not fasten off.

Sleeves (both alike): Make 35 ch and work in arabesque st for 14 cm (5½ in), ending with Row 1, then 1 row of dc worked into each 1-ch loop of previous row. Remove hook.

Join back to two fronts by sewing side seams, then join sleeve seams.

Yoke: Start by picking up working st with white wool on right front and work across right front, right sleeve, back, left sleeve then left front as follows: * 1 row in tr and 1 row in dc *. Rep from * to * twice more. Change to white wool and rep from * to *. At the same time dec evenly on each dc row until 53 sts remain.

Finish neck opening in blue wool by working a ribbon insertion row (1 tr, 1 ch, miss 1 st). Join back to 2 fronts by sewing side seams, then join sleeve seams. At each cuff work a ribbon insertion row, then 1 row dc and 1 row crab st.

With blue wool work 1 row of dc and

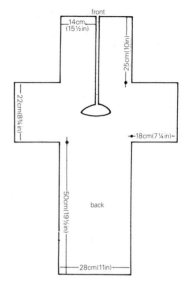

Diagram of baby's coat-bag

1 row of crab st round cuffs, down edges of both fronts and along lower edge. Make 3 cords, as described in previous pattern (optional), and thread through insertion holes. If preferred, ribbon can be used instead of crocheted cords.

Baby's coat-bag

Materials: 200 g white angora wool (used double); 100 g red angora wool (used double); 32 cm (12-13 in) heavyweight zip fastener; 4.00 mm (8) crochet hook.

Stitches used: Double crochet, crazy double crochet.

Make 44 ch and work in crazy double crochet for 50 cm (19½ in), alternating colours: 7 rows in white, 4 rows in red, 12 rows in white, 4 rows in red, 7 rows in white. Now make 30 ch in red wool for sleeves on each sides of work and continue 5 rows in red and 5 rows in white.

Baby's coat-bag

Work to centre 3 motifs miss 3 motifs, join in a 2nd ball of yarn and work 7 rows in white on each side separately. Now work 1 row in red and make 6 ch on inside edge for front neck-opening. Work 4 rows, still in red. Leave outer sts for sleeve and continue on 6 centre motifs, working 7 rows in white, 4 rows in red, 12 rows in white.

Collar: Work 30 dc in white wool round neck edge. Now work 7 more rows in dc, increasing 2 sts at beg of every row. Finish collar with 2 rows in dc (1 white, 1 red), working right round the collar to centre front. With red wool, work 2 rows in dc round wrists and down edges of both centre fronts. Sew zip fastener into cen-

tre opening. Join side sleeve seams, folding up the first 11 rows (7 white and 4 red) to meet lower edges of both fronts. Stitch top of flap to lower edges of each front.

Child's pink dress

Materials: 250 g 4-ply pink wool; small quantity of contrasting colour (brown is suggested); 1 small button; 3.00 mm (10) and 4.00 mm (8) crochet hooks.

Stitches used: Double crochet, simple shell, crab.

Front bodice: With 3.00 mm hook start at waist and make 110 ch. Work in simple shell st for 15 rows. Dec 2 shells on each side for armholes and

Child's pink dress

blue, green and yellow; 4.50 mm (7) crochet hook.

Stitches used: Double crochet, treble, elongated double crochet (ordinary dc worked into row *before* previous row, ie 2 rows back).

Back: With white wool, make 30 ch and work 6 rows in tr, starting Row 1 by working 1 tr in 4th ch from hook. Continue working as follows:

Row 1: ∗ 3 tr in blue, 3 tr in white ∗. Rep from ∗ to ∗ ending with 4 tr in blue.

Row 2: ∗ 3 tr in white, 3 tr in yellow ∗. Rep from ∗ to ∗ ending with 4 tr in white.

Row 3: Work in tr in green.

Row 4: ∗ 3 tr in yellow, 3 tr in white ∗. Rep from ∗ to ∗ ending with 4 tr in yellow.

Row 5: ∗ 3 tr in white, 3 tr in blue ∗. Rep from ∗ to ∗ ending with 4 tr in white. Work 5 more rows in white. Decrease 2 sts at each side for armholes on next row, then work 6 more rows.

Miss centre 7 sts and work 1 row on each shoulder separately for neck.

Half front: Make 21 ch and work 19 tr for the same number of rows and the same colour changes as on back. After armhole dec has been worked, inc 1 st at neck edge on next 5 rows for shawl collar.

Make 2nd half front to match, reversing shapings.

Sleeves: Make 21 ch and work 19 tr for 16 rows, repeating the same sequence of colours as for back. Shape top by dec 2 sts at each end of next row, then 1 st at each end of next and every alternate row until 7 sts remain.

Pocket: Make 8 ch in white wool and work in tr for 3 rows. Make another pocket to match.

Join side, shoulder, and sleeve seams. Join centre back collar.

Finish all edges with 1 row dc in white and 1 row in yellow as follows:

work 15 rows more. Miss centre 11 shells and work 1 row on each shoulder separately for neck. Fasten off.

Back bodice: Work as for front until 3 rows have been worked after armhole dec. Now divide for back opening and work each half separately.

Join side seams and turn work right side out.

Skirt: With no. 4.00 mm hook, work into foundation ch at waist and work 18 rounds in simple shell st. Work 1 row in dc and 1 row in crab st. Fasten off.

Finish neck edge, back opening and armholes by working 2 rows in dc and 1 row in crab st.

Make a cord in brown wool and thread through holes at waist. Sew button to left side of neck opening and make button loop at right side to correspond.

Child's jacket

Materials: 300 g double knitting wool; a few grammes of same in

✻ 1 dc, 1 elongated dc ✻. Rep from ✻ to ✻ for entire row. This border is worked round wrists, side fronts and collar edge; also along one edge of each pocket.

Sew pockets to each side of jacket, ensuring that they are evenly placed. Make two keepers for belt by making 2 lengths of ch each about 3 cm (1 in) and sew to side seams at waist level. Belt: With white wool make a chain 120 cm (46 in) long and work 2 rows in tr. Finish belt with 1 row in yellow as follows: ✻ 1 dc, 1 elongaged dc ✻. Rep from ✻ to ✻ all round belt. Thread through belt keepers at each side.

Sweater in houndstooth check

Materials: 150 g 4-ply beige wook; 200 g 4-ply rust wool, 4.00 mm (8) crochet hook.

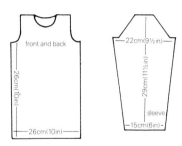

Diagram of sweater in houndstooth check

Stitches used: Half-treble, houndstooth check in 2 colours.

Back: Using rust wool, make ch 26 cm (10½ in) long and work 3 rows htr. Continue in both colours and work 24 cm (9½ in) in houndstooth check. Shape armholes by dec 3 sts at each side. Continue for a further

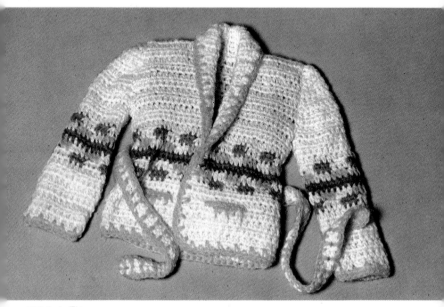

Child's jacket

17 cm (6¾ in) in houndstooth check. Miss centre 8 sts and work 1 row on each shoulder separately for neck.
Front: Work as for back until 2 rows less have been worked to neck shaping. Miss centre 8 sts and work 3 rows on each shoulder.
Sleeves: With rust wool make ch 15 cm (6 in) long and work 3 rows htr. Continue for 42 cm (17 in) in houndstooth check in both colours, increasing gradually on each side to a width of 22 cm (9¾ in). To shape top, dec 3 sts on each side and continue for a further 17 cm (6¾ in) in houndstooth check, decreasing regularly and gradually until 4 sts remain.
Join shoulder, side and sleeve seams. Insert sleeves. Using rust wool work 2 rounds, htr wool round neck.

Girl's dressing-gown

Materials: 350 g 3-ply red wool; 3.00 mm (10) crochet hook.

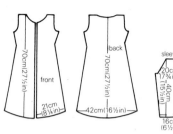

Diagram of girl's dressing-gown

Stitches used: Double crochet, simple shell, treble, crab.
Back: Make 68 ch and starting into the 3rd ch from hook, work ∗ 1 shell (= 1 tr, 1 ch, 1 tr), miss 1 st. ∗. Rep from ∗ to ∗ ending with 1 tr. Next row: 3 tch, 1 shell into 1-ch loop between the 2 tr of previous row, ending with 1 tr. Continue in this way for approximately 30 cm (12 in) then for a further 40 cm (15½ in) at the same time decreasing 1 st regularly at each side until 4 shells have been decreased at each side.

Sweater in houndstooth check

Girl's dressing-gown

Armhole: Row 1 – dec 2 shells at each side.

Row 2 – dec 1 shell on each side.

Rows 3-9 – work straight.

Miss centre 7 shells (back neck edge) and work each shoulder separately: 1 row of dc across all shells and 1 row across 3 shells only at neck edge. Fasten off.

Right front: Make 38 ch and work as for back, shaping on one side only.

Left front: as for right front, reversing shaping.

Sleeves (both alike): Make 28 ch and work 30 cm (12 in), increasing gradually until 1 extra shell has been completed on each side. Dec 2 shells in Row 1 of armhole and 1 shell in foll rows until 5 shells remain.

Collar: Make 40 ch and work 5 rows of shells.

To make up: Join shoulder side, and sleeve seams. Insert sleeves. Sew collar in position (from right side of work). Work 1 row of dc and 1 row of crab st round all edges. Make a cord in the same yarn and thread it through holes in pattern at waist.

TABLEMATS, TABLECLOTHS AND BEDSPREADS

The fascination of tradition

The patterns described in this section undoubtedly come within the most demanding area of this fascinating craft but also present the greatest challenge to the expert crocheter.

Perhaps the nostalgia conjured up by these designs for an age when it was the prerogative of rich and noble families to own such delicate and elegant work is part of the reason for its fascination. Or it may be that the meticulous workmanship, close attention to detail and patience involved are sufficient satisfaction in themselves, with the knowledge that the results will be imaginatively creative designs emerging from the simplest of materials – a fine thread and a small hook.

Tablemats, tablecloths, runners and bedspreads worked in either lacy patterns or in filet, with simple and complex stitches blended together, represent the most traditional, classical aspect of crochet. They remind us of elegant town and country houses of the past where gracious bedrooms would have been adorned by lovely bed coverings such as the 19th-century double bedspread described in the following pages, which originally came from one of the great homes belonging to the House of Savoy. Of course such a masterpiece represents many months of work and it is not simple; but the satisfaction of producing such a beautiful thing is sufficient reward for the patience and time expended.

However, the type of intricate work described here fits in just as well in modern settings as it did in times past. And with modern methods for laundering and conditioning fabric, combined with the beautiful crochet cottons now available, there is no reason why the old and the new should not live in harmony, for the one is complementary to the other.

One suggestion to ease the laundering problem is to place crocheted mats, traycloths, runners and the like under glass. It is a simple matter to have a piece of glass cut to fit a table top, tray or dressing-table and the mats stay fresh, with the design well displayed, until such time as you feel the need for a change. It is also a good way to cover a polished wood surface which may be less than perfect.

Centrepiece no. 1

Centrepiece no. 1

Materials: 50 g crochet cotton no. 12; 1.25 mm (4½) crochet hook.
Stitches used: Double crochet, treble, double treble.
(Replace first st of each round as follows: Tr by 3 ch, dtr by 4 ch. Close each round with a sl st.)
Make 8 ch and join with a sl st to form a ring.
Round 1: Work 1 tr, 3 ch into each ch.
Round 2: (3 tr, 5 ch) into each 3-ch loop.
Round 3: Sl st to 5th ch, *(1 dc, 9 ch, 1 dc) into same ch as 5th sl st, 5 ch. * Rep from * to * to end of round, working motif in brackets into 3rd of each 5-ch loop.

Round 4: (9 tr, 3 ch, 9 tr) into each 9-ch loop.
Round 5: Sl st to 5th tr, * 1 tr, 5 ch (1 dc, 3 ch, 1 dc) into 3-ch loop between tr, 5 ch. Miss 4 tr, 1 tr in 5th tr, 5 ch. * Rep from * to * end of round.
Round 6: Into each 5-ch loop of previous round work 4 dtr, separating each group of 4 dtr with 1 ch, and in each 3-ch loop work (1 dtr, 2 ch, 1 dtr).
Round 7: Sl st to first 1-ch loop, 1 dc into each 1-ch loop separating the dtr groups of previous round, 7 ch. *. Rep from * to *.
Round 8: Sl st to 4th ch, 1 dc, 7 ch, 1 dc into 4th ch of each 7-ch loop, 7 ch. Rep from * to * end of round.
Round 9: As Round 8.

Centrepiece no. 2

Round 10: ∗ (8 dtr, 3 ch, 8 dtr) into 7-ch loop, 1 dc into next 7-ch loop ∗. Rep from ∗ to ∗ to end of round.
Round 11: Sl st to 4th dtr, ∗ 1 tr, 5 ch, (1 dc, 3 ch, 1 dc) into 3-ch loop, 5 ch, 1 tr into 4th dtr, 5 ch. ∗. Rep from ∗ to ∗ to end of round.
Round 12: As Round 6.
Round 13: As Round 7.
Rounds 14, 15 & 16: As Round 8.
Round 17: ∗ 8 dtr separated by 1 picot (= 3 ch, 1 dc into dtr just worked) into first 7-ch loop, 1 dc into next 7-ch loop. ∗. Rep from ∗ to ∗ to end of round.
Fasten off.

Centrepiece no. 2

Materials: 70 g crochet cotton no. 8; 1.75 mm (15) crochet hook.
Stitches used: double crochet, half treble, treble, double treble.
Make 10 ch and join with a sl st to form ring. (Replace first tr with 3 ch at beg of each round. Close each round with 1 sl st into 3rd starting ch, except when working ch lace, round 5 when each round ends with 2 ch, 1 tr into first dc of same round).
Round 1: Work 28 tr into ring.
Round 2: Work 46 tr.
Round 3: Work 64 tr.
Round 4: ∗ 1 tr, 2 ch, miss 1 st. ∗. Rep from ∗ to ∗ to end of round.
Round 5: ∗ 1 dc, 5 ch. ∗. Rep from ∗

to * into each 2-ch loop.

Rounds 6, 7 & 8: * 5 ch, 1 dc into each 5-ch loop of previous round. *. Rep from * to * to end of round.

Round 9: * 6 ch, 1 dc into each 5-ch loop *. Rep from * to * to end of round.

Round 10: 6 ch, 5 tr into 3rd of 6-ch just worked, * 1 tr into 6-ch loop of previous round, 3 ch, 5 tr into tr just worked *. Rep from * to * to end of round, ending with 1 sl st into 3rd of 6 tch.

Round 11: Sl st to 3rd ch, * 5 ch, 1 dc into 3rd ch of next 5-tr group, 7 ch, 1 dc into 3rd ch of next 5-tr group *. Rep from * to * to end of round.

Round 12: * (1 dc, 1 htr, 4 tr, 1 htr, 1 dc) into 5-ch loop, (1 dc, 2 htr, 3 tr) into 7-ch loop, 4 ch, (2 unfin dtr, yoh, draw yarn through all 3 loops on hook) into back loop of 2nd of 3-tr group just worked, 4 ch, 1 dc into same 2nd tr of 3-tr group, (3 tr, 2 htr, 1 dc) into same 7-ch loop *. Rep from * to * to end of round.

Round 13: Sl st to first tr, * (1 tr, 3 ch, 1 tr) into 3rd tr of previous round, 5 ch, (1 tr, 3 ch, 1 tr) into closing st of 2 dtr cluster of previous round 5 ch *. Rep from * to * to end of round.

Round 14: * 1 dc into first 3-ch loop, ** (2 htr, 2 tr, 2 dtr, 2 tr, 1 htr, 1 dc) into next 5-ch loop **. (1 dc, 3 ch, 5 dtr, 3 ch, 1 dc) into next 3-ch loop, rep from ** to ** once *. Rep from * to * to end of round into first dc.

Round 15: Sl st to first dtr, * 1 dtr, 7 ch, 1 dc into 3rd ch of dtr group of previous round, 5 ch, 1 dc into last dtr of same group, 7 ch, 1 dtr between first and 2nd dtr of next group *. Rep from * to * to end.

Round 16: (1 dc, 1 htr, 5 tr, 1 htr, 1 dc) into each 7-ch loop of previous round.

Round 17: Sl st to 3rd tr of 5-tr group in previous round, * 1 dc into 3rd tr, 7 ch, 1 dc into first tr of next group, 7 ch, 1 dc into 4th tr of same group, 7

ch, 1 dc into 3rd tr of next tr group, 7 ch *. Rep from * to * to end of round finishing with 4 ch, 1 tr into first dc.

Rounds 18 & 19: * 7 ch, 1 dc into each 7-ch loop of previous round *. Rep from * to * to end of round.

Round 20: (2 tr, 5 ch) into each 7-ch loop of previous round.

Round 21: * 2 tr, 3 ch, 1 dc into 5-ch loop, 3 ch *. Rep from * to * to end of round.

Round 22: * 2 tr, 5 ch *. Rep from * to * to end of round.

Round 23: As Round 21.

Round 24: As Round 22.

Round 25: As Round 21.

Round 26: * 2 tr, 7 ch *. Rep from * to * to end of round.

Round 27: * 2 tr, 4 ch, 1 dc into 7-ch loop, 4 ch *. Rep from * to * to end of round.

Round 28: As Round 26.

Round 29: As Round 27.

Round 30: As Round 26.

Round 32: As Round 27.

Round 32: As Round 26.

Round 33: * 9 tr into 7-ch loop, 4 ch, 3 dc into next 7-ch loop, 4 ch. *. Rep from * to * to end of round.

Round 34: (1 tr, 1 ch) 8 times, 1 tr into 9 tr of previous round, (1 dc in space bet 2-dc) twice, 3 ch *. Rep from * to * to end of round.

Round 35: * (2 tr, 1 picot) (= 3 ch, 1 dc into 2nd tr just worked), 1 ch into each 1-ch separating the 9 tr (8 times in all), 2 ch, 1 dc bet 2-dc, 2 ch *. Rep from * to * to end of round. Fasten off.

Centrepiece no. 3

Materials: 60 g crochet cotton no. 12; 1.25 mm (4½) crochet hook.
Stitches used: Double crochet, treble.
(Replace first dc of each round by 1 ch, first tr by 3 ch. Close each round with a sl st).
Make 10 ch and join with a sl st to form ring.
Round 1: 1 ch (= 1 dc), 7 ch, ∗ 1 dc, 7 ch into ring ∗. Rep from ∗ to ∗ 10 times more.
Round 2: 3 sl st to central point of first 7-ch loop, ∗ 1 dc into loop, 3 ch ∗. Rep from ∗ to ∗ 11 times more.
Round 3: 2 sl st to central point of first loop ∗ 1 dc into first loop, 7 ch, 1 dc into same loop, 3 ch ∗. Rep from ∗ to ∗ 11 times more.
Round 4: 3 sl st to central point of first loop, ∗ 1 dc into 7-ch loop, ∗ 7 ch ∗. Rep from ∗ to ∗ 11 times more.
Round 5: ∗ 1 dc into dc, 5 ch, 1 dc into next 7-ch loop, 5 ch ∗. Rep from ∗ to ∗.
Round 6: ∗ (1 tr, 2 ch, 1 tr) into first loop (corner), (1 dc into next loop, 5 ch) 5 times ∗. Rep from ∗ to ∗ 3 times more.
Rounds 7 to 12: ∗ 1 corner into 2-ch corner round, (1 dc, 5 ch) into every following 5-ch loop ∗. Rep from ∗ to ∗ 3 times more.
Round 13: ∗ 1 corner into 2-ch corner loop, 1 ch, (5 tr, 1 ch into next loop) along one side ∗. Rep from ∗ to ∗ 3 times more.
Round 14: ∗ 3 dc into 2-ch corner loop, 1 dc into next 1-ch loop (5 ch, 1 dc into next 1-ch loop) along one side ∗. Rep from ∗ to ∗ 3 times more.
Round 15: Sl st to 4th dc, ∗ 1 dc into dc, 20 ch, miss three 5-ch loops, 1 dc into next dc, (5 dc into next 5-ch loop, 1 ch) 4 times, 5 dc into next 5-ch loop, 1 dc into next dc, 20 ch, miss three 5-ch loops, 1 dc into next dc, 6 ch,

miss 3 dc at corner ∗. Rep from ∗ to ∗ 3 more times.
Round 16: ∗ 24 dc into 20-ch loop, miss 1 dc (5 dc, 3 ch) 4 times, 5 dc, miss 1 dc, 24 dc into next 20-ch loop, 10 dc into 6-ch loop ∗. Rep from ∗ to ∗ 3 more times.
Round 17: ∗ 23 dc, 3 ch, (1 dc into next 3-ch loop, 5 ch) 3 times, 3 ch, miss first dc of 24 dc group, 23 dc, miss first dc of 10-dc group, miss 1 dc of 10-dc group and 1 dc of 24-dc group. Rep from ∗ to ∗ 3 times.
Round 18: ∗ 23 dc, 4 ch, (1 dc into next loop, 5 ch) 3 times, 1 dc into next loop, 4 ch, miss 3-ch loop and first dc of 23-dc group, 30 dc ∗. Rep from ∗ to ∗ 3 more times.
Round 19: ∗ 1 dc, 12 ch, miss 2 loops, 1 dc into next 5-ch loop, 12 ch, miss 2 loops, 1 dc in first dc of 30-dc group, 12 ch, miss 10 dc, 1 dc, 12 ch, miss 10 dc, 1 dc, 5 ch, miss 3 dc, 1 dc, 5 ch, miss 3 dc ∗. Rep from ∗ to ∗ 3 times more.
Round 20: ∗ (1 dc into 1 dc, 14 dc into 12-ch loop) 6 times, 2 dc into next dc, 8 dc into 5-ch loop, 2 dc into next dc, 8 dc into next 5-ch loop, 2 dc into next dc ∗. Rep from ∗ to ∗ 3 times more.
Rounds 21 & 22: 1 dc into every dc of previous round, working 2 dc into same st on each side of corner loops.
Round 23: ∗ 4 dc, 9 ch ∗. Rep from ∗ to ∗ 117 times more.
Round 24: 4 sl st to central point of 9-ch loop, ∗ 1 dc into 9-ch loop, 4 ch ∗. Rep from ∗ to ∗ to end.
Round 25: Sl st to central point of 4-ch loop, 1 dc into 4-ch loop, 5 ch ∗. Rep from ∗ to ∗ to end and close round.
Round 26: As round 25.
Rounds 27 to 31: St st to central point of 5-ch loop, ∗ 1 dc into 5-ch loop, 6 ch ∗. Rep from ∗ to ∗ to end.
Round 32: ∗ dc into each 6-ch loop ∗. Rep from ∗ to ∗ to end. Fasten off.

Centrepiece no. 3

Centrepiece no. 4

Materials: 70 g crochet cotton no. 20; 1.25 mm (4½) crochet hook.
Stitches used: Double crochet, treble, double treble.
(Replace first st of each round as follows: Tr by 3 ch, dtr by 4 ch. Close each round with a sl st).
This centrepiece is made up of 7 flower motifs worked separately.

First flower motif: Make 8 ch and join with a sl st to form ring.
Round 1: 1 ch, 24 tr into ring.
Round 2: * 1 tr, 2 ch, miss 1 st *. Rep from * to * 12 times.
Round 3: 6 dtr into each of the twelve 2-ch loops.
Round 4: * 1 tr into first dtr, 1 unfin tr into each of next 5 dtr, yoh, draw yarn through all 6 loops on hook, 8 ch *. Rep from * to * 12 times.

Round 5: 1 ch, 7 dc, into each 8-ch loop, 1 picot (= 3 ch, 1 sl st in 7th dc just worked), 7 dc. Cut off thread.
In working the rest of the flower motifs, make 2 joining loops in last round as follows: 7 dc, 1 dc (by inserting hook into picot of previous flower motif), 7 dc.

Chart for Centrepiece no. 4

Centrepiece no. 4

Centrepiece no. 5

Materials: 50 g crochet cotton no. 20; 1.25 mm (4½) crochet hook.
Stitches used: Double crochet, half treble, treble, double treble, treble treble.
(Replace first st of each round as follows: dc by 1 ch, dtr by 4 ch, tr tr by 5 ch. Close each round with a sl st).
Make 6 ch and join with a sl st to form ring.
Round 1: 12 dc worked into ring.
Round 2: * 1 tr tr into dc of previous row, 5 ch *. Rep from * to *.
Round 3: Sl st to 3rd of 5-ch of previous round, * (1 tr tr, 5 ch, 1 tr tr) into same 3rd ch *. Rep from * to * working 3rd ch of each 5-ch loop, to end of round.
Round 4: (1 dc, 1 htr, 2 tr, 5 dtr, 2 tr, 1 htr, 1 dc (= 1 scallop)) into each 5-ch loop between tr tr of previous round.
Round 5: Sl st to centre of first scallop, * 1 tr tr, 5 ch, 1 tr tr, 7 ch *. Rep from * to *.
Round 6: * (3 unfin tr tr, yoh, draw yarn through all 4 loops on hook, 3 ch)

3 times into 5-ch loop, 3 unfin tr tr, yoh, draw yarn through all 4 loops on hook (4 petals); 4 ch, 1 dc into 4th ch of 7-ch loop in previous round, 4 ch *. Rep from * to *.
Round 7: Sl st to 3-ch loop between 2nd and 3rd of 4 petals of previous round * into 3-ch loop between 2nd and 3rd petals work 4 petals as in Round 6, 4 ch, 1 unfin dtr into next loop, 1 unfin dtr into following loop, yoh, draw yarn through all 3 loops on hook, 4 ch *. Rep from * to *.
Rounds 8 & 9: As Round 7, but on Round 9 work 5 ch before and after the 2-dtr cluster.
Round 10: Sl st to 3-ch loop between 2nd and 3rd petals of previous round, * 12 dtr into 3-ch loop, 6 ch, 1 unfin dtr into first ch loop, 1 unfin dtr into 2nd ch loop, yoh, draw yarn through all 3 loops on hook, 6 ch *. Rep from * to *.
Round 11: * (1 dtr, 1 ch) 11 times into 1 dtr of previous round, 1 dtr, 4 ch, 1 unfin dtr into first ch loop, 1 unfin dtr into 2nd ch loop, yoh, draw yarn through all 3 loops on hook, 4 ch *. Rep from * to *.
Round 12: * (1 dtr, 2 ch) 11 times into 11 dtr of previous round, 1 dtr, 1 ch, 1 dtr into 2-dtr cluster, 1 ch *. Rep from * to *.
Round 13: 1 dc into ch loop preceding 12 dtr of previous round, 1 dc between first and 2nd of 12-dtr, (4 ch, 1 dc between next 2 dtr), 3 times, 4 ch, (1 tr, 4 ch, 1 tr) between 6th and 7th dtr, 4 ch, miss 7th and 8th dtr, (1 dc between next 2 dtr, 4 ch) 3 times, 1 dc between last 2 dtr, 1 dc into next ch. *. Rep from * to *. Fasten off.

Centrepiece no. 6

Materials: 50 g crochet cotton no. 20; 125 mm (4½) crochet hook.
Stitches used: Double crochet, tre-

Centrepiece no. 5

ble, double treble, treble treble, quadruple treble (see Round 6).
(Replace first st of each round as follows: Dc by 1 ch; tr by 3 ch; dtr by 4 ch; tr tr by 5 ch; quad tr by 6 ch. Close each round with a sl st.)
Make 8 ch and join with a sl st to form ring.
Round 1: Work (1 tr, 1 ch) 12 times into ring.
Round 2: 2 dc into each 1-ch loop of previous round.
Round 3: * 1 tr tr, 7 ch, miss 1 st. *. Rep from * to * to end of round.
Round 4: * 1 tr into tr tr (1 ch, miss 1 ch, 1 tr) 3 times, 1 ch *. Rep from * to *. (48 tr in all.)
Round 5: 2 dc into each ch of previous round.
Round 6: * 1 quad tr (= yoh 4 times, insert hook into next st or loop, as

instructed, yoh, draw yarn through, [yoh and draw through 2 loops on hook] 5 times), 5 ch, 1 dtr between 2nd and 3rd sts on stem of quad tr, miss 3 sts *. Rep from * to * (24 groups).
Round 7: Sl st to centre of first 5-ch loop, * 2 dtr into 5-ch loop, 7 ch, 1 dc into centre of next 5-ch loop, 7 ch *. Rep from * to *.
Round 8: * 2 dtr into each of 2 dtr of previous round, 7 ch, yoh twice, insert hook into next 7-ch loop, yoh, draw yarn through, yoh, draw yarn through 2 loops on hook, yoh, insert hook into next 7-ch loop, yoh, draw yarn through, yoh, draw yarn through 2 loops on hook, (yoh, draw yarn through 2 loops on hook) 3 times (1 group formed), 7 ch *. Rep from * to *.

Centrepiece no. 6

Round 9: ✲ 2 dtr in first of the 4-dtr of previous round. 1 dtr into each of next 2 sts, 2 dtr into 4th st, 7 ch, work 1 group inserting hook into next two 7-ch loops, 7 ch ✲. Rep from ✲ to ✲.

Round 10: ✲ 2 dtr into first of the 6 dtr of previous round, 4 dtr, 2 dtr into 6th dtr, 7 ch, work 1 group inserting hook into next two 7-ch loops, 7 ch ✲. Rep from ✲ to ✲.

Round 11: ✲ miss first dtr, 6 dtr, (7 ch, 1 dc into next 7-ch loop) twice, 7 ch. Rep from ✲ to ✲.

Round 12: ✲ Miss first dtr, 4 dtr, (7 ch, 1 dc into next 7-ch loop) 3 times, 7 ch ✲. Rep from ✲ to ✲.

Round 13: ✲ Miss first dtr, 2 dtr, (7 ch, 1 dc into next 7-ch loop) 4 times, 7 ch ✲. Rep from ✲ to ✲.

Round 14: Sl st to centre of 7-ch loop following 2-dtr of previous round, ✲ 1 dc into 7-ch loop, 7 ch, 1 dc into next 7-ch loop, 12 tr into next 7-ch loop, 1 dc into next 7-ch loop, 7 ch, 7 dc into 7-ch loop preceding 2 dtr of previous round, 7 ch ✲, miss 2 dtr ✲. Rep from ✲ to ✲.

Round 15: Sl st to first 7-ch loop, ✲ 1 dc into ch loop, into next 12 tr of previous round, work (1 tr, 1 ch) 11 times, 1 tr, 1 dc into next ch loop, 7 ch, 1 dc into next ch loop, 7 ch ✲. Rep from ✲ to ✲.

Round 16: ✲ 2 ch, (1 tr in 1-ch loop, 2 ch) 11 times, 1 dc in 7-ch loop, 7 ch, 1 dc in 7 ch loop ✲. Rep from ✲ to ✲.

Round 17: 1 ch, ✲ 1 dc into first 2-ch loop, (1 dc between the 2 tr, 4 ch) twice, 1 dc between next 2 tr, 5 ch, 1 tr between 5th and 6th tr, 4 ch, 1 tr, 1 tr between 6th and 7th tr, 5 ch, 1 dc between 7th and 8th tr, (4 ch, 1 dc

between next 2 tr), 3 times, 1 dc into
next 2-ch loop, (2 dc, 3 ch, 2 dc) into
next 7-ch loop *. Rep from * to *.
Fasten off.

Chart for Centrepiece no. 6

Section of Decorative pointed centrepiece

Decorative pointed centrepiece

Decorative pointed centrepiece

Materials: 60 g crochet cotton no. 8; 2.00 mm (0) crochet hook.
Stitches used: Double crochet, treble, double treble.
(Replace first st of each round as follows: Dc by 1 ch, tr by 3 ch, dtr by 4 ch. Close each round with a sl st.)
Make 15 ch and join with a sl st to form ring.
Round 1: Work 40 tr into ring.
Round 2: * 3 tr, 4 ch, miss 2 sts *. Rep from * to * another 7 times.
Round 3: Sl st to 4-ch loop, * (3 dtr, 2 ch, 3 dtr), 6 ch, into each 4-ch loop *. Rep from * to * to end.
Round 4: Sl st to 2-ch loop, * (3 dtr, 2 ch, 3 dtr), 5 ch into each 6-ch loop *.

Rep from * to * another 7 times.
Round 5: Sl st to 2-ch loop * (3 dtr, 2 ch, 3 dtr) into 2-ch loop, 4 ch, 1 dc under 6-ch and 5-ch loops of Rounds 3 and 4, 4 ch *. Rep from * to * another 7 times. (There will now be a star with 8 points.)
Round 6: Sl st to 2-ch loop, * 1 dc into 2-ch loop, 14 ch *. Rep from * to * another 7 times.
Round 7: * 1 tr into dc, 18 tr into 14-ch loop *. Rep from * to *.
Round 8: * 5 tr, 5 ch, miss 3 sts *. Rep from * to *.
Round 9: Sl st to 5-ch loop, (3 dtr, 2 ch, 2 dtr), 6 ch into each 5-ch loop.
Round 10: Sl st to 2-ch loop (3 dtr, 2 ch, 3 dtr), 5 ch into each 2-ch loop.
Round 11: Sl st to 2-ch loop, (3 dtr, 2

205

Fir-tree centrepiece

ch, 3 dtr), 7 ch into each 2-ch loop.

Round 12: Sl st to 2-ch loop, * (3 dtr, 2 ch, 3 dtr), 5 ch into 2-ch loop, 1 dc under ch loops of Rounds 9, 10 & 11, 5 ch *. Rep from * to * (19 pointed motifs).

Round 13: * 1 dc into 2-ch loop, 11 ch *. Rep from * to *.

Round 14: * 1 tr into dc, 12 tr into next 11-ch loop, 1 tr into dc, 13 tr into next 11-ch loop *. Rep from * to *.

Round 15: * 6 tr, 5 ch, miss 2 sts *. Rep from * to *.

Round 16: As Round 9.

Round 17: As Round 10.

Round 18: As Round 11.

Round 19: Sl st to 2-ch loop * (3 dtr, 2 ch, 3 dtr) into each 2 ch loop, 6 ch, 1 dc into ch loops of Rounds 16, 17 & 18, 6 ch *. Rep from * to * (32 points).

Round 20: As Round 13.

Round 21: * 1 tr into dc, 11 tr into next 11-ch loop, 1 tr into next dc, 12 tr into next 11-ch loop *. Rep from * to *.

Round 22: * 7 tr, 5 ch, miss 2 sts *. Rep from * to *.

Round 23: As Round 9.

Round 24: As Round 10.

Round 25: As Round 11.

Round 26: Sl st to 2-ch loop, * (3 dtr, 3 ch, 1 dc) into last of the 3 dtr just worked (= 1 picot), 3 dtr) into each

2-ch loop, 6 ch, 1 dc under ch loops of Rounds 22, 23 & 24, 6 ch *. Rep from * to * (45 pointed motifs). Fasten off.

Fir-tree centrepiece

Materials: 100 g crochet cotton no. 8 in écru; 1.00 mm (5½) crochet hook.
Stitches used: Double crochet, treble, double treble.
(Replace first st of each round as follows: Dc by 1 ch; tr by 3 ch; dtr by 4 ch. Close each round with a sl st.)
Make 12 ch and join with a sl st to form ring.
Round 1: Work 22 tr into ring.
Round 2: 22 tr (1 tr into each tr).
Round 3: 44 dtr (2 dtr into each tr).
Round 4: * 4 unfin dtr, yoh, draw yarn through all 5 loops on hook, 5 ch *. Rep from * to *.
Round 5: Sl st to first 5-ch loop, 9 dc into each 5-ch loop.
Round 6: Sl st to 5th dc of first loop, * 1 dc, 9 ch *. Rep from * to * into 5th dc of each of following loops.
Round 7: 13 dc into each 9-ch loop.
Round 8: Sl st to 7th dc of first loop, * 1 dc, 13 ch *. Rep from * to * into 7th dc of each of following loops.
Round 9: 17 dc into each 13-ch loop.
Round 10: Sl st to 9th dc of first loop, * (3 dtr, 2 ch, 3 dtr) into same 9th dc, 11 ch *. Rep from * to * into 9th dc of each of following loops.
Rounds 11 & 12: Sl st to 2-ch loop of previous round, * (3 dtr, 2 ch, 3 dtr) into 2-ch loop, 5 ch, 1 dc into 6th ch of 11 ch loop of previous round, 5 ch *. Starting in next 2-ch loop. Rep from * to *.
Round 13: As Round 12, working 5 ch instead of 2 ch between the 3 dtr.
Round 14: Sl st to 5-ch loop, * 11 dtr, 5 ch, (1 tr, 2 ch, 1 tr) into dc of previous round, 5 ch *. Rep from * to *.
Round 15: * (1 dtr, 1 ch) into each of 10 dtr of previous round, 1 dtr into

11th dtr, 4 ch, 1 dc into 2-ch loop between 2-tr of previous round, 4 ch *. Rep from * to *.
Round 16: * (1 dtr, 2 ch) 10 times, 1 dtr, 3 ch *. Rep from * to *.
Round 17: As Round 16.
Round 18: * 7 ch, 1 dc into next loop, miss 1 loop *. Rep from * to *.
Rounds 19 to 26: * 7 ch, 1 dc into next loop *. Rep from * to *.
Round 27: * 3 tr into 7-ch loop, 3 ch *. Rep from * to *.
Round 28: * 1 tr into 2nd of 3-tr of previous round, 1 ch, (1 tr, 1 ch, 1 tr) into 3-ch loop, 1 ch *. Rep from * to *.
Round 29: * (2 tr, 3 ch, 2 tr) into first loop, 3 ch, miss 1 loop, 20 dc (1 dc into each tr and 1 dc into each ch loop), miss 1 loop, 3 ch *. Rep from * to * (14 groups of 20 dc).
Round 30: Sl st to 3-ch loop between 4-tr *. ([2 tr, 2 ch] 3 times, 2 tr) into 3-ch loop, 3 ch, 18 dc into 2nd to 19th dc of previous row, 3 ch *. Starting into next 3-ch loop, rep from * to *.
Round 31: Sl st to first 2-ch loop, * 1 group (= 2 tr, 2 ch, 2 tr) into 2-ch loop, 3 ch, 1 group into next loop, 3 ch, 1 group into 3rd loop, 3 ch, 1 dc into 17 dc, 3 ch *. Starting into next 2-ch loop, rep from * to *.
Round 32: Sl st to first 2-ch loop, * 1 group into 2-ch loop, 3 ch, (1 group, 2 ch, 1 group) into 2nd loop, 3 ch, 1 group into 3rd group, 3 ch, 15 dc, 3 ch *. Starting into next 2-ch loop, rep from * to *.
Round 33: Sl st to first 2-ch loop, * 1 group into 2-ch loop, 3 ch 3 groups separated by 2 ch into next 3 loops, 3 ch, 1 group into 5th loop, 3 ch, 12 dc, 3 ch *. Starting into next 2-ch loop, rep from * to *.
Round 34: Sl st to first 2-ch loop, * 1 group into 2-ch loop, 3 ch, 1 group into 2nd loop, 2 ch, 2 groups separated by 2 ch into 3rd loop, 2 ch, 1 group into 4th loop, 3 ch, 1 group into 5th loop, 4 ch, 9 dc, 4 ch *. Starting

into next 2-ch loop, rep from * to *.
Round 35: Sl st to first 2-ch loop, * 1 group into 2-ch loop, 3 ch, 5 groups separated by 2 ch into next 5 loops, 3 ch, 1 group into 7th loop, 5 ch, 7 dc, 5 ch *. Starting into next 2-ch loop, rep from * to *.
Round 36: Sl st to first 2-ch loop * 1 group into 2-ch loop, 3 ch, 2 groups separated by 2 ch into next 2 loops, 2 ch, 2 groups separated by 2 ch in 4th loop, 2 ch, 2 groups separated by 2 ch into 5th and 6th loops, 3 ch, 1 group into 7th loop, 4 ch, 5 dc, 4 ch *. Starting into next 2-ch loop, rep from * to *.
Round 37: Sl st to first 2-ch loop, * 1 group into 2-ch loop, 3 ch, 7 groups separated by 2 ch into next 7 loops, 3 ch, 1 group into 9th loop, 4 ch, 2 dc, 4 ch *. Starting into next 2-ch loop, rep from * to *.
Round 38: Sl st to first 2-ch loop, *, **1 group with picot (= 2 tr, 3 ch, 1 dc into 2nd tr, 2 tr) into 2-ch loop, 3 ch **. Starting into next 2 ch loop, work from ** to ** into remaining eight 2 ch loops, 1 dc into next 4-ch loop before dc, 1 dc into 4-ch loop after dc *. Rep from * to *. Fasten off.

Rep from * to * 11 times more.
Round 7: Sl st to 3rd ch of 5-ch loop, * 1 dc into 3rd ch, 1 ch, ** 1 picot (= 3 ch, 1 sl st into first ch), 1 ch, 1 picot **, 3 ch, rep from ** to **, 1 ch, 1 dc into same ch, 4 ch *. Rep from * to * 11 times more.
Round 8: Sl st to 2nd st of 3-ch loop, * 1 dc into 2nd ch, 1 ch, ** 1 picot, 1 ch **, rep from ** to ** twice more *. Rep from * to * 11 times more. Fasten off.

Lacy motif

Materials: 10 g crochet cotton no. 20; 1.25 mm (4½) crochet hook.
Stitches used; Double crochet, ridged crochet.
(Replace first dc of each round by 1 ch; close each round with a sl st.)
Make 5 ch and join with a sl st to form ring.
Round 1: Work 9 dc into ring.
Round 2: 2 dc into each st, working only into the *back* loop of the sts (ridged dc) (18 sts).
Rounds 3, 4 & 5: Increasing 6 sts evenly in each round, continue in ridged dc.
Round 6: * 1 dc, 5 ch, miss 2 sts *.

Lacy motif

Rectangular mat

Rectangular mat

Materials: 120 g crochet cotton no. 5; 2.50 mm (0) crochet hook.
Stitches used: Double crochet, treble, double treble.
(Replace first st of each round as follows: tr by 3 ch; dtr by 4 ch. Close each round with a sl st.)
This mat consists of 96 identical motifs joined together in 8 rows of 12 motifs.
First motif: Make 8 ch and join with a sl st to form ring.
Round 1: Work 16 tr into ring.
Round 2: * 1 tr, 3 ch, miss 1 st *. Rep from * to * 8 times.
Round 3: * 4 dtr into first 3-ch loop, 9 ch, 4 dtr into 2nd 3-ch loop, 2 ch *. Rep from * to * 4 times. Fasten off.
Work the other 95 motifs in the same way but join each one, when working Round 3, to those already completed as follows:
Round 3 (joining round): * 4 dtr into first 3-ch loop, 1 dc into 5th ch of 9-ch loop of completed motif, 4 ch, 4 dtr into 2nd 3-ch loop, 1 ch, 1 dc into 2-ch loop of completed motif, 1 ch *. Rep from * to * to end of round. Fasten off.
When all 96 motifs have been worked and the rectangle completed, work border as follows:
Round 1: On each side work (4 dtr, 3 ch) into each loop and into each corner loop work: (4 dtr, 6 ch, 4 dtr).
Round 2: * (** 1 dtr, 1 ch ** 3 times, 1 dtr) into first 3-ch loop, 4 ch, 1 dc into next 3-ch loop, 4 ch *. Rep from * to * along each side, working ([1 dtr, 1 ch] 6 times, 1 dtr) into each 6-ch corner loop.
Round 3: * 3 dc into 4-ch loop after dc of previous round (1 dc, 1 picot, 1 dc) into 1-ch between each dtr, 3 dc into next 4-ch loop *. Rep from * to * along each side, working (1 dc, 1 picot, 1 dc) 6 times into each corner (picot = 3 ch, sl st into dc just worked). Fasten off.

Border in filet crochet for rectangular cloth and chart

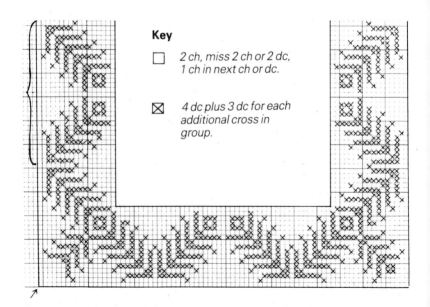

Key

☐ 2 ch, miss 2 ch or 2 dc, 1 ch in next ch or dc.

☒ 4 dc plus 3 dc for each additional cross in group.

Border in filet crochet for rectangular cloth

Materials: Crochet cotton no. 20; 1.25 mm (4½) crochet hook.
Stitches used: Mesh stitch with blocks and spaces.
Start at short edge of border and make 248 ch.
Row 1: 1 tr in 8th ch from hook (= 1 square), ＊ miss 2 ch, 1 tr ＊. Rep from ＊ to ＊ (= 81 squares).
Continue in pattern from chart (reading even rows left – right and odd rows right – left) until Row 17 has been completed.
Row 18 (wrong side): Pattern across 17 squares, miss 47 squares, join in a 2nd ball of yarn and pattern across remaining 17 squares.
Continue in pattern, working each side separately, until Row 56 has been completed.
Rep Row 27 to 56 (for a longer border these rows may be repeated once again).
To complete pattern sequence on sides, rep Row 27 to 33.
Row 34 (wrong side): Pattern across 17 squares, make 140 ch, taking care to keep chain untwisted, pattern across remaining 17 squares, breaking off 2nd ball of yarn.
Continue in pattern across all sts, working from Row 17 back to Row 1. Fasten off.
Lay finished border over fabric and stitch firmly together (using satin stitch or similar). Neaten edges of fabric and cut off surplus.

Square tablecloth

Materials: Approx 1700 g crochet cotton no. 5 in écru; 2.00 mm (1½) crochet hook.
Stitches used: Double crochet, treble, double treble.
(Replace first st of each round as follows: Dc by 1 ch, tr by 3 ch, dtr by 4 ch. Close each round with a sl st.)
Size: 170 × 170 cm (approx 66 × 66 in).
Cloth is made up of 324 large motifs worked separately and joined together, according to directions given after instructions for large motif, to form 18 strips of 18 large motifs. 255 small motifs are also worked to fill the spaces between.

Large motif

Make 5 ch and join with a sl st to form ring.
Round 1: Work (1 dtr, 3 ch) 8 times into ring.
Round 2: (5 tr, 2 ch) into each 3-ch loop (8 times).
Round 3: ＊ 1 tr into 5 tr, 1 tr into 2-ch loop, 5 ch ＊. Rep from ＊ to ＊ 7 times more.
Round 4: ＊ 6 unfin dtr, yoh, draw yarn through all 7 loops on hook (1 cluster), 3 ch, 5 tr into 5-ch loop of previous round, 3 ch ＊. Rep from ＊ to ＊ 7 times more ending round with 1 sl st into closing st of first dtr cluster.
Round 5: ＊ 1 tr into cluster, 3 ch, 1 tr into 5 tr, 1 tr into 3-ch loop ＊. Rep from ＊ to ＊ 7 times more.
Round 6: ＊ 11 ch, miss 1 tr, 1 unfin dtr into next 5 tr, yoh, draw yarn through all 6 loops on hook, 11 ch, 1 dc into tr ＊. Rep from ＊ to ＊ 7 times more. Fasten off.
The 18 motifs which are made into strips are joined together as Round 6 is being worked as follows:
Round 6 (joining round): 11 ch, miss 1 tr, 1 unfin dtr into next 5 tr, yoh, draw yarn through all 6 loops on hook, 1 dc into corresponding loop of motif to be joined, 5 ch, 1 dc into tr of previous round, 5 ch, 1 dc into next loop of motif to be joined, 5 ch; continue as for Round 6 of first motif. As the strips are made, the motifs will

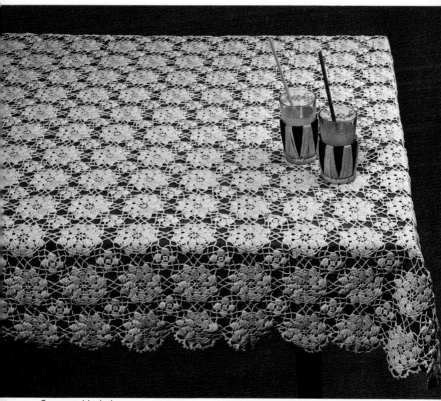

Square tablecloth

be joined to those on each side as well as to those above and below, but 2 loops will remain free between one join and the next. The spaces thus formed will be filled with small motifs, which are worked as follows:

Small motif

Make 4 ch and join with a sl st to form ring.
Round 1: Work 8 dc into ring.
Round 2: ∗ 1 tr, 5 ch, miss 1 st ∗. Rep from ∗ to ∗ 3 times more.
Round 3: (7 tr, 5 ch) into each of the 5-ch loops.

Round 4 (joining round): ∗ 1 unfin dtr into 7 tr, yoh, draw yarn through all 8 loops on hook, 1 dc into a free loop of large motif to be joined, 5 ch, 1 dc into 5-ch loop of Round 3, 5 ch, 1 dc into next free loop of large motif, 5 ch ∗. Rep from ∗ to ∗ 3 times more, thus joining the free ch loops of the large motifs. Fasten off.
Complete the tablecloth by working edging on all 4 sides as follows:
Into each 11-ch loop work (3 dc, 1 picot) 3 times, 3 dc, and into each 5-ch loop work (3 dc, 1 picot, 3 dc). Fasten off.

White rectangular tablecloth

Materials: 500 g crochet cotton no. 12; 1.25 mm (4½) crochet hook.
Stitches used: Double crochet treble, double treble.
Size: 150 × 200 cm (approx 60 × 80 in).
(Replace first tr in each round by 3 ch and first dtr by 4 ch. Close with 1 sl st into first starting st.
Round 1: Work 24 tr into ring.
Round 2: (1 tr, 1 ch) 24 times.
Round 3: 2 dc into each 1-ch loop.
Round 4: * 1 tr, 2 ch, miss 1 st *. Rep from * to * to end of round.

Round 5: 3 dc into each 2-ch loop.
Round 6: * 1 dc, 5 ch, miss 2 sts, 1 dc, 5 ch, miss 1 st *. Rep from * to * (28 loops) and continue with 1 dc into first loop without closing the round.
Rounds 7 & 8: * 1 dc into next loop, 5 ch *. Rep from * to *.
Rounds 9 & 10: * 1 dc into next loop, 6 ch *. Rep from * to *.
Round 11: * 3 tr, 5 ch, 3 tr (corner) into first loop, (6 ch, 1 dc into next loop) 6 times, 6 ch *. Rep from * to * 3 times more.
Round 12: * 3 tr into ch loop before corner, (6 ch, 3 tr, 11 ch, 3 tr) into 5-ch corner loop between 6-tr of previous

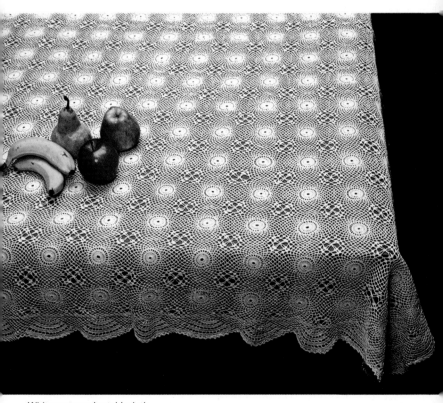

White rectangular tablecloth

round, 6 ch, 3 tr into next loop, (6 ch, 1 dc into next loop) 5 times *. Rep from * to * 3 times more. Fasten off. Work 279 more motifs in the same way, joining them to each other on Round 12 as follows:

Round 12 (joining round): * 3 tr into ch loop before corner, 3 ch, 1 dc into corresponding loop of first motif, 3 ch, 3 tr, 6 ch, 1 dc into 6th of 11 ch of motif or motifs to be joined, 6 ch, 3 tr, 3 ch, 1 dc into corresponding loop, 3 ch, 3 tr (3 ch, 1 dc into corresponding loop to be joined, 3 ch, 1 dc into loop of previous row) 5 times more, 3 ch, 1 dc into corresponding loop, 3 ch *. Rep from * to * on each side of the motifs to be joined. On the 4 motifs which form the 4 corners of the tablecloth, replace the 11 ch between the tr with 3 ch.

Complete the tablecloth by working the following border starting from one of the corners:

Round 1: ** (3 tr, 3 ch, 3 tr) ** into 3-ch corner loop, * 6 ch, 1 dc into each loop *. Rep from * to * along sides and from ** to ** into each remaining corner.

Round 2: Work (3 tr, 3 ch, 3 tr) into 3-ch corner loop, 4 tr into each 6-ch loop.

Round 3: (3 tr, 3 ch, 3 tr) into 3-ch corner loop, * 6 ch, 1 dc into first of next 4 tr. Rep from * to * along sides.

Round 4: 8 dtr separated by 2 ch into 3-ch corner loop, * 2 ch, (1 dc into next loop, 6 ch) 10 times, 1 dc into next loop, 2 ch, 4 dtr separated by 2 ch into next loop, 2 ch *. Rep from * to * along sides.

Round 5: 9 groups of 3 dtr clusters (= 3 unfin dtr, yoh, draw yarn through all loops on hook) separated by 2 ch into 2-ch loops before, between and after corner dtr of previous round, * 2 ch, (1 dc, 6 ch) 9 times, 1 dc, 2 ch, 5 groups of 3 dtr clusters separated by 2 ch worked before, between and

after 4 dtr of previous round, 2 ch *. Rep from * to * along remaining sides and work 9 groups of 3 dtr clusters separated by 2 ch at each remaining corner.

Round 6: 1 group of 4 dtr into each of the ten 2-ch corner loops, * (1 dc, 6 ch) 8 times, 1 dc, 1 group of 4 dtr into each of the following six 2-ch loops *. Rep from * to * along remaining sides and work 1 group of 4 dtr into each 2-ch corner loop.

Round 7: (1 dtr into first corner dtr, 3 ch, miss 2 sts) 13 times, 1 dtr, 3 ch * 1 dc, (6 ch, 1 dc) 7 times, (3 ch, 1 dtr, miss 2 sts) 8 times, 3 ch. Rep from * to * along remaining sides and work (1 dtr, 3 ch, miss 2 sts) 13 times 1 dtr, into remaining 3 corners.

Round 8: 1 group of 4 dtr into each of the thirteen 3-ch corner loops, * (1 dc, 6 ch) 6 times, 1 dc, 1 group 4 dtr into each of following eight 3-ch loops *. Rep from * to * along remaining sides and work group of 4 dtr into each of the thirteen 3-ch corner loop at remaining 3 corners.

Round 9: (1 dtr into first corner dtr, 3 ch, miss 2 sts.) 17 times, 1 dtr into each corner, 3 ch *, dc, (6 ch, 1 dc) 5 times, miss 1 dtr, (3 ch, 1 dtr, miss 2 sts) 10 times, 1 dtr 3 ch *. Rep from * to * along remaining sides.

Round 10: 1 group of 4 dtr into each of the seventeen 3-ch corner loops on each corner * (1 dc, 6 ch) 4 times, 1 dc, 1 group of 4 dtr into each of the following 10 3-ch loops *. Rep from * to * along remaining sides.

Round 11: (1 dtr into first corner dtr, 3 ch, miss 2 sts) 22 times 1 dtr, into each corner. 3 ch * 1 dc, (6 ch, 1 dc) 3 times, (3 ch, 1 dtr, miss 2 sts.) 13 times, 3ch, 1 dtr, 3 ch *. Rep from * to * along remaining sides.

Round 12: 1 group of 4 dtr into each of the twenty-two 3-ch corner loops, on each corner. * (1 dc, 6 ch) twice, 1 dc, 1 group of 4 dtr into each of following thirteen 3-ch loops *. Rep

from ✳ to ✳ along remaining sides.
Round 13: ✳ 1 dc, 6 ch, miss 3 sts ✳.
Rep from ✳ to ✳ for entire round.
Round 14: ✳ 1 dc into each 6-ch loop,
6 ch ✳. Rep from ✳ to ✳.
Round 15: ✳ (3 dc, 1 picot [= 3 ch, sl
st into first ch], 3 dc) into each 6-ch
loop ✳. Rep from ✳ to ✳. Fasten off.

Double bedspread

Materials: 2000 g white crochet cotton no. 3; 1.25 mm (4½) crochet
hook.
Stitches used: Double crochet, treble, double treble, treble treble.
Size: 739 hexagons joined in strips of
25½ motifs.
(Replace first stitch with 4 ch. Close
each round with 1 sl st).
Hexagon: Make 8 ch and join with a
sl st to form ring.
Row 1: Work 24 dtr into ring.
Row 2: ✳ (1 dtr, 4 ch, 1 dtr) into first
space between dtr, miss 1 st, 4 ch, 1
tr tr, 4 ch, miss 1 st ✳. Rep from ✳ to
✳ 5 more times (18 loops in all).
Round 3: ✳ (1 dtr, 4 ch, 1 dtr) into
4-ch loop between 2 dtr, 4 ch, 1 dc
into next 4-ch loop, 1 dc into tr tr, 1 dc
into next 4-ch loop, 4 ch ✳. Rep from
✳ to ✳ to end of round.
Round 4: ✳ (1 dtr, 4 ch, 1 dtr) into
4-ch loop between 2 dtr, 4 ch 1 dtr
into next 4-ch loop, 3 dtr, 1 dtr into
next 4-ch loop, 4 ch ✳. Rep from ✳ to
✳ to end of round.
Round 5: ✳ (1 dtr, 4 ch, 1 dtr) into
4-ch loop between 2 dtr, 4 ch, 4 dtr
into 4 ch loop, 5 dtr, 4 dtr into next
4-ch loop, 4 ch ✳. Rep from ✳ to ✳ to
end of round. Fasten off.
Work the rest of the hexagons in the
same way, joining them to each
other on Round 5 as follows:
Round 5 (joining round): ✳ (1 dtr, 2
ch, 1 dc into corresponding loop of
first hexagon, 2 ch, 1 dtr) into 4-ch
loop between 2 dtr, 4 ch, 1 dc into

first dtr of first hexagon, 7 dtr, 1 dc
into 7th dtr of first hexagon, 6 dtr, 1
dc into 13th dtr of first hexagon, 4 ch
✳. Rep from ✳ to ✳ on all sides to be
joined.
When the bedspread is complete, fill
in the empty spaces on the sides
with quarter hexagons worked in the
same way.
Complete by working 1 row of dtr
around the entire bedspread. Fasten
off.

The bedspread is illustrated on pages 216-217

Double bedspread in filet crochet

When working a filet crochet design in rounds, it is more satisfactory to complete each round, then turn and work back, rather than continue in the same direction. A treble, the basis of filet, is not absolutely vertical, and by working backwards and forwards each round corrects the slope of the previous round to give a slightly zigzag effect. To continue in rounds without turning leaves all the stitches sloping in the same direction, and the whole design will lean slightly to the right. A floral design could be acceptable worked by either method; a geometric pattern is better turned after each round, but whichever method is chosen, be consistent.

Materials: 1800 g crochet cotton no. 12; 1.25 mm (4½) crochet hook.

Stitches used: Double crochet, treble.

Size: 260× 280 cm (approx 102 × 110 in).

(Replace first tr in each round with 3 ch and close with 1 sl st into 3rd starting ch.)

Central square

First motif: Make 8 ch and join with a sl st to form ring.

Round 1: Work (1 tr, 2 ch) 8 times into ring.

Round 2: * 4 tr into first 2-ch loop, 5 ch, 4 tr into next loop, 1 ch *.

Rep from * to * 4 times more. Fasten off. Work the next motif, joining it to one side of the first motif while working Round 2 as follows:

Round 2 (joining round): 4 tr, 2 ch, 1 dc into 3rd ch in 5-ch loop of first motif, 2 ch, 4 tr into next 2-ch loop, 1 dc into 1-ch loop of first motif, 4 tr into next 2-ch loop, 2 ch, 1 dc into 3rd ch in 5 ch loop of first motif, 2 ch, then complete 2nd motif as first.

Continue until there are 40 motifs in the first strip.

Continue making the remaining 39 strips in the same way, joining the motifs on two sides until the square is completed.

Inner and outer borders

(Replace the first tr by 3 ch and close each round with a sl st into 3rd ch.)

Round 1: Rejoin yarn to 3rd ch of one 5-ch corner loop and work (1 tr, 5 ch, 1 tr) into same ch (= corner), * 3 ch, 1 tr into first tr of first 4-tr group, 3 ch, 1 tr into 1-ch loop, 3 ch, 1 tr into 4th tr of 2nd 4-tr group, 3 ch, 1 tr into dc joining motifs, 3 ch *. Rep from * to * on all 4 sides, working remaining 3 corners as before.

Round 2: (4 tr, 5 ch, 4 tr) into each 5-ch corner loop, 1 tr into each tr and 1 tr into each ch on all 4 sides.

Continue working in filet crochet following the chart on pages 224 and 225 for inner border and pages 222 and 223 for outer border.

Corners are formed as follows:

mesh ( ) = (1 tr, 5 ch, 1 tr) into 5-ch loop of previous round.

block ( ) = (4 tr, 5 ch, 4 tr) into 5-ch loop of previous round.

Openwork border for edging

Round 1: Starting from one corner, ** ([2 tr, 2 ch] 3 times, 2 tr) into 5-ch loop. Rep from ** to ** in each corner. * 7 ch, 1 dc into 3rd tr, 7 ch, miss next 2 sts, (3 tr, 2 ch, 3 tr) into next st *. Rep from * to * on all 4 sides.

Round 2: ** (2 tr, 2 ch, 2 tr) into each 2-ch loop **. Rep from ** to ** in each corner. * 5 ch, 1 dc into first 7-ch loop, 5 ch, 1 dc in next 7-ch loop, 5 ch, (3 tr, 2 ch, 3 tr) into 2-ch loop *. Rep from * to * on all 4 sides.

Round 3: Work corners as Round 2. * 7 ch, 1 dc into 2nd 5-ch loop, 7 ch, (3 tr, 2 ch, 3 tr) into 2-ch loop *. Rep from * to * on all 4 sides.

Round 4: ** ([2 tr, 2 ch, 2 tr] in 2-ch loop [2 tr, 2 ch, 2 tr] between 4-tr) twice, (2 tr, 2 ch, 2 tr) in last 2-ch loop **. Rep from ** to ** in each cor-

ner. Work sides as Round 2.
Round 5: Work corners as Round 2 and sides as Round 3.
Round 6: As Round 2.
Round 7: ✱✱ ([2 tr, 2 ch 2 tr] in 2-ch loop, 2 ch, 1 dc between 4-tr, 2 ch) 4 times, (2 tr, 2 ch, 2 tr) in last 2-ch loop ✱✱. Rep from ✱✱ to ✱✱ in each corner. Work sides as Round 3.
Round 8: ✱✱ ([2 tr, 2 ch, 2 tr] in 2-ch loop, [2 ch, 1 dc in 2-ch loop] twice, 2 ch) 4 times, (2 tr, 2 ch, 2 tr) in last 2-ch

Key for charts

☐ (space) 3 ch, miss next 3 ch or 3 tr. 1 tr in next st.

☒ (block) 5 tr, plus 4 tr for each additional block in group.

Chart for borders of double-bedspread in filet crochet, illustrated on pages 224-225. (Enlarged detail on pages 222-223).

Detail of chart for inner border in filet crochet

loop ✳✳. Rep from ✳✳ to ✳✳ in each corner. Work sides as Round 2.

Round 9: ✳✳ ([2 tr, 2 ch, 2 tr] in 2-ch loop, 5 ch, 1 dc in ch-loop between dc, 5 ch) 4 times, (2 tr, 2 ch, 2 tr) in last 2-ch loop ✳✳. Rep from ✳✳ to ✳✳ in each corner. Work sides as Round 3.

Round 10: ✳✳ ([2 tr, 2 ch, 2 tr] in 2-ch loop, [5 ch, 1 dc in 5-ch loop] twice, 5 ch) 4 times, (2 tr, 2 ch, 2 tr) in last 2-ch loop ✳✳. Rep from ✳✳ to ✳✳ in each corner. Work sides as Round 2.

Rounds 11 and 12: Rep Rounds 9 and 10.

Round 13: ✳✳ ([2 tr, 2 ch, 2 tr] in 2-ch loop, 5 ch, 1 dc in 2nd 5-ch loop, 5 ch [2 tr, 2 ch, 2 tr] in 2-ch loop, 5 ch, 1 dc in first 5-ch loop, 5 ch [2 tr, 2 ch, 2 tr] in 2nd 5-ch loop, 5 ch, 1 dc in 3rd 5-ch loop, 5 ch) twice, (2 tr, 2 ch, 2 tr) in last 2-ch loop ✳✳. Rep from ✳✳ to

✻✻ in each corner. Work sides as
Round 3.
Round 14: As Round 10, working 6
times.
Round 15: As Round 9, working 6
times.
Rounds 16 and 17: Rep Rounds 14
and 15.
Fasten off.

Yellow cot-blanket

Yellow cot-blanket

Materials: 400 g 3-ply yellow wool;
2.50 mm (12) crochet hook.

Stitches used: Double crochet, treble, raised shell.

Make a chain 80 cm (30 in) long and
work in raised shell st for 90 cm
(approx 36 in).

Complete blanket with this border
replacing first stitch as follows: dc by
1 ch, tr by 3 ch:

Round 1: 1 dc into each st, close
round with a sl st into first ch.

Round 2: * 3 tr into same st on corner, ** 5 ch, miss 3 sts, 4 dc into
next 4 sts, miss 3 sts, 5 ch, 1 tr into
next 2 sts **, *. Rep from ** to **
to next corner and from * to * to end
of round.

Round 3: * 7 tr into 3-corner-tr (work
1 tr in tr and 2 tr in sp between), ** 5
ch, 1 dc into 2 dc, 5 ch, 1 tr into 2 tr
**, *. Rep from ** to ** to next
corner and from * to * to end of
round.

Round 4: * (6 dc, 5 ch, 6 dc) into
7-corner-tr (work * 1 dc in tr, 1 dc in
sp * 3 times, 5 ch, miss 1 tr, * 1 dc in
sp, 1 dc in * 3 times), ** 5 ch, 1 dc

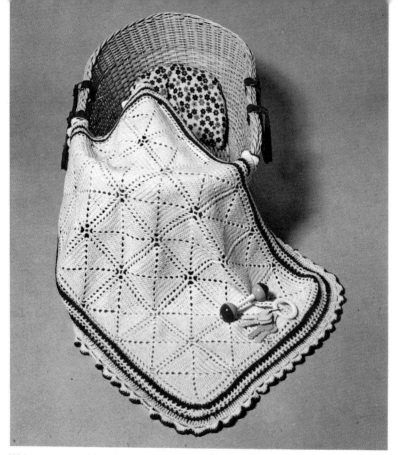

White pram rug with red border

between 2 dc of previous round, 5 ch, 4 dc, 5 ch, 4 dc between 5 tr ✱✱, ✱.

Rep from ✱✱ to ✱✱ to next corner and from ✱ to ✱ to end of round. Fasten off.

White pram rug with red border

Materials: 300 g 2-ply white wool; small amount of 2-ply red wool (or other contrasting colour); 2.00 mm (14) crochet hook.
Stitches used: Double crochet, half treble, treble, crab.

The rug consists of 24 squares, worked separately, sewn together invisibly.

Square: With white wool make 8 ch and join with a sl st to form ring.
Round 1: Into ring work 3 ch, 2 tr, ✱ 3 ch, 3 tr ✱.
Rep from ✱ to ✱ 3 times and close round with 1 sl st into 3rd starting ch.
Round 2: 3 ch, 1 tr into 2 tr of previous row, ✱ (2 tr, 3 ch, 2 tr) into 3 ch to form corner loops, 3 tr) ✱.
Rep from ✱ to ✱ to end of round, closing with 1 sl st into 3rd starting ch.
Rounds 3, 4 & 5: As for Round 2,

White cot-blanket

working tr into tr and the corners into 3 ch corner loops.

Round 6: ✽ 5 ch into corner, (1 tr, 1 ch, miss 1 st) along the side ✽. Rep from ✽ to ✽ to end of row, closing with 1 sl st. Fasten off.

Work another 23 identical squares. Join them together to form a rectangle of 6 × 4 squares with small, neat stitches which do not interfere with the design.

Complete rug with the following border, replacing first dc by 1 ch, first tr by 3 ch and closing each round with a sl st:

Round 1 (white wool): Work in dc with 3 ch into each corner.

Round 2 (white wool): 1 tr, 1 ch, miss 1 st; on the corners (3 tr, miss 2 ch, 3 tr).

Round 3 (red wool): 1 tr into tr, 1 tr into ch; 4 tr into each 2-ch corner loop ch.

Round 4 (white wool): As Round 2, working 7 tr into corners (1 tr in tr and 1 tr in each sp between 4-tr).

Round 5 (white wool): As Round 2, working 12 tr (2 tr in each sp between 7-tr).

Round 6 (red wool): As Round 2, working (1 tr, 2 tr in next tr) 6 times in 12-tr at corner.

Round 7 (white wool): 1 dtr into each st.

Round 8 (white wool): 1 dc, 6 ch, miss 5 sts ✽. Rep from ✽ to ✽.

Round 9 (white wool): (1 htr, 7 tr, 1 htr) into each ch loop.
Round 10 (red wool): Work in crab st for entire round.
Fasten off.

White cot-blanket

Materials: 300 g 4-ply white wool; 3.00 mm (10) crochet hook.
Stitches used: Half treble, large star, crab.
Make a ch 65 cm (25½ in) long and work in large star st for 115 cm (45 in).
Complete the blanket with 8 rows of htr, working 3 sts into same st on each corner. Finish with 1 row of crab stitch. Fasten off.

Cushion no. 1

Materials: 4-ply red wool and a small quantity in contrasting colour; 5.00 mm (6) crochet hook.

Stitches used; Treble, basket.
Make a chain to the length required, in multiples of 4 plus 2 sts. Work in basket stitch until the required size is reached.
For the cushion back, make the same number of ch and work in tr until back matches front.
Work 1 row of dc and 1 row crab st in contrasting colour round 4 sides, working in front only on 4th side.
Join front to back on 3 sides, insert cushion pad and sew 4th side.

Cushion no. 2

Materials: Navy, red and white crochet cotton no. 5; 3.00 mm (10) crochet hook.
Stitches used: Double crochet, treble.
(Replace first dc of round by 1 ch; first tr of round by 3 ch. Close each round with a sl st.)
With red cotton, make 5 ch and join with a sl st to form ring.

(Left) Cushion no. 1 (Right) Cushion no. 2

Round 1: Work 10 dc into ring.
Round 2: ∗ 2 dc into each dc of previous row ∗. Rep from ∗ to ∗ to end of round.
Round 3 (blue cotton): ∗ 1 hazelnut (= 3 unfin tr, yoh, draw yarn through all 4 loops on hook), 1 ch into each st of previous round ∗. Rep from ∗ to ∗.
Round 4: Sl st to first ch, ∗ 1 hazelnut (= 4 unfin tr, yoh, draw yarn through all 5 loops on hook) into 1-ch loop, 2 ch ∗. Rep from ∗ to ∗ to end of round.
Round 5: As Round 4, working 3 ch between each hazelnut. Fasten off.
Round 6: For this and next 2 rounds carry the cotton not in use through the work. To change colour, work the last stitch of the first colour until 2 loops remain on hook; now take the 2nd colour and draw through last 2 loops. ∗ (red cotton), 7 dtr into 3-ch loop of previous round (finish the 7th dtr with white cotton); with white cotton, work 1 group of 3 tr into each of the next four 3-ch loops (finish the last tr of the 4th group with red cotton) ∗. Rep from ∗ to ∗ to end of round.
Round 7: ∗ (red cotton) ∗∗ 2 tr between 2 dtr of previous row ∗∗ 6 times (12 tr now worked in red cotton), with white cotton work 1 group of 3 tr into each of next 5 spaces between groups ∗. Rep from ∗ to ∗ to end of round.
Round 8: ∗ (red cotton) (1 tr, 1 ch, 1 tr) between 3rd and 4th of 12 red tr of previous row, (1 tr, 1 ch, 1 tr) between 5th and 6th tr, (1 tr, 1 ch, 1 tr) between 7th and 8th tr, (1 tr, 1 ch, 1 tr) between 9th and 10th tr. Change to white cotton and 3 tr between 11th and 12th red tr, of 3 tr into each of next 4 spaces, 3 tr between first and 2nd of next 12 tr ∗. Rep from ∗ to ∗ to end of round.
Round 9 (white cotton): Starting from a corner, ∗ 3 tr between 3rd and 4th red tr of previous row, 2 ch, 3 tr between 5th and 6th red tr, 3 tr between 7th and 8th red tr, 3 tr into each of next 5 spaces, 3 tr between first and 2nd red tr ∗. Rep from ∗ to ∗ to end of round.
Round 10: Sl st to 2-ch corner loop, ∗ (3 tr, 2 ch, 3 tr) into 2-ch corner loop; 3 tr into each of next 7 spaces ∗. Rep from ∗ to ∗ to end of round.
Round 11: Sl st to 2 ch corner loop ∗. (3 tr, 2 ch, 3 tr) into 2-ch corner loop; 3 tr into each of next 8 spaces ∗. Rep from ∗ to ∗ to end of round.
Round 12: Sl st to 2-ch corner loop, ∗ (3 tr, 2 ch, 3 tr) into 2-ch corner loop; 3 tr into each of next 9 spaces ∗. Rep from ∗ to ∗ to end of round.
Continue working in the same way

until cushion is slightly smaller than required size (to allow for following 3 rounds of border).

Round 1 (blue cotton): ∗ (2 tr, 2 ch, 2 tr, 2 ch, 2 tr) into 2-ch corner loop; 1 tr into each st along side ∗. Rep from ∗ to ∗ to end of round.

Round 2 (red cotton): ∗ (2 tr, 2 ch, 2 tr) into 2-ch corner loop; 1 tr into each st along side ∗. Rep from ∗ to ∗ end of round.

Round 3 (white cotton): ∗ (2 tr, 2 ch, 2 tr) into 2-ch corner loop; 1 tr into each st along side ∗. Rep from ∗ to ∗ to end of round.

Make another square the same size in tr and join it to the front on 3 sides. Insert cushion pad and sew 4th side.

Table runner in filet crochet

Materials: Crochet cotton no 8; 1.25 mm (41) crochet hook.

Stitches used: Blocks and spaces in mesh st.

make 181 ch and work the first row in mesh st (1 tr in 7th ch from hook ∗ 2 ch, miss 2 ch, 1 tr ∗. Rep from ∗ to ∗) then continue as shown in diagram until required length is reached. (1 cross corresponds to 4 tr); for each additional cross in block and 3 tr).

Table runner in filet crochet (chart lower half of pages 232-233)

Border in filet crochet for towel

Materials: Crochet cotton no. 8;
1.00 mm (5½) crochet hook.
Stitches used: Mesh stitch (1 tr, 3 ch,
miss 3 sts, 1 tr), blocks and spaces in
mesh stitch.
Make 59 ch and beg with 1 tr in 7th
ch from hook. Work according to diagram until required length has been
reached (1 cross on the diagram corresponds to 5 tr; for each additional
cross in block add 4 tr).
Sew border to edge of towel and
make a fringe 15 cm (6 in) in depth,
knotting it 3 times.

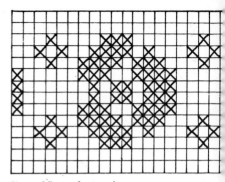

Chart of flower for towel

Chart for table runner in filet crochet

Towel with border in filet crochet

GIFTS AND THINGS TO MAKE

Easy-to-make patterns and practical ideas

So many useful and attractive things can be made with a crochet hook, some yarn and the simplest of stitches. Daily routines can be enlivened if unusual, colourful objects – made by your own hands or those of a friend – are used instead of machine-made things. For instance, brightly coloured potholders and ovengloves, shopping bags, little baskets or mats and so on can give an air of originality to every room in the home. The ideas covered in this section should be regarded only as suggestions – use your imagination to conjure up many more original schemes.

For the children there are toys reminiscent of the rag dolls of our grandparents' day. Crocheted toys can be as bright and colourful as rainbows and a child appreciates the individuality of handmade toys because no other child ever has one exactly the same; it is usually the handmade toy that becomes the favourite bedtime companion. Another advantage is that they are soft and, if stuffed with something like old tights (cut into small pieces), are washable.

Unusual materials can be used to make a gift that is quite out of the ordinary. Such things as cord, strips of leather or fabric, cobbler's thread, string, and so on, are only a few suggestions. It is up to you to develop the ideas we give you here to make something that reflects your very own personal taste.

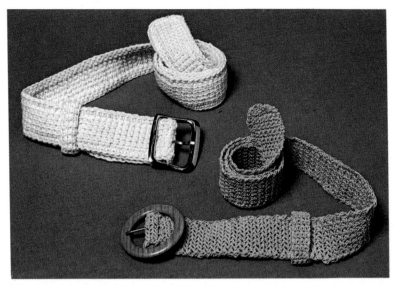

White belt and yellow belt

White belt in Tunisian stitch

Materials: 50 g dishcloth-type cotton; 1 belt buckle; 3.00 mm (3/0) crochet hook (Tunisian).
Stitches used: Double crochet, Tunisian.
Make 8 ch.
Starting in 2nd ch from hook, work in Tunisian stitch for 1 metre (approx 38 in). Fasten off.
For keeper, make 4 ch and, starting in 2nd ch from hook, work in Tunisian crochet for 10 cm (4 in). Fasten off. Work 1 row of dc right around the long strip.
Sew keeper in position and slip buckle over end of belt. Press the belt under a damp cloth.

Yellow belt

Materials: Cobbler's yellow thread or string; 1 belt buckle; 2.50 mm (0) crochet hook.
Stitches used; Double crochet, crab.
Make 9 ch and starting in 2nd ch from hook work in dc for about 1 metre (approx 38 in).
Shape point by dec 1 st at each end of next 2 rows to make 4 sts. Work 1 row in dc and 1 in crab st right around the strip. Fasten off. Make a keeper by making a 5 ch and starting in 2nd ch from hook in dc until strip is slightly longer than width of belt. Fasten off and sew to wrong side of belt. Slip the buckle over the end of belt nearest to keeper, fold end to wrong side and sew down on wrong side.

Red slippers

Materials: 50 gr 4-ply wool; 3.00 mm (10) crochet hook.
Stitches used: Double crochet, half treble, treble.
Begin at centre of sole and work in rounds, beginning each round with 1 ch and closing round with sl st into ch.
Make 20 ch.
Round 1: 3 dc in 2nd ch from hook, 4 dc, 8 htr, 5 tr, 5 tr in last ch to shape toe, then work back along 2nd side of foundation ch: 5 tr, 8 htr, 4 dc, 3 dc in last ch.
Round 2: 2 dc in first st, 19 dc, 2 dc in each of 5-tr group at toe, 19 dc, 2 dc in last st.
Round 3: 2 dc in each of first 2 sts, 19 dc, (2 dc in each of next 2 sts, 2 dc) twice, 2 dc in each of next 2 sts, 19 dc, 2 dc in each of last 2 sts.
Round 4: 2 dc in each of first 2 sts, 22 dc, 2 dc in next st, 3 dc, 2 dc in next st, 1 dc, 2 dc in each of next 2 sts, 1 dc, 2 dc in next st, 3 dc, 2 dc in next st, 22 dc, 2 dc in each of last 2 sts.
Round 5: 2 dc in each of first 2 sts, 10 dc, 8 htr, 9 tr, (2 tr in next st, 2 tr) twice, 2 tr in each of next 2 sts, (2 tr in next st) twice, 9 tr, 8 htr, 10 dc, 2 dc in each of last 2 sts (82 sts).
Round 6: In dc.
Round 7: In dc, working in back loop only of each st.
Rounds 8 and 9: As Round 6.
Round 10: 28 dc, (dec 1 [= insert hook into next st and draw yarn through, insert hook into following st and draw yarn through, yrh and draw through all 3 loops on hook, 1 st decreased], 2 dc) 6 times, dec 1, 28 dc (75 sts).
Round 11: As Round 6.
Round 12: 26 dc, (dec 1, 1 dc) 8 times, 25 dc (67 sts).
Round 13: As Round 6.
Round 14: 1 dc, dec 1, 19 dc, (dec 1, 1 dc) 8 times, 18 dc, dec 1, 1 dc (57 sts).
Round 15: As Round 6.
Round 16: 1 dc, dec 1, 11 dc, (dec 1, 1 dc) 10 times, 10 dc, dec 1, 1 dc (45 sts).
Round 17: 3 ch, miss 1 st, (1 htr, 1 ch, miss 1 st) 10 times, (1 htr, 1 ch) 4 times, (miss 1 st, 1 htr, 1 ch) 10 times, sl st into next ch.
Fasten off.
make a double crochet chain 50 cm (12½ in) long and thread through 1-ch loops in Round 17.

Baby's blue slippers

Materials: Approx 100 g 4-ply wool; 3.50 mm (9) crochet hook.
Stitches used: Double crochet, treble, double treble.
Each slipper consists of 8 squares.
Square: Make 4 ch and join with a sl st to form ring.
(Replace first tr with 2 ch and first dc

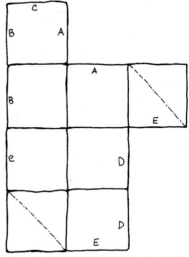

Diagram showing arrangement of squares for baby's blue slippers. Sew together as shown then sew sides together marked with the same letter, folding back at dotted lines.

Baby's red, blue and three-colour slippers

with 1 ch, closing each round with 1 sl st into starting ch).

Round 1: Work (3 tr, 2 ch *) 4 times into ring.

Round 2: * 3 tr into 3 tr, (2 tr, 2 ch, 2 tr) into 2-ch corner loop *. Rep from * to * to end of round (7 tr on each side).

Round 3: * 6 tr along side (2 tr, 2 ch, 2 tr) into 2-ch corner loop *. Rep from * to * to end of round (10 tr on each side).

Rounds 4 & 5: 1 dc into each st, 3 dc into 2-ch corner loop.

Fasten off.

Work another 7 squares in the same way and sew them together as indicated in diagram.

Finish the 4 turned-back edges as follows: * (1 dc, 2 ch, 1 dtr) into same st, miss 1 st *. Rep from * to * on all 4 edges and fasten off.

Make second slipper to match.

Baby's three-colour slippers

Materials: 4-ply wool used double (2 strands at a time); approx 100 g red, oddments of blue and white; 4.00 mm (8) crochet hook.

Stitches used: Double crochet, half treble.

Sole (starting from heel): Make 6 ch. Starting in 2nd ch from hook, work 5 dc, then continue in dc, beginning each row with 1 ch and increasing 1 st at each end of next and foll alt row (9 sts). Continue until work measures 8 cm (3 ins approx), then increase 1 st at each end of next and following alternate row (13 sts). Work straight until sole measures 14 cm (approx 5½ in) from beginning. Shape toe by decreasing 1 st at each end of next and following 2 alt rows. When sole measures 16 cm (approx 6¼ in), fasten off.

Upper: Maker 8 ch. Starting in 3rd ch from hook, work 6 htr (= 7 sts including starting ch). Continue in htr, starting each row with 2 ch and increasing 1 st at each end of next 4 rows (13 sts).

Join in blue and work 2 rows blue. Break blue.

Continue in red and increase 1 st at each end of next row (right side). Work 1 row.

Join in white and work 2 rows white. Break white.

Continue in red and increase 1 st at each end of next row (19 sts).

Work straight until upper measures 8 cm (3 ins) ending with a wrong side row.

Tomato- and vase-shaped potholders

Continue in htr on first 5 sts *only* for back of upper and work a further 10 cm (4 in). Fasten off.

With right side facing, miss centre 9 sts, rejoin yarn to next st, 2 ch, 4 htr. Continue on these 5 sts and work 10 cm (4 ins). Fasten off.

Tomato-shaped potholder

Materials: Crochet cotton no. 5 (approx 50 g red, oddments of green); 2.50 mm (0) crochet hook.
Stitches used: Double crochet, crab.
With red cotton, make 4 ch and join with a sl st to form ring.
Round 1: Work 10 dc into ring.
Shape tomato by working turnings rows:
Round 2: Working only on 5 sts, work 1 ch, 6 dc, turn.
Round 3: 1 ch, 10 dc, turn.
Round 4: 1 ch, 14 dc, turn.
Round 5: 1 ch, 22 dc, turn.
Round 6: 1 ch, 24 dc and, without turning, work 7 dc over sts of first round left unworked, sl st into first ch, turn.
Continue working complete rounds, joining with a sl st into first ch and increasing a few stitches on each

round (to keep work flat) for a further 14 rounds and turning work at end of every round.
Round 21: Work in crab st.
With green cotton, work 2 leaves as follows: Make 7 ch and work 1 round in dc (continue along 2nd side of foundation ch). Work 3 rounds more, increasing 2 sts at the sides and 2 sts in the centre.
Make another leaf in the same way.
Stem: Make 23 ch and starting in 2nd ch from hook, work in dc, continue and form loop by working 10 ch and joining to top of stem with a sl st. Work 1 row dc into 10-ch loop and fasten off.
Stitch the leaves and stem onto the potholder.

Vase-shaped potholder

Materials: Crochet cotton no. 5; 50 g light green and oddment of dark green; 2.50 mm (0) crochet hook.
With light green cotton make 8 ch and join with a sl st to form ring.
(Replace first dc of each round by 1 dc and close round with a sl st into starting ch.)
Round 1: Work 12 dc into ring.

Acorn- and square-shaped potholders

Round 2: (1 dc, 2 dc in next st) 6 times (18 sts).

Round 3: (2 dc, 2 dc in next st) 6 times (24 sts).

Round 4: (3 dc, 2 dc in next st) 6 times (30 sts).

Round 5: ✻ (1 ch, 1 group [= 4 tr all worked into next st in Round 3, leaving thread fairly loose to avoid pulling, remove hook from work and insert it in the 1-ch worked at beg of sequence; pick up working loop again and close it tightly with 1 ch], 2 dc) twice, 1 ch, 1 group, 3 dc ✻. Rep from ✻ to ✻ to end of round (9 groups).

Round 6: ✻ (2 dc in group, 1 dc in dc, 1 dc between dc, 1 dc in dc) twice, 2 dc in group, 3 dc ✻. Rep from ✻ to ✻ to end of round (45 sts).

Round 7: (8 dc, 2 dc in next st) 5 times (50 sts).

Round 8: (4 dc, 2 dc in next st) 10 times (60 sts).

Round 9: (dc, 2 dc in next st) 6 times (66 sts).

Round 10: ✻ 1 ch, 1 group (see Round 5), 2 dc ✻. Rep from ✻ to ✻ to end of round (22 groups separated by 2 dc).

Round 11: (2 dc in group, 1 dc in dc, 1 dc between dc, 1 dc in dc, 2 dc in group, 2 dc) 11 times (99 sts).

Round 12: (10 dc, 2 dc in next st) 9 times (108 sts).

Round 13: (11 dc, 2 dc in next st) 9 times (117 sts).

Round 14: (12 dc, 2 dc in next st) 9 times (126 sts).

Rows 15-18: Work 20 dc only. turn. Break light green. Join in dark green.

Row 19: With dark green cotton, ✻ 1 dc, 1 dc made by inserting hook 1 row below, 1 dc made by inserting hook 2 rows below, 1 dc made by inserting hook 1 row below ✻. Rep from ✻ to ✻ 4 more times.

Rows 20 & 21: 20 dc.

To make 2 loops on each side to form handles, make 15 ch and join to appropriate point on vase. Work 20 dc into loops. Fasten off.

Acorn-shaped potholder

Materials: Crochet cotton no. 5 used double; 100 g brown; 50 g yellow; 3.00 mm (3/0) crochet hook.

Stitches used: Double crochet, half treble, treble, double treble, elongated double, crab.

With strands of brown make 13 ch.

Round 1: Starting in 2nd ch from

Little chef and white and green potholder

hook, 12 dc on one side of ch and 12 dc on opposite side.

Round 2: As Round 1 inc 3 sts at each end.

Round 3: Work in elongated dc (thus covering the dc of Rounds 1 and 2), inc 5 sts at each end.

Rounds 4 & 5: Work in dc.

Round 6: Work in elongated dc (thus covering the dc of Rounds 4 and 5), inc 3 sts at one end and 5 sts at the other.

Rep Rounds 4, 5 and 6 three more times, increasing the elongated dc to 5, 7 and 9 sts respectively at one end and to 7, 9 and 11 at the other.

Work 1 round in crab st and fasten off.

With yellow cotton (2 strands) work 2 leaves as follows: Make 12 ch and work 2 dc, 2 htr, 2 tr, 4 dtr, 1 tr, 2 htr, 2 dc; move work round and work along opposite side of base ch, 2 dc, 2 htr, 1 tr, 4 dtr, 2 tr, 2 htr, 2 dc. Work another leaf in the same way.

Sew the leaves to the widest part of the potholder. Between the 2 leaves work a ring of 10 ch with 2 strands of yellow cotton and join with a sl st.

Square potholder

Materials: 50 g 8-ply cotton; 3.00 mm (3/0) hook.

Stitches used: Double crochet, ridged double crochet.

Make 12 ch and join with a sl st to form ring.

Round 1: Work 18 dc into ring. This

Two-colour Catherine Wheel potholder

forms the hanging ring and is the only round as the rest of the potholder is worked back and forth as follows:

Row 2 (right side): 1 ch, 4 dc, 3 dc into 1 st (corner), 4 dc, turn.

Row 3 (wrong side): 1 ch, 5 dc, 3 dc into centre corner st, 5 dc, turn.

Row 4: 1 ch, 6 ridged dc, 3 ridged dc into centre corner st, 6 ridged dc.

Rep Rows 3 and 4, working 3 sts into centre corner st and 1 additional dc on each side until work measures 20 cm (8 in) across. Fasten off.

Little chef potholder

Materials: crochet cotton no. 5: 20 g ball each white and red, oddment of black; 2.50 mm (0) crochet hook.

Stitch used: Double crochet.

With red cotton make 11 ch.

Row 1: Starting in 2nd ch from hook, work 10 dc.

Continue in dc, increasing 1 st at each end of every row until there are 32 sts. Work 10 rows straight. Break red and join in white and work 17 rows straight. Inc 5 sts on each side and work in dc for 6 rows.

Make loop: 21 dc, 12 ch, 21 dc.

Next row: 21 dc, 18 dc in 12-ch loop, 21 dc.

Fasten off.

With black crochet cotton, embroider the main features of the face.

White and green potholder

Materials: Crochet cotton no 8 used double; 50 g white, 20 g green; 2.50 mm (0) crochet hook.

Stitch used: Double crochet.

With white cotton make 4 ch and join with a sl st to form ring.

(Replace first st of each round by 1 ch; Close round with a sl st).

Round 1: Work 8 dc into ring.

Round 2: (1 dc, 2 dc in next st) 4 times (12 sts).

Round 3: (2 dc, 2 dc in next st) 4 times (16 sts).

Continue until Round 12 has been worked, increasing a few sts regularly spread on each round to ensure that the disc remains flat, break white; join in green.

Two-colour Catherine Wheel potholder

Materials: Crochet cotton no 5; 50 g each white and green; 2.50 mm (0) crochet hook.

Stitches used: Double crochet.

(Replace first st of each round by 1 ch, close round with a sl st into starting ch.)

With white cotton, make 8 ch and join with a sl st to form ring.

Round 1: Work 14 dc into ring.

Round 2: 28 dc.

Round 3: * With green cotton work 4 dc, 2 ch, miss 1 st; with white cotton work 4 dc, 2 ch, miss 1 st *. 3 times altogether (the strand not in use is carried under the sts).

Round 4: * With green cotton miss 1 st, 3 dc of previous row, 2 dc into next 2-ch loop, 2 ch; with white cotton miss 1 st, 3 dc, 2 dc into 2-ch loop, 2 ch *. Rep from * to * 3 times altogether.

Continue in this way, increasing 1 st on each whorl in every round until there are 114 sts (19 sts to each whorl).

Make 12 ch and join with sl st into base dc. Work 18 dcs into ring and fasten off, making sure that join to main fabric is neat and strong.

insert hook into work 2 rounds back and work 3 dc in same st (keeping yarn loose), miss 1 st *. Rep from * to * to end of round.

Round 14: Work in dc.

Rounds 15 & 16: With white cotton, work in dc.

Rounds 17, 18 & 19: With green cotton, work in dc.

Round 20: With white cotton, as Round 13.

Round 21: Work in dc, ending with 15 ch joined with a sl st to form ring for hanging. Work 20 dc into ring. Fasten off.

Square lettuce-shaker or shopper

Materials: 100 g of crochet cotton no. 5; 2.50 mm (0) crochet hook.
Make 180 ch.
Row 1: 5 ch (= 1 tr and 2 ch), miss 2 ch, 1 tr into 3rd, * 2 ch, miss 2 ch, 1 tr *. Rep from * to *.

Row 2: 5 ch, * 1 tr into tr, 2 ch *. Rep from * to *, ending with 1 tr into 2nd of 5 starting ch of previous row.

Rep Row 2 until a complete square is obtained.

Work 2 rounds of dc along all 4 sides of square, with (2 dc, 1 ch, 2 dc) into each corner space.

Finish with the following scallops worked over 8 sts: * 1 dc, 2 htr, 2 tr, 2 htr, 1 dc *. Rep from * to * round square. Fasten off.

Rejoin yarn to 1 corner and make a ch 15 cm (6 in) long. Join to 2nd corner with a sl st, then work back across ch in dc. Fasten off. Join remaining 2 corners in the same way.

Square lettuce-shaker or shopper

Vegetable or shopping bag

242

Decorative basket no. 1

Vegetable or shopping bag

Materials: 100 g crochet cotton no. 5; 2.50 mm (0) crochet hook.

Stitches used: Half treble, treble, crab.

Make 6 ch and join with a sl st to form ring.

Round 1: 5 ch (= 1 tr and 2 ch), * 1 tr, 2 ch *. Rep from * to * 9 times more into ring and close with 1 sl st into 3rd of 5 starting ch.

Round 2: 5 ch, 1 tr into first space, 2 ch, * 1 tr into next sp, 2 ch *. Rep from * to * to end of round, increasing 1 sp in round as follows: (1 tr, 2 ch, 1 tr) into 1 sp where inc is to be worked. Close round with 1 sl st into 3rd starting ch. (Work inc spaces evenly in following round).

Rounds 3 & 4: As Round 2, inc 7 spaces in each round.

Round 5: As Round 2, inc 5 spaces.

Round 6: As Round 2, inc 4 spaces.

Round 7 & 8: As Round 2, inc 4 spaces.

Round 9: As Round 5.

Round 10: As Round 6.

Rounds 11 & 12: As Round 5.

Continue for a further 25 rounds, working as for Round 2 but without increasing.

Work 1 round in htr (1 htr into each sp and 1 htr into each tr).

Complete bag by working 3 rounds of htr, decreasing 5 sts evenly in each round. Fasten off.

Make 30 ch and work 5 rows of htr. Fasten off (1 handle).

Make another handle to match. Sew both handles to top of bag, evenly spaced, and finish all edges with 1 row of crab st.

Decorative basket no. 1

Materials: 100 g crochet cotton no. 5 used double; 3.00 mm (3/0) crochet hook.

Stitches used: Double crochet, crab.

First, select a bowl in a shape you like, as this will be the 'mould' on which the basket will be based.

Using the instructions for white and green potholder as a guide, make a circle in dc the same size as the base of the bowl. Fasten off.

Make a length of ch in multiples of 12 plus 9 plus 2 (for selvedges) plus 1 t ch, equal to the circumference of the disc already worked.

Row 1: 1 dc in 2nd ch from hook (selvedge), * 9 dc, 8 ch, miss 3 ch *.

243

Decorative basket no. 2

Rep from * to * ending with 1 dc.

Row 2: 1 ch, 8 dc, * 5 ch, 1 dc into 4th ch of 8-ch loop, 5 ch, miss 1 dc of previous row, 7 dc, miss 1 dc *. Rep from * to * ending with 1 dc and 1 dc for selvedge.

Row 3: ch, 1 dc, 2 ch, * miss first dc of previous row, 5 dc, 5 ch, 3 dc (= 1 dc to right of next dc of previous row, 1 dc into st itself, 1 dc to left of same st), 5 ch *. Rep from * to * ending with 5 dc, 2 ch and 1 dc for selvedge.

Row 4: 1 ch, 1 dc, 3 ch, * 3 dc (missing first and last dc of previous row), 5 ch, 5 dc (= 1 dc to right of 3-dc of previous row, 3 dc, 1 dc to left of same 3-dc), 5 ch *. Rep from * to *, ending with 3 dc, 3 ch, 1 dc for selvedge.

Row 5: 1 ch, 1 dc, 5 ch, * 1 dc into centre of 3-dc of previous row, 5 ch, 7 dc (as worked in Row 4), on 5-dc of previous row, 5 ch *. Rep from * to * ending with 1 dc into centre of 3-dc of previous row, 4 ch, 1 dc for selvedge.

Rounds 6, 7 & 8: Work in dc.

Fasten off.

Press both pieces of basket under a damp cloth. Sew the strip to base with invisible stitches and join the two selvedges together. Complete the basket by working 1 round of crab st. round top edge.

To keep the basket firm, immerse in a strong solution of starch or sugar dissolved in water. For this make a thick syrup by boiling some sugar in 2 breakfast cups of water (bring to boil slowly, stirring until sugar is dissolved). To avoid crystallization while boiling, add a small quantity of glucose or a pinch of cream of tartar. When syrup is clear, leave until completely cold and then immerse the basket, making sure the syrup penetrates right into the fabric. Mould it around your chosen bowl and leave to dry (ideally upside down, with bowl supported on top of a saucepan stand or similar).

Decorative basket no. 2

Materials: 100 g crochet cotton no. 5, used double; 3.00 mm (3/0) crochet hook.

Stitches used: Double crochet, treble, crab.

Follow directions for basket no. 1 for base.

Side strip: Make 8 ch and join with a sl st to form ring.

Work 18 tr into ring, turn. Work 1 dc into each tr, * turn, 8 ch and form ring by working 1 sl st into 4th dc of semicircle just made, turn, 18 tr into and ch ring and link with 1 sl st into corresponding st of previous semicircle, turn, 18 dc into tr, with 1 sl st into corresponding st of previous semicircle *. Rep from * to * until length corresponds to circumference of base disc. Fasten off.

Press both pieces carefully under a damp cloth and sew the strip to base with invisible stitches. Use a flat seam to join ends of strip. Finish top edge with 1 row of crab st.

Stiffening: See directions under basket no. 1.

Mophead in loop stitch

Materials: Approx 150 g chunky wool, small quantity in contrasting colour; 5.00 mm (6) crochet hook.

Stitches used: Treble, loop.

Make 54 ch and work in loop st for 15 cm (6 in).

Now work in rounds, 1 tr into each st, for 10 rounds to make a bag which will cover a mophead.

In a contrasting colour, make a ch about 1 metre (38 in) long and thread it through a row of trebles. Place over mophead, draw up cord and tie in a bow. Ends of chain may be finished with small tassels or pom pon.

Oven glove

Materials: Coloured ribbon, tape or strips of cotton fabric, small quantity in second colour; 6.00 mm (4) crochet hook.

Stitches used: Double crochet, crab.

With main colour make 25 ch and join with a sl st to form ring.

Work 1 round in dc into ring.

Continue with 1 round of dc in 2nd colour, then 9 rounds in main colour, without increasing.

Leaving 8 sts unworked, continue in rounds on remaining sts, inc 2 sts on next round (19 sts). Work 8 more rounds straight and another 3 rounds, decreasing 5 sts evenly in each round so that all sts have been

Mop-head in loop stitch

Oven glove, potholder and saucepan mat in coloured ribbons or tape

Oval bedside or bathroom mat

worked off at end of 3rd round. Fasten off.

Return to the 8 unworked sts for thumb. Working in rounds, continue for 3 rounds, decreasing 2 sts evenly in last round.

Round 5: Hold work so that front and back of thumb are together and work a sl st through front and back sts. Fasten off.

Finish wrist with 1 row of crab st.

Potholder and saucepan mat

Materials: Coloured ribbon, tape or strips of cotton fabric, small quantity of second colour; 6.00 mm (4) crochet hook.

Stitches used: Double crochet, crab.

Make 3 ch and work in dc for 3 rounds, increasing as necessary to keep work flat.

* Work 1 round in 2nd colour. Return to main colour and work 1 round in dc and 1 round in crab st, making a hanging loop with 6 ch before fastening off. *

For saucepan mat, work 9 rounds in main colour, increasing to keep work flat. Continue from * to *.

Oval bedside or bathroom mat

Materials: Coloured ribbon, tape or strips of fabric, small quantity in 2nd colour; 6.00 mm (4) crochet hook.

Stitches used: Double crochet, crab.

Make 45 ch. Work in dc, (1 dc, 1 ch, 1 dc) into last ch, work in dc along opposite side of foundation ch, ending with (1 dc, 1 ch, 1 dc) into last ch.

Continue in dc for another 12 rounds, increasing from time to time on the sides to maintain oval shape (for the increases, instead of working 2 sts into the same st, work 1 st and 1 ch then work 1 dc into 1-ch loop on following round).

Work 1 round in second colour.

Work another 6 rounds and finish with 1 round in crab st.

White and blue bag

Materials: White ribbon, tape or strips of cotton fabric; small quantity in blue; 6.00 mm (4) crochet hook.

Stiches used: Double crochet, ridged double crochet crab.

Make 15 ch. Work in dc, working (1 dc, 1 ch, 1 dc) into last st. Then continue in dc along opposite side of ch, ending with (1 dc, 1 ch, 1 dc) into last st.

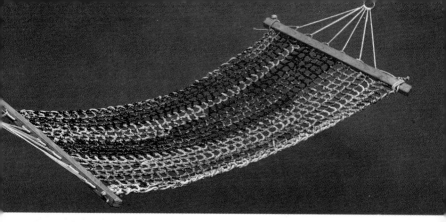

Hammock

Work another 4 rounds in dc, increasing 3 sts evenly on the sides to maintain oval shape (for the increases, see previous pattern).
Work 1 round, without increasing, in ridged dc to form edge of base.
Continue straight in dc for 16 rounds.
Work 1 round in 2nd colour.

Work another 5 rounds in main colour.
Finish the bag with 1 round of crab st.
Make 2 handles in 2nd colour: 40 ch, 1 dc into each ch.
Stitch them securely, evenly spaced, at right angles to the line in 2nd colour, as in illustration.

White and blue bag

Hammock

Materials: 850 g coloured tape or string; 2 wooden crosspieces with 16 evenly spaced holes; synthetic cord or rope and strong synthetic string; 2 steel rings; 6.00 mm (4) crochet hook.
Make 100 ch.
Row 1: * 5 ch, 1 dt, miss 5 ch *. Rep from * to *.
Row 2 and following rows: * 1 dt into dt, 5 ch, miss 5 sts. *. Rep from * to *.
The hammock should be a rectangle of 20 × 50 spaces. Weave a strong cord round all loops on one long edge. Continue along short edge, taking it through holes in wooden crosspieces as shown in illustration *. Rep from * to *. Insert one end of a strong piece of cord through first hole in one of the crosspieces. Knot end firmly. * Weave round all loops

along 1 short end of hammock, carrying cord through holes in crosspiece to anchor crochet.

Continue to weave cord down one long side of hammock *. Rep from * to *, ensuring that end of cord is firmly lashed to crosspiece.

Where the cord emerges on outside of crosspieces, thread the string through these large stitches into a large steel ring. Fastened firmly.

Funny bunnies

Materials: 150 g wool in pink or beige, oddments in several colours; material for stuffing; 3.00 mm (10) crochet hook.

Stitches: Double crochet, treble.

The head is formed from 2 circles worked as follows: Make 5 ch and join with a sl st to form ring. Working first round in dc into ring, continue in dc, increasing evenly to keep work flat, until circle measures 15 cm (6 in) in diameter. Fasten off. Sew circles tog, leaving small space for stuffing at neck edge.

Body: Starting from seat, make a flat circle in dc 12 cm (4¾ in) in diameter. Continue for another 14 rounds, decreasing evenly until 30 sts remain. Fasten off.

Arms (work 2): Make 5 ch, join with a sl st to form ring and work 8 dc into ring. Work a second round increasing 6 sts evenly. Then work 12 more in dc without shaping. Fasten off.

Legs (work 2): Make 9 ch and, starting in 2nd ch from hook, work 7 dc, 3 dc into last ch, and then work 7 dc along opposite side of foundation ch, ending with 3 dc into last ch. Work 2 rounds without increasing, then dec on next 3 rounds at the front for foot until 14 sts remain. Work another 11 rounds straight. Fasten off.

Ears (work 4): Make 18 ch, 1 tr in 4th ch from hook, 14 tr, 5 tr into last ch and then work 15 tr back on opposite side of foundation ch. turn and work 1 row in dc all round. When second piece has been made, join it to the first by working 1 row of dc in contrasting colour all round, working through edge sts of both pieces tog, leaving lower end open. Stuff head, body, arms and legs and sew tog.

For the girl bunny, make a dress as follows: Make 30 ch, join first ch with a sl st to form ring. Work 1 tr into each ch and continue straight for 5 rounds, changing colours on each round. Work 1 row in dc. Make 2 short lengths of ch and work 1 row in dc for shoulder straps. Sew these to the skirt and slip bunny into dress.

Clowns in colourful discs

Materials: 100 g of oddments of double knitting wool in 6 colours; fine string; a number of round beads with holes 2 or 3 little bells; 3.00 mm (10) crochet hook. If the toy is for a young child, the bells can be discarded and pompons used instead of beads.)

Stitch used: Double crochet.

The clown is made of 15 yellow, 12 orange, red, pink, blue, green circles.

Circle: Make 6 ch and join with a sl st to form ring. Work 7 rounds in dc, increasing evenly to keep flat.

Thread string through first bead and then, using it double, through the centre of the circles.

Arms and legs: Alternate 3 circles in one colour with a bead ending with 1 yellow disc at ends of both. Thread string from both legs (4 strands) through remaining 11 yellow circles for body and tie with ends of arm string. Make 2 circles for neck frill by working as above in dc for 10 rounds and then 2 dc in every st for 2 rounds. Thread all strings through both circles and fasten through a bead or button.

Funny bunnies

Clowns in colourful discs

249

Work a ball or 2 circles for head in dc, using head as a guide. Stuff and sew into top bead or button.

Make a hat, using all the colours, starting from centre top. Make 9 ch, join with a sl st to form ring and work in dc alternating colours. Continue straight until a few rounds of each colour have been worked.

Turn edge up to form a brim, sew onto head and decorate. Embroider face with black wool or felt.

Heat-resistant mat in cord

Materials: Fine picture cord or ordinary string; 3.00 mm (3/0) crochet hook.

Stitches used: Double crochet, ridged double crochet.

The mat is made up of 6 leaves.

For each leaf, make 11 ch.

Row 1 (wrong side): Starting in 2nd ch from hook, work 9 dc, 5 dc into last ch, 9 dc on opposite side of foundation ch, turn.

Row 2 (right side): 3 ch, miss first st, 9 (ridged dc ridged dc is used in *each* row and is abbreviated to rdc), 5 rdc into 3rd of 5-dc of previous row, 9 rdc along 2nd side, turn.

Row 3: 3 ch, 10 rdc, 5 rdc into 3rd of 5-rdc of previous row, 10 rdc along 2nd side, turn.

Rows 4 to 8: As Row 3, increasing 1 st on each side and working 5 rdc into central st. In Row 8 there will be 15 sts on each side and 5 on centre st. Fasten off.

Carnation keyring

Materials: Crochet cotton no 5 (50 g in red, 25 g in green); 2.00 mm (1½) crochet hook.

With green cotton make 4 ch and join with a sl st to form ring.

Round 1: Work 10 dc into ring, closing with a sl st.

Round 2: In dc, increasing 6 times evenly (16 dc).

Continue straight on these 16 sts until Round 12 has been worked. Break green, join in red.

Rounds 13, 14 & 15: With red work 3 dc into each dc of previous round.

Round 16: * 3 dc, 1 picot (= 3 ch, 1 dc into last dc worked) *. Rep from * to *. Fasten off.

With green cotton make 40 ch, work 1 row dc. Thread through key and sew both ends to carnation.

Heat-resistant mat in cord

Carnation keyring

Index

alternating stitch, no.s 1, 2, 38, *38*
Antonella's stitch *48,* 49
arabesque stitch 75, *75*

bag, white and blue 246-7, *247*
basket, decorative 243-5, *243-4*
basketweave stitch 39, *39*
　ridged 43, *43*
belt
　white, in Tunisian stitch 235, *235*
　yellow 235, *235*
bib
　blue and white no. 1 164, *165*
　blue and white no. 2 165, *165*
　white and red 166, *166*
bikini swimsuit 180-2, *181*
blanket
　pram, white and red *227*, 227-9
　cot, white *228*, 229
　cot, yellow 226-7, *226*
block and cluster stitch 68, *69*
borders
　for rectangular cloth in filet crochet
　　210, 211
　for towel in filet crochet 232, *232*
　no.s 1-12 133-42, *133, 135, 137-8,*
　　140-2
　for towel in filet crochet 232, *232*
　no. 13 with corners 142, *142*
bunnies, funny 248, *249*
buttonholes 30-2, *31*

cap, lurex *179*, 180
centrepieces
　decorative pointed 205-7, *205*
　fir-tree *206*, 207-8
　no.s 1-6 193-202, *193-4, 197, 199-*
　　201
chain stitch 17
close bobble stitch 42-3, *43*
cloth with border in filet crochet 211,
　211
clowns in colourful discs 248, *249*,
　250
coat, woman's 174, *175*
coat-bag, baby's 186-7, *187*
collars, child's no.s 1-3 166, *166-7*,
　167-8
column stitch *49*, 50
Common crochet 11-12

cornflower stitch 44-5, *44*
coverlet
　double bed 215, *216-17*, 218
　double bed in filet crochet 218-19,
　　220-21, 224-5
crochet, history of 7-11
crochet, starting 16-17
crochet, types of 11-12
crochet hook
　how to hold 16
　types of 11-12, 23
crossed bar stitch *46*, 47
cushion 229-31, *229*

daisy stitch 45-6, *45*
decreasing 25-7
　of blocks on mesh or filet 28
　on mesh and filet 27
　on outside edges 25, *25*
　on outside edges of Tunisian stitch
　　28, *29*, 30
　within rows 26, *26*
　within rows of Tunisian stitch 30,
　　30
diamond
　halved 97-8, *97*
　halved, lower or upper part 98, *98*
　in double crochet *96*, 97
double crochet 18, *18*
　crazy 42, *42*
　crossed 36, *36*
　elongated 37, *37*
　fancy 41-2, *40, 41*
　knotted 48-9, *48*
　ridged, with openwork 75, *75*
　ridged, crazy 42, *42*
double crochet pyramid stitch 67-8,
　67
double treble 20, *20*
dress, child's pink 187-8, *188*
dressing-gown, girl's 190-1, *191*

edgings
　with chain lace crochet 155, *154*
　crabstitch 33-4, *33*
　with fan design *153*, 153
　no.s 1-6 *148*, 149-50, *150-52*, 152
　picot 34, *35*
　scalloped 34, *34*
　shell 34, *35*

twisted cord 34, *35*

fabric, texture of 34
fan stitch 47-8, *47*
fancy stitch 41-2, *40-1*
filet stitch *see:* mesh stitch
flower, stylized *115*, 116-17
flower stitch
    double 45, *45*
    open 69, *69*
forget-me-not stitch 46-7, *46*
four-leaf clover stitch 68, *68*
Friulian crochet 12

German crochet *see:* Common
    crochet
Graziella's stitch 76, *76*

hairpin crochet 12
hammock 247-8, *247*
hat, woman's 178, *178*
hazelnut stitch 91-2, *91*
hexagon
    with star design 114-16, *114*
    two-colour 94-5, *94*
houndstooth check 55-7, *55, 56*

increasing
    of blocks on mesh or filet 28
    on mesh or filet 26-7
    on outside edges 24, *24*
    on outside edges of Tunisian stitch
        28, *29*
    within rows 24-5, *25*
    within rows of Tunisian stitch 28,
        29
insertions, no.s 1-9 *155*, 156-9, *157-62*, 161-2
Irish crochet 10
Irish loop lace stitch 71, *71*

jacket
    child's 188, *189*
    woman's 176, *177*
    man's 183, *184*

Kairomanta stitch 61, *60*
key to symbols 113
key-ring, carnation 250, *250*

lace stitch, Irish loop 71, *71*
Lacy motif 208, *208*
lattice stitch 21-2, *21*
Lella's stitch *76*, 77
lettuce-shaker, square 242, *242*
loop stitch 63, *63*

Martha's stitch 77, *77*
mat
    bedside or bathroom 246, *246*
    heat-resistant, in cord 250, *250*
    saucepan 246, *245*
matinée coat
    blue 184-5, *185*
    white 186, *185*
medallion
    with central flower 121-2, *121*
    with eight-petal flower 122-3, *124*
    for four-leaf clover design 108-9,
        108
    with four-pointed star and four
        rays 126-9, *128*
    multicoloured strip 106-7, *106-7*
    with interwoven centre *119*, 120
    with lacy flowers 111-12, *111*
    large circle 110-11, *110*
    'Old America' in four colours *104*,
        105
    'Old America' strip for a rug *104-5*,
        105
    'Old America' in three colours 103,
        103
    small circle 109-10, *110*
    small square 117-18, *117*
    square woollen 100, *100*
    with star 131, *131*
    with star design 123-7, *127*
    three-colour *118*, 119-20
    with triangular design 130, *130*
mesh stitch 22, *22*
    blocks and spaces 22-3, *22*
    broken 72, *72*
    double (no. 1) 72-3, *72*
    double (no. 2) 73-4, *73*
    hazelnuts on 73-4, *73*
    with picots 71, *71*
mophead cover 245, *245*

netting stitch 70, *70*

open lacy stitch 74, *74*
openwork stitch 81-88, *81-88*
oven glove 245-6, *245*

plaited stitch 50, *50*
pockets 32-3, *32-3*
poncho 173-4, *173*
popcorn stitch, alternating 48, *48*
potholder
  acorn-shaped 239-40, *239*
  little chef *240*, 241
  square *239*, 240-1
  tomato-shaped 238, *238*
  two-colour Catherine wheel *240*, 241
  vase-shaped 238-9, *238*
  white and green *240*, 241

rectangular mat 209, *209, 210*, 211
rib stitch 49-50, *49*
ribbon insertion stitch 78, *78*
ridge stitch 37, *37*
  with chain 40, *40*

sample 34
Sara's stitch 79, *79*
saucepan mat 245-6, *245*
Sayonara stitch 79, *79*
scarf, mohair 169-70, *169*
Scottish tartan in two colours 57-8, *57*
shawl
  black in filet crochet 172-3, *172*
  cream triangular 170, *170-71*
shell stitch 44, *44*
  alternating 66, *66*
  no.s 1-4 64-6, *64-5*
  raised 93, *93*
  simple 64, *64*
shopper, square 242, *242*
shopping bag 243, *242*
skirt, white and gold 178, *179*
slip stitch 17
slipover, white and gold sleeveless 178-80, *179*
Slippers
  baby's blue 236-7, *237*
  baby's red 236, *237*
  baby's three-colour 237, *237*
smocking stitch 78, *78*

square shape from circles 98-100, *99*
star stitch 54-5, *54*
  large 92, *92*
stole, cream 168, *168*
sweater
  mauve 176, *177*
  two-colour 189-90, *190*
Sylvia's stitch 79-80, *79*

table runner in filet crochet 231
tablecloth
  square 211, *212*
  white rectangular *213*, 213-15
tension 13
three-colour stitch 58-60, *58-9*
top, silver evening 180, *181*
towel with border in filet crochet 232, *233*
transverse stitch *50*, 51
treble crochet 19, *19*
  crossed 21, *21*
  diagonal *66*, 67
  half 18-9, *19*
  ridged no. 1 39-40, *39*
  ridged no. 2 *39*, 40
  two-colour *52*, 53
trellis stitch *see*: mesh stitch
tricot crochet *see*: Tunisian stitch
trimmings no.s 1-10 with corners 143-6, *143-7*
Tunisian check 60-1, *61*
Tunisian stitch 12, 23, *23*
  broken 62, *62*
  fancy 58, *59*, 60
Tunisian tweed 61-2, *61*
turning chain 14
two-colour interweave *51*, 52
two-colour wavy chevrons *53*, 54
two-colours with clusters 53, *53*

V-stitch 44, *44*
vegetable bag 242-3, *242*
Vera's stitch 51-2, *51*

waistcoat *182*, 183
Wanda's stitch 80, *80*

zigzag strip, multicoloured 101, *102*